THE LAST RUN

THE LAST RUN

The Dramatic True Story of an American Woman's Escape from a Colombian Cocaine Family

Kay Wolff and Sybil Taylor

B
BERKLEY BOOKS, NEW YORK

Many of the people you will meet in this book are composite portraits. The names, backgrounds, and physical descriptions of all the characters have been changed to protect the privacy of the people whose stories are included in this book. "Kay Wolff" is not only a pseudonym, but, wisely, the author has also never revealed her true name to anyone in Colombia.

For the children of Colombia

ACKNOWLEDGMENTS

The authors are very grateful to Reid Boates, Sheila La Farge, Barbara S. Bull, Ben Barenholtz, Janet Cole, and Pamela Dorman for their interest, time, and help.

Special thanks from Kay Wolff to Janey Schaefer, Bill Hahn, Carol Graham, Pat Bond, and Sergio Silva, as well as to Jean, Robin, Brooke, Jeanne, Andrea, Anne, Heidi, Linlee, Giuliana, and Gisela.

For their constancy and individual contributions, heartfelt thanks from Sybil Taylor to William Saw, Erika Taylor, Scott Taylor, June Sanders, and Judy Richheimer.

THE LAST RUN

PART ONE

THE ROAD DOWN

The First
Step

I FIRST HEARD about Kay Wolff (a pseudonym) in 1983 through friends. Kay's was a seventies tale of cocaine and redemption that began with a move to Colombia in search of fortune and ended with a run for home with two abandoned street children.

Fascinated, I tried to arrange an interview with her, but though she wished to tell her story, she was wary of any stranger who knew her true identity. Even after fourteen years she still felt echoes of paranoia concerning the Colombian drug "family" she had deserted.

The more I learned about her, however, the more interested I became. During the 1960s, even before her sojourn as an international smuggler, Kay had become a legendary West Coast character: she had transformed herself from a California Okie farm kid working night shifts in a peach-canning factory to the radical star of the UCLA Art Department; she had earned her tuition for a master's degree by modeling outrageous clothing at a hip sixties leather boutique; her uncannily intelligent dog, which appeared to be a husky, was in fact ninety percent wolf.

With all this input I had my own image of Kay, which was instantly shattered when we finally did meet. The woman I found waiting for me in a small Greenwich Village café looked like a successful lawyer. In her late thirties, she had pale blond hair cut crisply short, and a quiet elegance that was sparked with superbly designed silver jewelry.

She was waiting for me at a table that allowed her an unobstructed view of the door. As we began to talk, I realized that behind the apparent ease and charming friendliness of her manner, her extraordinary green-and-gold-spangled eyes assessed me coolly.

It was to take yet another year of working on the book and a trip together to Bogotá before I could be certain that I had earned, to a large extent, her true trust and friendship. It was not only the mafiosi of Colombia who haunted Kay and kept her wary. For vague and deeply felt reasons of her own, she would always maintain one last protective veil between herself and the world.

I asked Kay, on that first day, what had made her finally come forward and interrupt her present peaceful life, her job working at a small university; what had motivated her to agree to relive her seventies outlaw memories in a book that could still pose some risk to her?

"I've had certain pictures in my head for years and I wanted to get them down on paper. Speaking of pictures . . ." She smiled, opened her purse, and took out a photo.

"These are my children, Blanquita and Esperanza [pseudonyms]." She handed me the photo. Two dark-haired little girls, pants and T-shirts hanging on spider-thin bodies, stood looking very small in front of a flowering bush. "That was in Bogotá fifteen years ago," Kay said.

She returned the photo to her purse. "They don't remember anything about their country, about where they came from, and now that they've grown up I want them to have something they can hold in their hands, you know, a record of how they came into my life and what they've meant to me." She paused, thinking a moment.

"And then, too," she went on, "I was lucky enough to get out of cocaine addiction alive. A lot of other people were not. In this country we know a lot more about drugs now than we did in 1967, when I first went to Colombia. Cocaine wasn't killing basketball stars then. I think my experiences in Colombia relate to how dangerous innocence can be, and that's part of what I want to say.

"Because, remember back in the seventies? We didn't think cocaine was addictive then. We thought it was a great new creative tool, 'the Light and Magic of the Andes,' and then we got greedy and suddenly it was tragic magic.

"I think my story is about the one way it happened, how it

became tragic, not only for us but for the Colombian people too."

I noticed how compelling her eyes were, and her flat, matter-of-fact way of speaking, the diction very precise but with a faint California drawl. Later I was to learn that she had worked hard with a speech coach to erase her Okie twang.

"You were an artist during the 'Magical Mystery Tour' of the sixties," I said, "so I can understand how you became familiar with cocaine. But what made you go to Colombia? How did you get involved in that life?"

She sighed. There was a lot of reasons. South America had always been an obsession with her. She had been fascinated by the Mexicans she worked with in the fields and orchards of her childhood, and then, too, for herself and the college students of the early sixties, the "Gringo Trail" held far more mystery and appeal than the familiar sights and predictable youth hostels of Europe.

Just after graduating, she took a student loan and went off on a summer trip with friends to explore Ecuador, the Galápagos Islands, Peru, and Colombia. In the high mountain villages of the Incas, she had fallen in love with the Andes, with the colors, the art, the music, the people. She had stayed up all night chewing their magic coca leaves, certain that someday she would have to return.

Three years later, in the summer of 1969, she was given the opportunity. A young man, the friend of a friend, made her an offer that was to change her life—a free round-trip ticket to Colombia, all expenses paid, plus three thousand dollars. All she had to do was accompany him to Bogotá and bring back a kilo of cocaine, carrying it taped to her body. The trip was completely planned, the man said, and had been successful many times before. He would have "carried" himself, but he needed someone with a fresh passport.

It was the eve of the seventies. The buoyant optimism of the sixties was over and Kay was feeling an overwhelming sense of malaise. Thirty thousand had already died in the Vietnam war, and there didn't seem to be any end in sight. It seemed to her that Nixon had no time for the youth of America—"America love it or leave it" was a message that seemed meant for her personally. Everything had died; the Kennedys, King, Joplin, and there she was, reporting every day to a boring job dressing windows for a department store.

The trip to Bogotá had come like a gift of fate, she told me, but the adventure itself turned out to be a near disaster. The young California dealer's behavior was a lesson in what not to do on a smuggling mission. Kay was horrified by his carelessness; he was all high visibility and "ugly Americanism," getting drunk, picking up teen-age prostitutes, and telling people his business. On the trip home via Canada (the safest route, he thought) he disappeared somewhere on the train with the luggage, leaving her alone with a kilo of cocaine strapped to her body under her clothes and the job of explaining to the customs official what she was doing with only one tiny suitcase and a fresh Colombian stamp on her passport.

"I'm taking time off from school just to travel around and visit friends. I like to travel light," she had said, smiling up at him and opening the little suitcase cooperatively for inspection. He had smiled back and moved on. Beginner's luck.

Once safely home in Los Angeles, however, Kay could not stop thinking of Bogotá, a moody Andean city of sudden lightning and equally sudden rainbows, of orchids and beggars, of bowler-hatted Indians driving mules through downtown traffic and emerald merchants peddling their wares in the streets.

She could picture herself living there, exploring the countryside. There was money waiting to be made in Bogotá, and beauty and adventure.

So in September of 1969 she left her gray life behind for the vibrant colors and the mysteries of Colombia. Packing up her few things, selling her '68 Mustang, and leaving her wolf-husky behind in her apartment with her best friend, Maggie, she set off on the journey that was to become at once a personal, yet singularly American odyssey.

—Sybil Taylor

Chapter
One

Bogotá is the mourning widow of the Andes; the gaunt city whose university was in full swing long before the Pilgrims set out for the New World; Bogotá is the peak of achievement of the Spanish Conquistadores, hacking their way through the jungle up the mountains. In Bogotá you will find the most charming people in the world. You will find terror and gaiety.

—Virginia Paxton,
Penthouse in Bogotá

THE HOTEL BATHROOM had a little slit of a window, just big enough for a hand to fit through. Kay opened it and peered out at sunset over the Andes, steep mountains looming darkly against a flamingo-neon sky. A cold, misty wind blew a few raindrops into her face, chilling her, and she closed the window again. The only sure thing about Bogotá's weather, Kay thought, was that you could never be sure about it.

Bogotá is both fire and ice, a paradox 8,700 feet high in the Andes yet only a few degrees from the equator. The sun shines so fiercely it almost crackles, yet cold rains blow in over the mountains and the temperature is never much above 58 degrees Fahrenheit.

Kay's bathroom was tiny, a shower in the ceiling and a drain in the floor with toilet and sink crowded in. It was also cold. No building in Bogotá had heat, due partly to technological lag and partly simply to custom. Even those who could have afforded to heat the Taj Mahal shivered unquestioningly in their luxurious mansions.

The face that looked back at her from the bathroom mirror

was scrubbed clean. She appraised it thoughtfully, an artist contemplating a fresh canvas upon which to work. It was an old business with her, this act of creating herself, a chameleon who changed to fit her environment. Her face was strong-boned and angular, an "Okie puss," she used to say disparagingly, and the eyes were intense, an unsettling gold-flecked green with small pupils. "If you don't want people to notice you, you'd better hide those eyes behind glasses," her friend Maggie had warned her.

She began her toilette, accenting the cheekbones with a dusky makeup, heightening the eyes with green liner. Leaning in, Kay worked impersonally, with the same cool concentration she gave to her paintings back home in L.A.

She brushed out her hair, which hung long and smooth to just below her shoulder blades, and went into her room to check out the total effect, a tawny California beauty in a splashy print dress, five feet nine inches, leggy, and broad-shouldered. By standing on the bed and twisting around, she could see various parts of herself in the mirror above the bureau. She felt oversized for the room, the narrow bed, the cramped wooden desk.

On the bureau was an official-looking engraved invitation. Kay stuck it into her bag as though it were a pearl-handled revolver. She was on the hunt.

Stepping into the lobby, she saw Señor Schneider, the hotel's chunky proprietor, soothing a thin, dark-haired girl who seemed upset. He was talking to her in French, but when he saw Kay he switched effortlessly to English.

"Oh my, oh my, Señorita Wolff, whose heart will you break tonight?" he said to her.

Schneider had emigrated to Bogotá from Frankfurt in 1950. He had stayed on in the Norte section of Bogotá, joining other Germans, Swedes, Danes, and Americans in this cozy enclave with its cafés offering cappuccinos and pastries and foreign-language newspapers sold in its gossipy shops.

His soft, insinuating voice and German accent reminded Kay of Peter Lorre's, except that with Schneider there were no sinister overtones. In fact, his very air of bourgeois comfort-ableness, his ordinary quality, had been part of Kay's decision to move into his hotel.

She had been looking for a base of operations, a safe harbor in the alien and treacherous currents of Bogotá life, and Schneider's hotel turned out to be just that. It was perfect.

Señor Schneider stood guard at the desk while his fussy wife ruled over the clean little dining room, the German and Colombian staff, and the prominently displayed refrigerator. Refrigeration was not something to be taken for granted in the Bogotá of 1969, and Kay felt secure in the knowledge that at least here she would not get served a dose of food poisoning.

And finally, she liked the location. The Norte was the safest section of Bogotá, residential and fashionable, far away from the town center where hungry pickpockets and lightning-fast thieves stalked the crowds for victims.

On this early evening in October, Kay bid Schneider farewell, left the hotel, and turned right onto Carrera 15. The mountains were like a presence above the street, the sky turning purple, the great white church on the summit of Monserrate starkly illuminated. She took a couple of deep breaths; the thin air of the Andes still made her dizzy, and from the lush gardens behind the mansion walls came the earthy smell of flowers watered at evening: bougainvillea, roses, orchids, hibiscus, freesias.

Carrera 15 was the main street of the section, and all along the road the fancy boutiques, the jewelry stores full of Colombian emeralds, and the galleries of pre-Colombian art were closing shop for the night. An old man, wearing a blanketlike *ruana* against the cold, was sweeping the patterned sidewalk in front of the Club Nocturno. Kay began to feel the buzz, the mood of anticipation in the street, the pause between night and day.

She loved Bogotá, loved its strong colors, its subterranean Indian beat, its brooding edginess, the strange way that brutality and beauty intermingled, like an orchid with a deep drop of blood at its heart. In Bogotá she felt a constant sense of eerie premonition, like turning in a crowd to see who had called her name and finding no one. Bogotá challenged Kay, seduced her with its paradoxes.

Turning the corner onto Calle 85, she saw a number of expensive cars parked under the tall mimosa trees in front of the gallery. A taxi pulled up with a man and woman inside. Suddenly two scruffy beggar children materialized from an alley and began clamoring around the car window while the man paid the driver. The gallery owner came out and waved them irritably away, as if they were merely annoying flies. Turning, they spotted Kay and began running toward her, shouting, one of them holding up a battered box of Chiclets.

"*¡Señora! ¡Señora! ¡Chiclets, señora! ¡Una moneda por favor!*"

Then they were standing in front of her, staring up at her with a kind of terrible strained attention, like starving dogs looking at a plate of food. Kay winced. They were barefoot, their skin mottled gray with filth, no older than six. The boy had a scabby swelling on the side of his head, and the girl's face was screwed into a grimace that Kay guessed was meant to be a winning smile. Silently Kay reached into her bag and emptied her change purse into the girl's outstretched hand. The coins showered into the street and the children grabbed at them.

"*Gracias, señora, Dios le pague, señora,*" they kept intoning. The intensity of their gratitude shamed her, and she could barely look at them as they ran along at her side, still thanking her all the way to the gallery.

They were all over Bogotá, ratpacks of these homeless kids, thousands of them inhabiting a Dickensian world of squalor and crime, haunting the alleyways and side streets, living and dying in the gutters and garbage-choked courtyards behind restaurants, begging, thieving, selling whatever they could lay their hands on just to stay alive. The United Nations estimated that in Colombia in 1970, two hundred fifty children under the age of five died every day, mostly of malnutrition.

The gallery echoed with the well-bred roar of an elegant cocktail party. The crowd looked promising and very conservative, not a beaded necklace or a fringed leather jacket in sight. Waiters moved like acolytes, offering champagne. Kay thought they looked uncomfortable, their broad, Indian features and sturdy bodies at war with the formal abstraction of their black-and-white uniforms.

Several men had tuned to stare at her as she came in, and she felt the women prickle, aware of but refusing to acknowledge her. Now, Professor Guzmán lumbered toward her, a short, freckled man with salt-and-pepper crinkly hair and a neat reddish beard.

"Ah, Kay," he said, and then, as she suppressed an astonished laugh, he actually bent over her hand and brushed it lightly with his lips. "I'm so glad you received my invitation. What do you think of the show?" His English was oddly stilted.

"Well," she shrugged lightly, then leaned toward him, smiling. "Exciting and splashy, isn't it? The artist is French?"

"Yes," he said, taking her arm and moving through the crowd toward the end of the room, "abstraction is very fashionable here in Bogotá now, but perhaps not so interesting for an avant-garde American like yourself."

Guzmán was looking over her shoulder. Kay had the feeling he was subtly signaling someone. She tried to shift so she could see, but Guzmán, with his hand still on her arm, had turned her toward one of the large red-and-white canvases.

A few weeks earlier, newly moved to Bogotá from L.A., Kay had learned his name and gone to see him at the university in Bogotá. He was chairman of the Art Department. In Colombia, a man of education was highly regarded and Kay thought Hector Guzmán would know a lot of high-powered people. He would have to be a good contact, she reasoned, so she had gone to ask him about teaching art.

"So have you found a good teaching job for me yet, Professor?" Kay asked.

"Ah no, señorita, but I am thinking of something. You are a smart woman. I feel there are many things you could do in Bogotá with your excellent fine-art background, no? And alas, of course, as you know, teaching is an honorable profession but it does not pay well."

Kay looked down at the hand on her arm. Something was obviously helping the professor's own teaching salary along: he was wearing a Rolex watch and an expensive European suit.

"*Gracias, Ricardo. ¿Qué tal?*" Guzmán said to a young man who had appeared beside him and was handing him a glass of champagne. "I know you did not come over here to talk art to an old man." The two men exchanged a swift glance. "May I present," Guzmán said, "Señorita Kay Wolff, Ricardo Alvarez."

Now here, Kay thought, was a really great-looking young guy. Just turning the corner from boy to man, he was so handsome it was almost ridiculous, like a cartoon hero. Kay put him at somewhere around nineteen or twenty. His hair was soft and straight and he had a nervous habit of flipping back a dark

wing of it that kept falling across his forehead. Clearly
well-connected, she thought. He was dressed with the almost
obsessive neatness of the Latin upper class, a starched collar
and conservative tie showing above the neck of a maroon
cashmere sweater.

"Hi, Kay," Ricardo said, being cool and American.

"*Hola, Ricardo. ¿Qué tal?*" Kay countered.

"So, you speak Spanish." He grinned.

"Not yet, but I'm willing to learn." She was demure, but
implicitly provocative. He clicked his fingers for one of the
waiters. Kay hated the gesture.

"*A sus órdenes,*" the waiter said.

"More champagne. We must not allow this beautiful woman's glass to run to dry."

"Run dry," she corrected. He looked blank. "We say 'run
dry.'"

"Señorita Wolff is the American I told you about," the
professor said. "She loves our pre-Columbian art and our
Indian *típicos*, and she even knows something about them. Oh,
will you pardon me please, I must go and speak to someone."
Guzmán turned to Kay, and bowed slightly. His expression
remained blandly polite, but one eyelid fluttered down in what
could have been a wink.

Kay watched him nod and greet his way through the crowd,
finally stopping to talk to a heavy, balding man with a smiling
face. Guzmán said something to him and the man looked over
at Kay and held her glance. He lifted his champagne glass to
her in a small toast and Kay could see that the woman beside
him was annoyed.

The women, Kay noticed, were dressed to kill. She had not
seen anything like it in years; spike heels and plunging
necklines, black net and little hats, like the Barbie dolls her
older sister used to play with in the fifties. With animated
chatter and rapt attentive eyes, they concentrated on the men
and ignored each other. Kay felt for a moment as if she were in
a room full of caged exotic birds.

"Do you know Bogotá well?" Ricardo asked.

"Not really. I was here a little while ago, on business. I liked
it so much I just packed and moved."

"I can't believe that." Ricardo shook his head. "You really
like Colombia better than the States?"

"Yes, I do."

"Maybe you would like to see some real Bogotá nightlife? Do you know how I mean, I could show you something different—not for tourists."

"I like to dance," she said.

His hand was very warm as he pressed her arm to his side and began maneuvering them toward the door. The heavy man interrupted a conversation he was having to call out "*Pórtate bien* [Behave yourself]."

Outside it was raining. Ricardo kept his arm around Kay, and guided her toward a sky-blue customized VW with chrome running boards and white leather upholstery.

He saw them even before she did, three teen-age street boys coming out from behind a black Mercedes. "*Pendejos,*" he said, trying to unlock the door as fast as he could. "Get in, get in!"

The boys had begun to run toward them, and as Ricardo started up the engine, she saw at her window a distorted face in a tattered straw hat, mouth open, yelling obscenities.

The car pulled away and gunned down the empty street. There was no one out. It had stopped raining as suddenly as it had started, and an orange quarter moon shone above the trees that ran down the center of the street.

Ricardo shoved a Jimi Hendrix tape into the deck and hummed along with the riff. He pushed the VW up to seventy, running the deserted intersections. Kay said nothing, sitting with her hands folded in her lap.

"It is dangerous to stop for lights," he explained. "Sometimes you can be robbed." He glanced at her face. "Don't worry about it, *bonita*," he said, taking her hand. "In Bogotá you have to be fast sometimes, and keep the eyes open."

Traffic was heavier in the International section of town. The Tequendama and Hilton hotels, and the Avianca building rose incongruously, like tall interlopers, from the surrounding Andean town of low, red-tiled roofs.

Ricardo drove down a few twisting side streets just wide enough for the car. They passed the city bull ring, empty and massive under the moon, its flags snapping in the silence. He parked nearby, across from a doorway with a flashing red sign of a charging bull and the words DISCOTECA EL BULLRING.

"I have something to make you feel good," he said, and

took out an ornate silver vial with a tiny spoon on a chain. Leaning toward her in the dark intimacy of the car, he held a spoonful of coke tenderly to each of her nostrils. She saw his eyes, very close, very brown and solicitous, felt the slightly perfumed, breathing warmth of his body—then the hit. Jackpot!

It was extraordinary—the best she had ever had. There was no burn in it at all, the coke slipped up her nose smooth and cool, a little blast of euphoria. If she could get to the source of this, it would be like finding El Dorado.

She took the vial from him and repeated the ritual, this time for him.

"This is really *puro*," she said. "I found everyone here has stuff to sell, but nothing like this." She screwed the cap on the bottle and handed it back to him.

He curled his fingers around it. "Keep it, *bonita*. It's beautiful, like you."

"*Muchas gracias, Ricardo.*" She made a business of putting the little vial in her purse, asking casually, "You can get more easily?"

"It is not a problem." He was equally offhand, and opened the door to get out.

A skinny doorman stood guard under the sign of the flashing bull. He looked young, in a rumpled, slightly dirty uniform with epaulets and gold braid. Kay thought of a kid dressed up to play a general in a school play. Ricardo spoke a few words to him, pressing some money into his hand.

Inside the disco it was black as a closet, except for the strobes on the dance floor. The rock music was so loud, Kay could feel it vibrating through all the bones in her body. The place was an uncanny imitation of an early sixties American black-light club with a lot of heavy action going on under cover of darkness.

A hostess, plump in a tight red mini-skirt, came to guide them to their table. They followed her flashlight, moving among the dim shapes of people sitting silently in the dark. Two merged shadows parted, and one of them, a woman, slipped purposefully under the table between the knees of her date.

The hostess led them to a table by the dance floor and Ricardo ordered drinks, his mouth close to her ear. Almost as soon as the hostess was gone, a man materialized in front of them, his face a dark blur above a white shirt. He pushed back a sleeve and displayed a row of watches, one above the other, on a muscular forearm. Ricardo shook his head. Next, the man took a white handkerchief from his pocket. Kay thought of a magician as he opened the kerchief to reveal a clutch of different-sized green stones nestled there. Ricardo waved his hand, no. The man was tireless. He brought his fingers up to his nose and made snorting gestures. Finally, he melted away into the music.

Their drinks came, and as Kay watched the packed dance floor, she thought she recognized the thin French girl Schneider had been comforting in the lobby of her hotel.

"It's too crowded here," Ricardo shouted into her ear. "Enough of the underbelly of Bogotá. I am going to take you to dinner."

The Roof Room of the Bogotá Hilton was still serving when they arrived at eleven o'clock, not at all unusual in a Latin city where people always eat late. From the windows, draped in brocade, the city's lights swept in a starry drift in all directions. A group of fifteen people in evening clothes laughed and sparkled around a long table in the reflected glow of chandeliers and red damask walls. The nineteenth century on the forty-second floor, Kay thought.

"Para servirle, Señor Alvarez," the maître d' murmured, seating them at the best window table in the room.

Ricardo had glanced at her to see if she was impressed, but Kay kept her face expressionless.

One of the women at the long table waved to Ricardo. He smiled and waved back. *"Hijo de puta,"* he said. *"Son of a bitch,* by tomorrow morning my mother will know I have been here with you." He recovered himself. "May I order for you?" he said. She nodded, amused.

No one had ordered a meal for her since she was a kid. She could hear the cries of "Male chauvinism" back home. She looked at Ricardo studying the wine list, doing what a Colombian male is brought up to do. He wouldn't even know what the word *chauvinism* meant.

"So, Señorita Kay Wolff, what are you doing here—really?" He folded his arms on the table and leaned toward her, his voice playfully conspiratorial.

"I'm looking for adventure, Señor Alvarez," she picked up his tone. "I have come to seek my fortune, as they used to say in the old days."

"Have you found anything yet?"

She looked for a flicker in his eyes, but he was keeping himself a cipher.

"Maybe." She was leaning forward toward him now, quizzical, one elbow on the table, her chin resting on her hand.

"Good," he said.

He ordered caviar with toast points, tournedos du boeuf, a bottle of Château Lafite Rothschild '52, and a bottle of champagne, Louis Roederer. Afterward, they settled into the tiny adjoining bar.

Conscious that their legs were almost touching, they talked American cars and rock bands, Indian legends and Bogotá's museums; a protective smoke screen of conversation behind which they watched each other. Finally, a small band came in, dressed in black dinner jackets and ruffled shirts. With their hair greased back and their large gold cuff links, they seemed to shine all over. They began playing tangos and rhumbas, the fast rhythms of the *cumbia*, Columbia's sexy national dance, and an occasional Beatles tune.

Ricardo got up and held out his hand to her, and Kay was glad for those Arthur Murray lessons she had taken in the days when she had taken lessons for everything, including, most especially, the removal of her Okie twang.

The dance floor was very small and only one other couple was dancing. Ricardo pulled Kay to him and held her firmly, pressing her against the length of his body. They swayed and turned in perfect unison, Ricardo guiding her effortlessly to the flow of the music. She felt the heat of him through his clothes, and when the music stopped they embraced tightly.

"Is this something we should be doing in public?" she asked, leaning back from him and laughing.

He got them a suite on the thirty-second floor. In a mirrored cabinet was a well-stocked bar. He poured the clear fire of aguardiente into two glasses, brought them to the coffee table, and began laying out some lines on its glass surface.

Kay had kicked off her shoes and was leaning back against the cushions of the couch, watching. He wasn't talking and he looked very nervous, avoiding her eyes, his head bowed over the lines he was arranging. He *is* just a kid, she thought, and impulsively she left the couch and knelt next to him.

"Ricardo," she said, and put her hand to his cheek.

It was all very urgent and awkward, his hands touching her frantically, pushing up her dress, his mouth biting her neck, her ear, and then it was over.

They lay on the floor afterward. Ricardo put two cigarettes in his mouth, lit them both, and passed her one—Paul Henreid style. In the silence, breathing out the smoke, Kay was working out what to say. Finally, she reached across him and stubbed out her cigarette in the ashtray on the floor.

"Ricardo," she said, "that was—"

He interrupted her, his face bright red. "I was not very good with you, I know. I am sorry. It is my first time."

"What?" She pulled herself up on an elbow.

"No, no. My first time with a *real* woman, I mean."

"A *real* woman? You mean you've been . . . imagining?" She made a gesture with her hand.

"No, no," he said, alarmed, sitting up, "not *that*."

She looked at him blankly, and he pushed on. "You don't understand, you are an American. For you it is different, you all sleep with each other."

He lay down again, one arm across his eyes. "Here, in Colombia, you can't make love with a real woman until you marry her. To do that is a big sin, an insult. So"—he rolled over and busied himself prying another cigarette out of the pack of Marlboros—"I have never had a real woman. I have been to bed only with whores."

I don't believe this, Kay thought. The sixties had obviously never arrived here. The only thing to do was to sweep it all aside. "Come on," she said. "Let's go into the bedroom and have a meaningful cultural exchange."

His body was as sleekly muscled as a swimmer's, and his skin, the color of dark honey, was smooth as a woman's. A *dije* hung from a thin gold chain around his neck, a gold fist with the thumb sticking out between the first and second fingers. It chilled Kay, yet, at the same time, it excited her, a touch of perverse menace swinging against the innocent curve of his naked chest.

She switched on the radio. "Do it the way you dance," she

said, her lips against his shoulder. The bedside light was on and they made love, open-eyed.

Dawn came. Outside, clouds had begun to pour down the flanks of the mountains. An Indian woman, a muffled shape in a black shawl, baskets at her feet, sat motionless against the white-washed wall of a closed restaurant. The sun rose higher and she was gone.

At breakfast in the Hilton coffee shop, Kay drank her coffee with one hand while Ricardo held the other. Coffee was more than a drink in Colombia, it was a ritual. She signaled the waiter for more, and caught the musky smell of the night that still lingered in her clothes.

"We have everything we need here," Ricardo said. "Why don't we stay for a month."

She sighed, squeezed his hand, then took hers away. "Our coke supply would run out," she said lightly, "and it's such great stuff. Actually I would love to buy a kilo."

He went back to his breakfast, taking his time wrapping a piece of pancake around a bite of blood sausage.

"Let's take a walk and talk about it," he said. She could see that the guard dog in his head had sprung to attention.

Outside the Hilton, people were hurrying to work wearing brightly colored *ruanas* against the chill morning drizzle. Indian women were hanging leather bags, sandals, and jackets on the makeshift walls of the street stalls and even at eight in the morning, the sweet carts were already rolling.

It was as if all Colombia had a massive, collective sweet tooth, and candies and pastries were everywhere, in every shape and size: sweet yeast pan *dulces*, tiny candy *bocadillos*, *roscón* rolls loaded with guava jelly, brown sugar *panela* squares, milk and honey *tungo* buns, crystallized guava jelly squares, *canasta de coco* (coconut custard), *hinchares* (cream puffs), bonbons, *confitados* (candy), and *helados* (ice cream).

Kay and Ricardo drifted down Carrera 7 toward the Tequendama Hotel. This was the International section and Carrera 7 was a modern boulevard lined with shops and airline offices like any in Europe. It was, however, only a superficial swath of modernity cut through the cobbled warren of the old city. Just off the boulevard, narrow passageways led past ancient houses of quarried stone. A smell of smoke and mold rose from the courtyards and just up one of these steep, weed-cracked lanes, Kay saw a half-starved mutt poised on top of a wall. He stood motionless, staring down the street toward her.

The image had a kind of surreal, shadowless clarity, alien and yet oddly familiar. At that moment the fierce Andean sun burst through the clouds and, feeling its heat on her back and shoulders, she felt more intensely alive than ever before.

They had been walking along in silence. Now they stopped in a little square with palm trees opposite the Tequendama. They sat down on a white stone bench near the fountain.

"So, what are we talking about exactly?" Ricardo asked briskly.

"A kilo *puro*."

Neither of them said anything. They looked across at the Tequendama where the young American dealers were hanging around, stoned, trying to be cool.

"I don't run mules like those hippie dudes do," Kay said contemptuously. "They're sloppy and dangerous. Look at them, they're not fooling anybody. With those pale necks the whole world can see they've just cut off their long hair. No, with me there are no problems, no rip-offs."

"You know something, even if you are careful, I still don't need the risk or the business," Ricardo said.

"Fine with me. Bogotá has other places to find good coke." She smiled sweetly.

Ricardo shook two cigarettes out of his pack and offered her one. "*Bueno,* I can get you a kilo *puro* for six thousand dollars."

The parameters for bargaining had been set up: she wanted the coke, he wanted to keep her in his life. The rest was form.

"Six thousand dollars?" Kay said incredulously. "I think the price should be more like five thousand."

"Oh, certainly," Ricardo was indignant. "There are deals for even less if you do not mind borax and ground glass. The sample, of course, would be perfect."

"I've got five thousand dollars," she said firmly.

They sat for a moment without speaking.

"How is the carrying done?" he asked.

"Why do you want to know that, Ricardo?"

"I'm still worried about you."

"All right," she conceded, "suitcase concealment."

"Who fabricates?"

"I do."

Kay knew he had plenty of reason for being cautious about dealing with an American. The papers were full of horror stories, she had just read of two cases recently:

Two girls from Montana had been promised five thousand dollars by a Mexican phone contact. The contact never materialized, but in their hotel room they found seven kilos hidden under their pillows. They were caught with the cocaine and sentenced to thirteen years in a Mexican jail.

A Minneapolis high-school teacher and former social worker for the Chippewa Indians was teaching five days a week and driving a cab nights to make ends meet. When his wife became pregnant, he accepted a three-thousand-dollar offer to smuggle a kilo, was unsuccessful, and found himself pleading his case in court.

"Bueno," Ricardo said finally, "five thousand. I have to say you drive a good bargain and you have an interesting way of doing business. Shall I meet you at your hotel tomorrow?"

"No. Not there. Around the corner. Will you be in your car?"

"A different one, a black Mercedes." He glanced at her and smiled, breaking the mood. "What about last night?"

"It was a great tour of Bogotá," she said, trying to keep the tone light. She wasn't prepared for the sudden shift in his mood.

"I had hoped it would be more," he said morosely. He stared down at his shoes. "Are you going to be an American women's lib and sleep with everyone? I don't want you to. I want you to be for me, Kay."

"I didn't come to Bogotá to fuck men, Ricardo, so one should be more than enough." She could hear the sudden intake of his breath as he stared at her and then he began to laugh.

They got up, crossed the street, and Kay felt a subtle tremble in the pavement beneath her feet as though a subway had passed underground. It was a familiar feeling for a Los Angeles native, the faint reminder that this was earthquake country.

Chapter Two

Smuggling is one of the folkways of Colombia, a nation with sparsely settled borders . . . thousands of miles of coastlines on two oceans, and an estimated 7,000 unregistered dirt strips long enough to accommodate small planes.

Smugglers have an economy all their own—a major industry not reflected in government growth statistics. Everything from emeralds to beef on the hoof goes out. Everything from television sets to Scotch comes in.

In context, cocaine, a drug distilled from the leaf of the Andean coca plant, is only the latest in a long line of goods passed along by Colombian smugglers.

—*The Miami Herald,*
April 25, 1974

ON THE WALLS of Kay's room at Schneider's were her postcards, her sketches of Indian street vendors, and a large map of the constellations. A woven blanket of deep purples and blues had been thrown over the fat, upholstered hotel chair. There were a tiny kitchenette and a balcony, with bars that had obviously been added as an afterthought—for security. Life in a birdcage, Kay thought.

She turned off the little TV set and went downstairs to the desk to get her mail. Schneider's wife loved plants and the small lobby was homey, crowded with pots of begonias. The white tile floor was mopped to a shine. Near the arched doors to the restaurant stood a low couch and a coffee table loaded with ashtrays and travel folders.

The glass door to the street was open, and Kay noticed that the air outside was unusually still.

Behind the desk Señor Schneider held her letter and slowly examined the stamp and return address. "Ah ah," he said, "and who is this 'Etta Raisin' from Los Angeles? A boyfriend maybe?" He was nosy. "I like to know what's going on in my hotel" was how he had explained it to Kay. "My wife and I, we have always run a nice place here. . . ."

Kay reached out silently for her letter. She had been nervously awaiting it for a week and was in no mood to play Schneider's little games. At that moment, a hollow, rumbling sound, like a huge truck going by, came from the open door, and she turned her head to look out into the street.

Not more than a second later, there was a boom and another rumble and suddenly Schneider was shouting "¡Terremoto!" Kay bolted, seeking cover under a mahogany table, a reflex drilled into her by years of civil-defense instructions in her California grade school. Schneider intercepted her and dragged her, struggling, into the street. "Leave me alone! Are you crazy?" she kept shouting.

People were running out of buildings like panicked ants, and almost immediately Kay and Schneider were swept helplessly down the street, trapped in the middle of a shoving, screaming mass of human bodies. At the next rumble, the street seemed to tremble and a high, terrified wailing rose from the crowd, as if from one human throat.

Bricks and stones began to rain down, and Schneider, his face inches away, his body pressed against Kay by the crowd, kept repeating, "Don't be afraid, this is not a bad one. It will pass; don't be afraid."

At last the mob spilled into a park and Kay and Schneider came to rest under an acacia tree loaded with yellow blossoms. People stood, stunned and silent among the lush shrubs and bright flowers. It seemed to Kay the rumbling had stopped, yet no one was leaving.

"We have to wait," Schneider said. He explained that sometimes the worst tremors came at the end, collapsing the city's buildings in upon themselves like so many ruined cakes.

"I am sorry I had to become rough with you before," he said, "but in South America, when you hear a quake coming, you get out into the street as fast as you can. This is not the

USA. Down here there is no building code, no reinforced concrete. After each earthquake, they just level the rubble and build another badly made building . . . sometimes right on top of the dead." He sighed.

"How do you know when it's over?" Kay asked, looking at the crowd that had began to stream back into the street.

"You don't know. You just believe it is and then hope there will be no bad aftershocks the next day."

He wanted Kay to walk back to the hotel with him. But even under ordinary circumstances she hated getting caught in a crowd. Claustrophobia, feeling trapped, panicked her: she always needed to be sure there was a way out.

"Thanks, Señor Schneider, but I think I'd rather stay here and recover for a while." She tried to laugh away the queer and uncomfortable intimacy that had sprung up between them.

"Well," he said, patting her shoulder, "you'd better start getting used to it, my dear." He nodded his large head, and blinked his round, pouchy eyes. "So then, I will see you later," he said, and went off.

She sat down and leaned her back against the tree trunk. Trees had been the solid comfort of her childhood. When she was in trouble, she would run and hide in her grandfather's orchard, lying safe along an accommodating branch while from down below, through the leaves, came the sounds of people calling for her.

Now, with the bark pressing against her back, the sturdiness of the tree seemed illusory, the invisible roots stretching out beneath her were vulnerable and tenuous.

Maggie's letter was still clutched in her hand, a message from another world. She looked at the red-white-and-blue stamp and the neat round letters of Maggie's handwriting and opened the envelope.

Sept. 10, 1969

Dear Lucy Furr,

Must dash this note off before you forget my face. I despair of ever having the luxury of writing you a proper letter. Not that writing you a proper letter was ever easy. First the mulling of the wine, then finding the record with the wolf howls etc. Setting the mood is so important.

Speaking of wolves, Teddy is all right and most people think he's some kind of shepherd-husky mix. The only thing is, he's learned to open the fridge door. Why can't you just get a normal dog like everyone else.

Thoughts of taking a vacation are making things at work tolerable. I am marking the days off of my calendar at the Salt Mines and dreaming of my escape.

The show is definitely on the road. The tour begins Tuesday the 19th booked out of LAX on the usual carrier. It's not a direct flight, but one stop in the West. It's been a lot of work getting ready with the usual people being the usual pains in the familiars.

Gossip? The Jones sisters have hit a new high or low, depending. . . . Just when we thought they could go no further out with health food and Bach Flower Remedy cures, they discovered colonics and were standing in line to have their insides washed out. They got tired of standing in line and bought a machine and now they are giving the treatments to their friends, for a small fee, should anyone wish for that kind of a high.

They rave on about how *really* good and clear they feel now. And, my gad, they took the damn machine over to Hawaii with them. Would like to see the face when someone in the airport opens that looking for Kono Gold. Must close now with a "wish you were here!"

Love Etta Raisin not brown rice

Kay laughed out loud, pleased with the information that Maggie had managed to embed within her bizarre L.A. social report.

Maggie always said that when she and Kay met it was hate at first sight. It was the summer of 1963 and they were both seniors at UCLA. Maggie was a serious student of film and photography, with a minor in anthropology. She was famous as the campus photographer whose face, half hidden behind an ancient Leica and a snaky tumble of flaming red hair, was part of every radical event and civil rights march from Berkeley to L.A.

Kay, the unpredictable darling of the Art Department, traveled with the cool-eyed hipsters of the latter-day "beat" crowd, taking off for San Francisco and preferring the coffee-houses and the waterfront dives to the emerging "flower scene" in Haight-Ashbury. Even though Kay and Maggie went to the same bars and stood in the same lines to hear Peter, Paul and Mary, the fact that their paths crossed was a fluke.

It was at a party thrown by the campus newspaper on a hot afternoon, with the music of Bob Dylan and Joan Baez booming out of all the open windows. Kay had come to the party with a friend but she didn't know anyone else. She had gotten a little too high and had crawled out of an upper-story window onto the shingled roof of the porch to catch the breeze and get away from the noise.

But the porch roof was already occupied. Maggie was sitting there leaning her back against the wall of the house. Neither was pleased to see the other. They sat in silence until Maggie asked for a cigarette.

"I don't have a cigarette but I have some grass," Kay said.

"Thanks." Maggie stretched out her hand and lit the joint Kay passed her. "This is really good," she said, and turned to look at Kay, surprised. Kay immediately recognized the clear, clipped sound of money in her voice—an upper-class accent.

"Where are you from?" Kay asked.

"Bel-Air."

"Oh, then of course you play tennis and all that," Kay said.

"Are you always this bitchy?" Maggie said, "or do I rate some kind of special privilege?"

They laughed and kept talking till the party was over.

The park was empty now. It was time to go back to the hotel. There was a deal on.

While Kay sat in her room waiting for Schneider to ring her back with her call to the States, she made a list of what she wanted to say.

Carrying: Maggie was going to be packing cash down. Kay wanted ten thousand dollars, five thousand for the deal with Ricardo and five as backup for living expenses. Maggie's look would have to be perfect and she would have to carry without discomfort. A custom-sewn long-line bra would do it.

Equipment: Kay needed another Samsonite suitcase to work on. Maggie could buy one and fill it with stuff Kay needed anyway.

Finally, after an hour, the call came through, the operator verifying the Stateside number and then, as the ringing started, Kay heard a little click, meaning a Colombian government ear had just joined them on the line. A lot of calls to the United States were monitored, Ricardo had told her. They weren't exclusively looking for drug traffickers, it was a sort of generalized spying, a way of keeping track of what was going on in all quarters.

"Etta, darling," Kay rushed in as soon as Maggie said hello, "it was so great to hear from you, loved your funny stories, keep them in the act."

Not giving Maggie a chance to answer, she went right on. "Do you have a pencil handy? These lines are always very full of static so we have to talk fast, know what I mean?"

There was a second's pause and then Maggie's unruffled California drawl, "It's so good to hear you, Lucy, although you sound like you're talking from the bottom of some kind of rabbit hole. But don't worry, I read you."

Kay could hear rustling and imagined Maggie riffling through her desk for a pencil, the phone clamped between her raised shoulder and her round Irish mug with its frame of wild red hair.

When the rustling stopped, Kay said, "Ready? You'll need all your own traveling money. I'm broke. Could you bring me some cash! We can work out how I'll pay you back when you get here.

"Next make a shopping list, okay? There's a lot of stuff I can't get down here. Jack La Lanne protein bars, peanut butter, vitamins, rolling papers, Scotch, and Tampax. They don't have Tampax here; I think it's considered sinful. So is birth control, so you might as well include some of those pills too. Anything can happen down here, and let's at least not let *that* happen.

"Oh, and could you please bring *Beggars' Banquet, Electric Ladyland,* and anything by Led Zeppelin. And please bring me a couple of pairs of men's Levi's, twenty-six by thirty-two. Buy another big brown to carry all that stuff in. I'll pay you back when you get here. Got it?"

"Got it!"

"Oh yes, and listen, I hope you haven't gained any weight, I bought you a ball gown but the sizes are smaller here. So why don't you squeeze yourself into one of your custom long-lines, just to make sure you'll fit.''

Maggie was right there for it all. "Thanks a lot, Kay. You make me feel like a tank, but I can't wait to see the gown. I'll wear the damn long-line. Do you need to tell me anything else, because this call is really costing you mucho, no?''

"*Sí, sí.* I think that covers it. And Etta, darlin',' she reverted mockingly to the old Okie twang, "take good care of yourself now, hear?''

"You too, and I guess you're already taking care of whoever fits into the twenty-six, thirty-two, so bye-bye, Lucy." Maggie hung up.

Kay didn't break the connection but continued to sit on her narrow bed listening to the dead air rushing in her ear through the chunky, fifties receiver. Then came the faint click of the government tap going off the line. The room felt cold. She got up and put on her purple *ruana.*

On her way to the dining room, Kay saw the French girl hanging around the desk talking to Schneider as usual.

"Are you all right now?" he called out.

Kay went over to them. The girl was wearing widely cut, sailor-style jeans that hung off bony hips. Her thin, triangular face was curtained on both sides by smooth black hair and her mouth, outlined in pale, almost white lipstick, had a chapped look.

"I'm Nadine Hubert," she said in English. "I see you look often for your mail—like me."

"Always. Are you going in to dinner?"

"No. I'm not so hungry yet. But why don't you come to my room for coffee after?"

Not so hungry yet, Kay thought. This girl had better watch it. She had a gaunt look, an edgy brightness that spelled out coke as obviously as a neon sign. It was like asking to be arrested or killed. She was appealing, though, Kay thought, but in an unreal way, like one of those wistfully sentimental paintings of clowns in costumes too big for them.

After dinner, Kay found she really wanted to go up to Nadine's room. Success in the smuggling business meant it was best to keep to yourself, to make no imprint that might trip you up later, but after three weeks alone in Bogotá, Kay felt like a ghost. She wanted to talk to someone.

Anyway, she told herself, it might be useful to check out Nadine's Bogotá scene, find out what she knew about Señor Schneider . . . like did he expect a bribe.

Nadine's room was oddly impersonal, nothing lying around, as though she was only staying overnight and had not bothered to unpack. She offered Kay the only chair. "I'll sit on the bed," she said, "it's a lot like a bench anyway. You can't find a thinner mattress anywhere in the world, except maybe in a South American jail." Her eyes were challenging and she seemed beyond caring that she was being indiscreet.

"You've been in jail?" Kay asked.

"Just once, in Brazil. My boyfriend got into trouble with a local man over some business and ended up losing all of his money, but they let us out after two days."

"That's an experience I've missed," Kay said and smiled, "so far."

Nadine eased up. "Well," she laughed, "make sure you keep it like that." Her English was surprisingly good, the pronunciation British with just the trace of a French accent.

"I have instant coffee if that's what you *really* want, but I also have something better . . ."

From a drawer, Nadine produced a silver mirror with an onyx handle, and expertly laid out the coke with a series of rapid chops and swirls of a razor.

The stuff had a burn, and Kay did only half a line and then passed the mirror back. "Thank you."

"I'm sorry," Nadine said, "this is not the best. I bought it in a disco last night, good price but no quality. You never get the best buying a gram, but still, it's better than street coke in Paris, or even in L.A., no?"

Kay thought of the bottle of Ricardo's coke in her purse, but she didn't want to have to answer any questions about it.

"I've been waiting to hear from my boyfriend for days now and I'm beginning to run out of money," Nadine said, making little sniffing noises. "He is back home in France. I know it wouldn't take this long unless he is with someone else now or something. It's the waiting that gets me down, you know? The waiting and not knowing."

Kay said, "I know. You're waiting for the man, the money, and the run. Right?"

Nadine looked at Kay.

"Sure," Kay went on. "I understand. I worked with a guy like that once, waiting for him, being dependent on his judgment and knowing how fucked up he was most of the time." She shook her head. "I dropped him after one time. If I take the fall, I want to do it myself. What's in it for you, Nadine?"

"I don't know anymore really," Nadine said flatly. She bent her head, holding the plastic straw to her nostril for the last line, laid out clean and cold in the mirror. Her hair, slipping down across one cheek, hid her face from Kay.

"I was not a good student," she said, putting the mirror down on the faded blue carpet. "I failed my baccalaureate, and I never wanted to study those things anyway. I like to sail, you know? I used to hang around the yachts in St. Tropez. Everybody got to know me and I used to hitch rides—that's how I learned. And then, when I crewed on a yacht going to Greece, I met Daniel. We decided we wanted to buy our own boat, sail around the world, maybe do chartering later on, for a business. So he knew some people, 'connections,' and it seemed like a good way to make the money for the boat. But now . . ." She trailed off, then picked up again.

"Daniel always says not to worry if I get caught. He says he'll get me lawyers, get me off, but sometimes, like now, I really wonder if he would be there for me. I know someone else in town who would possibly fix me up with a run, Rio to Paris. He only pays eighteen hundred dollars, but it's a body carry and he only puts a pound on you. But he never has the money to pay right away, and he won't pay in coke, so you have to wait for him to turn it and then you have to keep going to him for the money. Finally you get it, but you usually have to fuck him a few times before he'll give you what he owes you. I wish I could get home some other way, but I may be stuck with no money, so I don't know, maybe I'll have to do it."

Nadine made Kay wonder. Would her own fate be better than Nadine's lost dreams of romance, Nadine with her pale, chewed lips and her empty waiting room of a hotel room? Kay had heard of other girls like her, mules, members of an international underground sorority. Lured by private visions of glamour, or money, they found themselves trapped instead in a kind of twilight life. They were the pack animals of the outlaw subculture, drifting around the world from one city to another, counting relief in the number of lines they could snort a day.

Nadine told her about one time, when she had contracted to body-carry, and the coke was packaged in a long length of plastic wrapping rubber-banded off like a string of beads. The beads were shoved into her rectum and vagina, forced to capacity, and then cut at the last link. "It was"—Nadine paused, looking for the right word—"obscene," she finally said, avoiding Kay's eyes. "And the rest of the links, those left over," she went on, "go to stuff the next mule." She glanced up at Kay now and was silent for a moment.

"Of course, if the plastic breaks inside of you," she continued, "you're dead." As she talked, Nadine's hands fiddled with the plastic straw. "But you don't think about that so much because of the pain and trying to look normal. . . . It gets so bad that you almost wish—" She shrugged and said, "Oh well. They wanted me to do it again, but I told them, no. Only fat pigs make any money on a sausage run anyway. The more links you stuff, the more money at the other end, if you get there. And I am petite Nadine."

Nadine was messed up, but Kay could see she wasn't dumb. She told Kay all the ways she had smuggled coke: in Kotex, in padded bras, in radio batteries, sewn into clothes and concealed in high-heeled shoes, in aerosol cans of hairspray, in stuffed lizard souvenirs with their little parasols, so ridiculous that no one could suspect. She was using techniques that would not become familiar to customs until the mid-1970s.

And she knew her way around the routes.

All airport customs were tough on flights coming from South America, but some she dreaded more than others. Berlin was more difficult than Frankfurt, and Paris was tougher than London. In Nadine's opinion, the best way into Europe was via Lisbon or the African coast, with a flight originating in Rio, when one could be found.

As far as the United States went, she said, Miami and Los Angeles were to be avoided, San Francisco and New Orleans were still the least sophisticated, although the airports were all beginning to realize that drug traffic was becoming a growing problem. Mexico City was totally out. They did stop-and-search on virtually anyone who was young, long-haired, or stood out in any way. Nadine had heard they had a lucrative extortion business going for themselves, taking bribes from the worried friends and family of the young Americans they caught.

"Fine," Kay said, "so you know the routes and you have the perfect concealment. But what about the 'x factor'?"

Kay had thought a lot about this thing she called the x factor: it was the danger of the unexpected, the random element loose in the world, and it gave her a hollow feeling in her stomach.

It could be anything, she explained to Nadine: a terrorist bomb scare that suddenly causes all the luggage to be pulled apart, a thunderstorm or an airline strike that forces a change of destination, a customs clerk new on the job and trying to prove his worth.

"You can plan all you want to," Kay said, "but you always have to figure in the x factor, and in the end, that's the real measure of how good you are."

"I know what you mean," Nadine said, "but for me, I don't care about that. To me, the hard thing is the loneliness—you can never show your real self to anyone." She tilted her head to one side and squinted at Kay, half-mocking. "For instance, to be safe, I should never have even started this conversation with you. Right?"

"What can I say?" Kay grinned. "Here we are."

Nadine laughed and shrugged. In the bathroom she lifted the top off the toilet tank. "I do not like this Colombian custom of warm beer," she said, taking two dripping bottles of Costena from the water, "so I make my own fridge. And—*voilà*." She presented a bottle to Kay, holding it elaborately against her arm like a fine champagne.

The next day, Kay looked around for Nadine but she didn't see her. A few evenings later, when she was going upstairs after dinner, Schneider called to her from his spot behind the desk.

"Your friend," he said, raising pale eyebrows, "she is gone. After a phone call. Very quickly. She paid her bill but left behind her suitcase. 'Hold it for me,' she said to me, but she never came back for it." He shrugged—disappearances were hardly uncommon in Bogotá. Then, his face looming closer across the desk, he said, "Between us, I'm not surprised. I don't usually like that type in my hotel. By the way, you have a message.''

''I know what you mean, Señor Schneider,'' Kay said. She reached out for the envelope in her box, giving him her sunniest California smile. The envelope was from Ricardo: ''I'll be at the Mont Blanc Coffee Shop downtown tomorrow at two. The car is on Calle Ninety-three. Here are the keys. Drive carefully and don't get hurt, because I have many plans for us.'' The handwriting was tall and angular. Kay noticed that some of the letters at the ends of words stopped short with a bitten back sort of look.

When she stepped into her room, there was something subtly wrong. She looked around, opened drawers, checked the positions of things. Nothing had been disturbed, but her uneasiness wouldn't go away. Nadine's disappearance was a shadow, a question to which Kay knew, even then, there wasn't ever going to be an answer. She went to the door and slid the bolt into place, perfectly aware that the flimsy lock was no barrier against anyone who wanted in.

There was a chair in the corner with a padded back and seat. Kay knelt in front of it and, with a small metal nail file, began slowly and carefully to rip open a seam in the seat, one stitch at a time. When the upholstery gaped, she reached in and removed a green canvas tool kit and a plastic bag of cocaine, leaving behind another plastic bag containing her papers, passport, and a roll of American currency.

She laid out her tools on the floor with the care of a surgeon: C-clamps, needle-nose pliers, glass rolling pin, pinking shears, various sizes of scissors, matte knife, sable brushes, cans of casein glue, tubes of paint, plastic and balsa-wood sheets.

There wasn't much left to be done on the brown Samsonite suitcase. The lining had been carefully removed and most of the coke was already in place on the bottom. She turned on the TV. ''I Love Lucy'' dubbed in Spanish had become her daily Spanish lesson. She began working. Like baking, she thought, pouring some of the coke onto a plastic sheet, rolling and pressing it out, thin and even, just like pie dough.

On the small, flickering black-and-white set, Lucy was running around, eyes popping. ''¿Dónde están los niños?'' she cried hysterically. ''¿Dónde están los niños?'' Kay repeated.

"Ricky, yo no tengo la culpa." Lucy was hanging her curly head.

"Ricky, yo no tengo la culpa." Kay heat-sealed the flat package of cocaine with a Seal-A-Meal tool that made her think of putting up tomatoes in her grandmother's kitchen, something she hadn't done in ten years. Her mind was filled with memories.

To Kay, her grandmother had always been the unchanging rock around which history flowed. A piece of history herself, Grandma had arrived in the San Joaquin valley in 1934 with her husband and children, one family among the hundreds of "Okie" refugees fleeing the dry winds of the Dust Bowl.

She and Grandpa had settled into the clapboard house in Bakersfield, with the orchard and the vegetable garden that ran down to the tracks. There Kay and her cousin Ray would go and stand breathlessly among the weeds waiting for the train to roar by.

Kay liked looking at the framed photo of the Oklahoma farmhouse that hung on Grandma's wall beside the pictures of Grandpa with the big fish, Kay's mother on her honeymoon vamping like Lana Turner, and Grandma herself at a picnic, her round face shaded by a checked poke bonnet.

She hadn't realized until she went to school that her grandmother was special, an American myth like Norman Rockwell, only more true—taking care of all her grandbabies, praising the Lord, sewing blazingly beautiful quilts, keeping her husband's fiddle under the bed. And she didn't realize either, until she went to school, that "Okie" was a bad word, a word that meant you were dirt-poor and low, almost as low as a Mexican.

Kay hated the snobby, rich kids at the high school. She washed and curled her hair every night and took care to come to school looking extra clean, her blouse meticulously ironed. She was not any dumb trash, she would say fiercely to her mirror self, and she was going to get out of the Valley someday and show them. She would do something and be famous or rich herself.

She knew Okies were supposed to hate Mexicans, especially the *braceros* who came to town to compete for every job, for every space in the migrant labor camp. But she didn't hate the Mexicans at all; they fascinated her.

She wondered about the strange people who lived close enough to be driven to work in the Valley in big buses yet could not speak a word of English. She loved their hats and bright scarves and the way they would stick their heads out of the bus windows and yell in Spanish to her, passing her as she walked down the road to Uncle Avril's house.

She took books out of the library to read about Mexico, and even that last day home before leaving for Colombia, when she had driven to Bakersfield to say good-bye, Grandma had said, "So you're goin' away to the south. Well, isn't that fine, Kayleen, honey. You were always dreamin' about faraway places."

And Kay had looked down at the secret nick she had made in the leg of the kitchen table when she was six, and knew that nowhere in the world would there ever be more love and more safety. She felt full of bittersweet remorse that she couldn't tell her grandmother what she was about to do "down south."

Kay pressed the last package into the suitcase bottom, fitted a thin balsa-wood board on top, repainted bottom and sides with glue, and then, meticulously avoiding the slightest telltale drip, bubble, or wrinkle, replaced the lining. Next, she put C-clamps around the sides to hold the lining in place while it dried, cushioning each clamp with a piece of foam and a handkerchief so the mark wouldn't show.

It was late by the time she finished. Shoving the suitcase under the bed, she considered the room, the gaping chair, the tools on the floor, the merciless ceiling light glaring down. On the TV, two elderly men in tuxedos were singing a sentimental ballad: "¿Dónde estás, mi dulce encanto? ¿Dónde estás que no te veo?"

Her shoulders ached, and she wanted nothing more than to sleep, but she began the hour-long process of cleanup anyway. To leave things out, even overnight, was just asking for trouble. And after another line of coke, it was suddenly not so bad. Energy sparkled through her veins, and her head felt as clear and clean as the Andean air outside. Magic.

In the morning Kay checked the flights. For once, Braniff

was on time. Getting past Schneider with the suitcase would be a problem, but she was prepared for him.

"Don't you worry, Señor Schneider," she said, laughing. "I'm not Nadine. I'll be back—I won't leave you with my suitcase and then disappear." He was looking at her coolly. "I'm just loaning some clothes to a friend. She's going to the coast and wants to look good. You know how it is." "No," Schneider said, finally smiling, "how is it?"

"Here." She handed him an envelope. "I just wanted to say thank you for taking such good care of me, watching over my mail and keeping an eye out for me on my first time in Bogotá. I really appreciate it. Well, see you later." She walked away, carrying the suitcase and leaving him holding the envelope filled with one hundred dollars in American cash.

Ricardo had left his blue VW around the corner as they had agreed. It looked like a car in a children's book, with a smiling bumper and round headlight eyes. She put the suitcase in the front seat beside her and drove the ten miles to El Dorado airport.

It was an infamous airport. Parts of wrecked airplanes that had exploded, flaming in the tall weeds, were left to rust where they had landed, grisly reminders of El Dorado's black-star status as one of the most dangerous landing strips in the world. Through the windshield Kay looked up into a sky of piled clouds, thinking of Maggie's plane, a tiny gnat descending through the lethal air currents of the Andes. Her stomach tensed. Kay was always more nervous about Maggie's safety than her own.

Extremely close friends, even after their college days, Kay and Maggie had been smuggling partners before, mainly grass from Mexico, with Kay scouting the source and Maggie dealing. When Kay returned from that first nightmarish trip to Bogotá with Joel, they decided to go into the import of Andean Magic themselves. They had already made one run, a suitcase pass to Maggie in Puerto Rico.

In Bogotá, it's best never to leave anything in a car, locked or not, so Kay took the suitcase with her into the weathered, peeling terminal. Inside, the air was thick with dust. Armed soldiers patrolled the hall. Barricades and signs were everywhere. NO ENTRAR. MILITARES SOLAMENTE. It was like a war zone. A few months ago, on that first trip, she had thought something terrible had happened, a bomb scare, an assassination, a battle.

She was just beginning to understand now that in Colombia political unrest had become a part of the fabric of life. Although no Colombian president had ever been assassinated, the country had suffered one hundred fifty revolutions in the past thirty years.

There was no announcement that the plane had landed, only the sudden rush of the porters—desperate, bony men and ragged boys fighting for the best position outside the closed gates. They waited, staring hungrily through the iron bars at the passengers going through the slow ritual of showing their papers, passports, and visas.

Finally, two soldiers opened the gates. There were a few tourists sprinkled among the stream of Colombians now pushing each other to claim their luggage and head for customs, dragging home their precious cargos of American toasters and TV sets. One of the tourists was a stocky midwestern society matron. Her dyed brown hair was teased into a varnished helmet, her feet were sensible in two-hundred-dollar Ferragamo shoes, and her bosom was expensively encased in an I. Magnin silk blouse with a bow. For a split second, Kay didn't recognize her.

Maggie had aged herself twenty years and could easily have passed in any exclusive country club, from Grosse Point to Palm Springs. No Colombian customs inspector in his right mind would dream of questioning her.

In an instant, the porters were upon her, pulling at her sleeves, a mass of frantic hands and pleading voices, *"Señora, aquí, aquí. Tiquetes por favor."* Two of the boys, one around eight, the other five, were jumping up and down in front of her. They were scrawny and chicken-breasted, and the older one was missing two fingers. Maggie gave her tickets to them.

"What's your name?" she asked the smaller one.

He told her, "Condorlito [little condor]."

"I'm so glad you're here. How was your flight?" Kay asked Maggie, firmly planting kisses on both her cheeks. But there was no conversation till they got to the car. Talking in airports was a sloppy thing for a smuggler to do. It left you open to chance conversations with strangers, and conversations led to questions and questions to lies. Chance, Kay knew, had a way of breeding disaster. It was the quirky x factor again, the unforeseeable accident that could destroy even the most perfect plan. You could never avoid it entirely, but you could keep a low profile.

"Where'd you get this cartoon car?" Maggie asked from the back seat where she sat jammed between her suitcase and its identical twin, the one Kay had spent the night "loading." "A customized VW?"

"I borrowed it from a guy I know. VWs are a big deal for the young guys down here," she said lightly.

"So the car goes with the Led Zeppelin and the twenty-six, thirty-two jeans?"

Kay smiled. "Hey, Maggie, I'm just glad you're back there where I can't see you. You look so much like your mother it scares me. Are you sure you're not your mother?"

"No, I'm not sure, and it scares me too. What's our story?"

"Your connecting flight to Santa Maria is still on time, right? In three hours?"

"Uh-huh," Maggie affirmed.

Kay went on, "I got the car so we could drive around, see some of Bogotá, and then back to the airport. So let's get the pass over with now." She patted the suitcase beside her. "Here's your boy."

"I don't know, Kay," Maggie was grunting as she wrestled with the suitcases, banging her elbows and head in the small car, "this is an amusing little pass and I like its witty style, but hotel rooms are easier." She opened both suitcases and transferred her clothes into the one loaded for the "carry." The case she had brought down with her was now empty except for the things Kay had requested on the phone. It would go back with Kay to the hotel to be loaded for the next trip.

"How does my work look?" Kay asked, glancing at Maggie in the rearview mirror.

"Finally, a master's degree in fine arts put to good use. No, really, it's perfect, not a lumpy seam, not a drop of glue anywhere."

Traffic was heavy and Maggie fell silent looking out the window. A patchwork of discarded junk lined the road, crude shacks pulled together out of rusty car doors, beaten fenders, bits of burlap, and parts of packing crates. Indians leading heavily burdened horses fought for space with donkey carts, cars, and buses. A convoy of twenty brand-new Ford trucks, transports, their backs loaded with military men in green uniforms, tried to move through it all, horns blasting.

"What's going down with the military?" Maggie said. "Are things heating up here?"

"Things are always hot here," Kay said. "There have been a lot of student strikes lately. Last March, President Lleras Restrepo closed all the schools and warned the students to behave themselves or he would close the universities indefinitely."

"Nixon would probably like to close the schools indefinitely, too, if he thought he could get away with it," Maggie said.

Ricardo was waiting for them at the Café Mont Blanc. He was drinking one of those endless demitasse cups of *tinto* ("ink"), coffee essence that the Colombians are never without. He got up and bowed over Maggie's hand.

The Mont Blanc restaurants were a chain of medium-priced coffee shops in Bogotá. This one was the nicest, with a chaletlike flavor and black-and-white tile floors that were scrubbed by hand every day. There were lace curtains on the windows and doilies on the tables. Customers were served by an Indian-looking woman in a white uniform and a starched white cap.

"Please excuse us," Kay said to Ricardo.

She took Maggie down the long hall to the *damas*, with its tiny open window near the ceiling and its damp floors. They locked themselves in. Maggie took off her blouse, unhooked the front fasteners of the long-line Maidenform, and gave Kay the ten thousand dollars she had carried in the bra's secret muslin stash pockets.

Their business agreement was simple. Kay was the supplier and Maggie the runner and source man to the dealers back home. Maggie dealt only in quantity and quality, and she was expensive, one thousand dollars an ounce, because her cocaine was guaranteed one hundred percent pure and free of the synthetic additives dealers often used to stretch their product. For each run, Maggie received a flat three thousand dollars. Any money she invested or lent to Kay for the procuring of the cocaine was returned to Maggie in product, which was then hers to sell outright.

"I have something nice here for you," Kay said, taking a vial out of her purse.

Maggie finished buttoning her blouse and took a hit.

She whistled. "More than nice," she said. "Anything to do with that Latino baby movie star out there?"

"Don't worry about it, Mags. He's just part of the deal."

"Yeah," Maggie said, rolling her eyes, "I noticed."

A few months after Kay and Maggie met, the landlord of Maggie's clapboard rooming house on Yucca Street asked her to leave, telling Maggie she needed the room for the crop of orchids she intended to raise there. "I don't think she likes 'me or my kind,'" Maggie had said.

Kay had immediately invited her to move in with her. For the next year they lived in the fifty-foot barn Kay had rented and converted into a studio, and which she kept filled with a kaleidoscopic circle of friends, gigantic paintings, parachute silk ceilings, papier-mâché sculptures, and a wood, shrub, and earth environment she had created at one end for her numerous stray cats.

Maggie and Kay were an odd pair as they themselves were the first to admit. Maggie's conservative family was proud of their Scotch-Irish heritage and wore their own clan tartans for special occasions. Her grandfather had started the toy company which was later to turn the family name into a household word and Maggie's playroom into a den of enormous stuffed animals presided over by a British nanny.

She was driven to grade school by a chauffeur, but she had him stop blocks away rather than be seen arriving in a limousine. One morning when she was fourteen, the family awoke to the shock of finding a shark in the Olympic-sized swimming pool of their estate. She denied having anything to do with it, but her mother said that Maggie was "just trying to make some kind of an idiotic rebellious statement."

She had grown up with the pool and was a superb swimmer as well as a professional-quality tennis player, with a roomful of trophies. Kay was secretly impressed.

Maggie and Kay presented powerfully exotic and magnetic extremes to one another, in which strange undercurrents of guilt and anger were at play as well as a profound mutual understanding and sympathy. Although they each had different male lovers in the lighthearted sixties, when sex was almost a mandatory part of friendship, they remained bonded in an intense relationship that, for a time, even involved them in their own exploration of physical love with each other.

But Kay, always elusive, remained so, and in the end they moved into separate apartments, with Kay working in the window-dressing department of a store while Maggie became the darkroom assistant for a well-known photographer.

The three of them drove around the city for Maggie's sight-seeing tour. Kay was uneasy, caught between Ricardo, who was talking too much and too brightly, and Maggie, who was too reserved behind the façade of her disguise. By the time they were on the road back to the airport they had all fallen into a tired silence.

At the terminal, Ricardo waited in the car while Kay went and stood at the gate with Maggie. "Gook luck, puss," Kay said. Maggie hugged her and walked away. Without turning around, she raised two fingers over her head in the peace sign.

Kay got back into the VW. She and Ricardo drove to the Hilton for a drink and ended up in a room on the nineteenth floor.

Before they went upstairs, Ricardo stopped in at the lobby florist and bought her a dozen roses. Kay was finding out young Colombian men were extravagantly romantic, verbal, and gallant. In bed, Ricardo would cry out, *"Mi tesoro, mi preciosa, mi vida."* He called her his sun and moon, gazing at her with yearning eyes. He never appeared without a present—candy, flowers, an expensive leather purse, a hand-embroidered lace blouse.

Kay knew he liked to show her off to his friends. He took her to the discos and the cafés where the young rich guys sat and scanned the personals in *El Espacio:* "Estrella, I am pleased with the sight of you and I long to make you happy. Will you let me know? Philosopher."

She knew she made him look good, an older mistress, but better than that, an American one. The young men were eager for anything American, even though they were usually a couple of years behind the latest American trends. While Ricardo could talk for hours about international soccer teams, Colombian bicycle races, and Italian fashions, what really grabbed

him was hearing about American cars, about *Easy Rider* and
Jimi Hendrix. He wanted to know all about Kay's L.A. life, yet
at her slightest personal probe, he would twist expertly aside.
His family? Import-export, he said. A family business.

They had been together for about a month when, one
afternoon, everything suddenly changed. Kay was in her room
working on the Samsonite Maggie had left her for the next trip,
when she heard footsteps in the hallway outside. They stopped
at her door and she sat motionless, a pair of pinking shears in
her hand.

There was a knock, then Ricardo's voice, muffled, as though
he had his mouth to the door. *Bonita,* are you there?'' Silently,
Kay slid the bolt, and Ricardo stepped in.

He started talking immediately. ''Please, Kay, I am in
trouble. I need to ask you a big favor.'' His eyes flicked from
the half-finished suitcase and the tools on the floor to the
disemboweled chair in the corner.

Kay went and stood in front of it. ''What are you doing
here?'' she said, coldly furious. ''You know you can't come
here. Now there'll be questions. The man at the desk—''

''I know,'' he interrupted, ''I'm so sorry, but I had to see
you. I'm short a kilo, you see. That could be very bad for me,
very serious, you understand.'' He was looking at her intensely, trying to hold her eyes. ''So I am asking you, can I
have the kilo back? I will make it good to you, you have my
word.'' He raked his hands anxiously through his hair, then
jammed them into his pockets.

She picked up the sealed plastic bag of coke from the floor,
wrapped it in newspaper and a brown paper bag, and handed it
to him.

He didn't kiss her but stood at the door. ''Did you do that to
the chair yourself?''

''Yes,'' she said, wondering at his speculative glance.

''Where did you learn?''

''I taught myself. I worked for a decorator once. Why are
you so interested in my chair?''

He shook his head and smiled. ''Nothing. *Gracias, bonita
mía, para todo, muchas gracias.*'' He closed the door.

After he had left she paced around the room unable to settle
down, prowling from dresser to chair to dresser in her

nervousness. His sudden demand had thrown her off course. She was short a kilo now. She was going to have to cancel the run. She hated feeling simultaneously angry at Ricardo and concerned about him. There was nothing to do but wait till the time was right to phone Maggie, wait for the next kilo, wait for Maggie to set up things again at her end.

It seemed to Kay that half the smuggling business was waiting and coping with your nerves while you waited. You waited for the deal to go down, sometimes for days. You waited for hours in hotel rooms for the phone to ring with necessary information. You waited on customs lines trying to be cool with coke on your body or loaded in suitcases.

Kay sighed and went to the closet to get a small watercolor of the Andes she was working on. In the cloudy sky over the mountains she placed a tiny airplane.

Chapter
Three

Few efforts have been made to deal with the gamines. Well-meaning citizens offering [them] food soon learn that they are "suckers." Casual relationships with gamines generally end in exploitation or mutual loss of trust. The primary relationship with the adult world has been broken, leaving a wound that kindness and trust threaten more gravely than hostility.

For this reason, attempts by social service agencies to work with [them] in traditional forms of rehabilitation have been marked by failure. . . . Gamines so provoke and threaten Colombian institutional workers that they elicit continually those same authoritarian and rigid responses that convince the children, again and again, of the basic meanness of adults.

—Cynthia Monahon,
Special to *The Christian Science Monitor*,
August 15, 1974

KAY HAD SPENT a bad morning downtown looking for casein glue. The clerks in the old-fashioned wooden-walled *tiendas* shook their heads politely. *"No tenemos eso,"* they said, as though she had asked for a diamond. Realizing she was late, she had begun to walk rapidly along Carrera 7, past the dark eighteenth-century façade of the Iglesia de las Nieves, its steps crowded with beggars and cripples, past the loitering young hoods who made kissing sounds and called out *"muchacha pendeja* [fuck-girl], *muchacha pendeja,"* as she walked toward the Parque de Independencia.

The shoulders of the Andes were half hidden in a rainy mist, and the giant blooms of the rhododendrons glowed like purple lamps. Black smoke rose from a cooking cart where an ancient woman sold skewered corn cobs, bits of beef and pork, and the light blue eggs of the Araucana chicken. Behind her, in the park, a knot of five or six street *gamines* were shouting. As Kay approached, she saw that a fight had broken out.

Two small, haggard boys faced each other, crouched and tense. Both had wrapped their left arms in jackets for protection; knife blades flashed in their right hands. They began to circle slowly, each of them looking for an opening. One of them wore a filthy baseball cap with a leaping orange tiger on the front; PUT A TIGER IN YOUR TANK was written on the back. Kay looked around for someone to help stop the fight, but the bystanders were all shouting encouragement.

Suddenly, the boy in the Esso cap cried out in pain as the other's knife plunged deep into his side under his right arm. He slumped to the ground, blood oozing through his ragged shirt. The other boy backed off, but the wounded boy kept trying to stagger up, moaning and cursing, wild to go on.

Before Kay could move forward, two of his friends had quickly dumped him—covered with blood and screaming obscenities—into a battered wooden cart. Seconds later, they were running away, wheeling him down the street. Only then did Kay realize that the two friends were not boys, but young girls, no more than nine or ten. It was all over very fast.

The question of the *gamines*, the countless homeless children roaming the streets, had begun to haunt Kay. They were everywhere. She kept candy and change in her purse for them, but could get no answers to her inquiries about them. To most Bogotanos, *gamines* were simply a fact of life, as inevitable as stray dogs. There was nothing one could do, there were just too many of them.

They were even regarded with a certain tolerant fondness. Walking past a tour group, Kay had overheard the petite and smiling Colombian tour guide refer to the fountain in front of the Tequendama Hotel as "the *gamines'* swimming pool."

But these children were also considered a dangerous nuisance. Car windows were kept rolled up even on the hottest days to avoid having a wristwatch or necklace torn off at a stop signal. On the street, just a moment's inattention could mean a snatched purse. Valuable jewelry was left at home.

Kay thought of her sister's kids in Bakersfield, California, waiting for the school bus, watching "Gilligan's Island" on TV, and eating Reese's peanut butter cups. They were the same age as these desperate kids, who had just scattered into the park. The image of the bloodied *gamine* was still in her mind as she passed the inevitable epauleted young doorman in his slightly shabby uniform, on her way into El Fuego Restaurant.

El Fuego was one flight up, a place where women were seldom seen. The big Avianca office building was nearby, and men met each other here when they had business downtown; the emerald trade, the coke trade, the government, the airlines—all were interrelated.

The stairwell was cold, and Kay was conscious of the loud echo of her heels on the polished wooden steps. The host waited, beaming, at the top. He ushered her ceremoniously into the small reception area. *"Espere un momento, señorita,"* he said, bowing, and disappeared through a curtain.

Kay stood in the vestibule looking at a strange display of breads and fruits decoratively arranged around a large piece of cooked steak. On a table opposite was a tall vase with a flamboyant spray of spidery, striped orchid blossoms. The murmur of conversation and the clink of silverware came from the other side of the curtains.

"Hola, Kay," said Ricardo, coming through them. He looked different, nervous and formal in a gray suit with side vents and an Italian silk tie.

"I have a surprise for you," he said quickly. "We will not be having lunch alone. I have brought you to meet my father. He is in the dining room, waiting for us."

"How nice," she said, "but I want to go to the *damas* first."

Actually, she was upset. She hated being caught off guard. Kay was like a creature that changes color for camouflage. To feel effective she needed to feel secure in the image she was projecting, she needed to know that her clothing and makeup were perfect for the situation. The camel-colored wool pantsuit and white cashmere sweater she had on were not quite right. It was a classic look, but she knew that men in South America frowned on women in pants.

In the cramped, cold little room she tried to build her confidence, combing her hair and applying fresh makeup. She undid the long chiffon scarf she wore wrapped around her neck and draped it loosely to show off her slim throat and gold jewelry. Better, she thought, opening the door. She was about to meet, she was sure, a very major source of the best cocaine that could be had in Colombia.

In the dining room it could have been any time of day. The curtains were drawn and candles burned in heavy, carved sconces on the tables. The room was half-empty, and in a corner, well away from the other tables, was a group of five men.

They all stood up when Kay arrived, their eyes openly appraising, but Ricardo only introduced her to one of them. "May I present," he said, stiffly ceremonial, "my father, Señor Roberto Alvarez, Señorita Kay Wolff."

Roberto Alvarez was a surprise to Kay. He was about five foot eight and he looked, she thought, like a museum curator at a meeting of the board, all starched white cuffs and impeccable British tailoring. His dark, thinning hair was combed straight back from a high, tranquil forehead, and his eyes were a very light gray. Just beside the left one was a small, dark mole.

He pulled out one of the cowhide chairs for Kay, and as he motioned the men to sit, she caught a faint trace of musky cologne.

"So," he said, folding manicured hands on the table in front of him. The men came to attention in their chairs, except for a thin-nosed blond in his late twenties who lolled back and examined Kay from under half-closed lids.

"You are the woman with whom my son has been doing business." His glance shifted briefly to Ricardo, who was looking down at his silverware, and then back to Kay again.

Kay said, "Yes," and smiled politely. He waited for a fraction of a second, but she just smiled, giving away nothing more. He snapped his fingers for the waiter.

Roberto waved aside the menus the waiter proffered and ordered for the whole group as though they were children: *carne bien asada* (well-done meat) and a bottle of Vino Rojas de Chile.

"Now," he said, "let me see." He drew Kay's hands together in his and squeezed them delicately. "I like your hands." He turned them over, palm side up. "They're small and pretty. I may have a job for them." With a pat, he laid her hands back on the table and looked around at his men. They leaned forward, relaxed now, as if slipped from a leash. Ricardo alone sipped his wine with careful indifference.

Under the table Kay clenched and unclenched her left hand as they began to grill her, closing ranks in a succession of rapid-fire questions.

They took turns: Can you stitch-sew? Have you ever worked in leather? What kind of glues have you used? Have you ever reupholstered a car? What suitcases have you worked with? Do you have any tools?

Roberto sat back and smoked a cigarette, listening and watching.

Her answers were cool and precise. Hair-trigger alert, she felt the solidity of her back against the chair, her feet on the floor. She had entered a state of calm euphoria, a heightened reality that comes only in moments of true challenge. It was a state she had discovered young, taking on a dare, and had never stopped seeking since.

Kay felt sure she had seen one of the men before but couldn't remember where. He was stocky, with a round head, very short neck, and a jowly face. There was something familiar about him and the humorous, insinuating way he looked at her. His English was good and he translated for the others when necessary.

Roberto held up his hand. The meal was arriving; the beef, like that displayed in the vestibule, was two inches thick and served on a wooden cutting board with a slot for a sharp knife at one end and a trough to catch the juices at the other. It came with *chimichurri,* a spicy green sauce.

"Well," Roberto said, cutting a piece off his steak and fastidiously inspecting it on his fork, "you seem to know a few things. Let me be honest with you." He popped the piece of meat into his mouth and chewed silently, his eyes closed. When he opened them again, he was looking directly at Kay.

"At first, when Ricardo told me he was doing business with you, I was not pleased. We are strictly a family"—he paused, looking for the right English word—"enterprise. You understand? We do not admit outsiders. However, now that I have met you myself, I can no longer blame Ricardo." He smiled and the men chuckled dutifully.

"We are in the middle of a big job and we have just lost one of our men," he went on. "We need someone who knows fabrication, someone who can learn quickly. I think, since you are so close to my son, we can call you a friend of the family and make an exception to our rule.''

Subject closed. He went on to ask Kay about her painting, which Ricardo had obviously mentioned to him. He had many fine antiques, Roberto said, and a rare coin collection, including coins made from revolutionary cartridges.

Kay was having trouble concentrating on what he was saying. Obviously, he was assuming that some sort of a deal had just been made, but what was it? What were the terms? What had she agreed to? What had happened to the man who was "lost"?

The jowly man named Carlos was lifting a glass to her in a tiny toast. Suddenly she remembered him from the gallery opening. She looked across the table, trying to catch Ricardo's eye, but his face was closed, a stranger. She felt like a surfer, just beginning to see coming toward her the magnitude and force of the wave she had been waiting to ride for a long, long time.

The lunch was over abruptly. Roberto put his napkin on the table and got up. Immediately, the men pushed back their chairs and stood, too. *"Muy buenas tardes, Señorita Wolff,"* he said formally. In Spanish he told Ricardo to escort *la señorita* home and left, the men filing out behind him. There was no bill.

"I don't know about you," Kay said to Ricardo after they had all left, "but I want a drink after that."

Ricardo was in a black mood. "Bring us two double Scotches, pronto," he snapped at the waiter.

The man lowered his eyes. *"Sí, Señor Alvarez. A sus órdenes."* Kay was thinking she would slip him a big tip.

"What's the problem, Rick?" she said, using the Americanization of his name she knew he liked.

"I'm sorry, *bonita.*" He frowned, looking for the right words. "My father is difficult for me. He shows me no respect. For him I am still a child, the oldest son."

The waiter came with their drinks. After he left, Ricardo said, "And now that I see you with him it worries me. I am not so sure I have done the right thing." He poured a double shot over the ice in his glass and knocked back half of it.

"I know this is what you said you were looking for in

Bogotá, but you don't really understand our ways and that makes me afraid. My father is not a very bending man, you understand? If anything goes wrong you will have to leave Bogotá immediately."

"I have no plans for anything going wrong," Kay said.

"Please, *bonita*, listen to me. You are an American woman and you are used to different ways. Women have never had a place in our business. With you, my father has made an exception—for his own reasons. You have to be very careful around him and around my Uncle Carlos. Don't speak your mind without talking to me first."

"Of course." She took his hand. "You're my guide, so don't worry. You'll be surprised how well I'll fit in."

She felt high, full of adrenaline. "Do you think your father would allow me to continue the runs with Maggie?"

"I think for now that will be okay, but you have to understand you're working for the family now. Your first responsibility is to the work he will have for you. You'll be paid well, and in return he will expect complete loyalty and secrecy. The family always comes first. Don't take that lightly."

The candles were dripping low now, and Ricardo took a small piece of the hot wax and began rolling it absently, nervously, between his thumb and forefinger.

"People have lost their lives because they made mistakes in these areas or were not loyal. When you work for the family, you work only for the family. Someone else here in Bogotá might offer you work too. If that happens, you turn it down—act as if you don't really understand what they're talking about. How you say no is as important as saying no.

"This is like a small town in respect to the business, and there has been trouble here over the years with fabricators . . . some like to move around. But that is a very dangerous thing to do." He took the little ball of wax and started flattening it on the table, smoothing it like a penny. When he looked up at Kay there was nothing boyish about him at all. "I hope you don't mind my giving you this advice?"

"Go on," she said.

"If you become a good fabricator, my father will guard you like a jealous husband. So don't be tempted by more money with someone else. It will bring big trouble. For the most part, you will be thought of as my woman, and that will help you, but there are limits to that. So remember to be careful what you say and do or we will both have a problem."

"Now, my Uncle Carlos . . ." he began. He put the little bit of wax back into the top of the candle, watching as the flame instantly melted it. "Carlos can teach you. He is a master. If you become a good fabricator he'll think it is all because of him. Let him think that. Let him think he has taught you everything. Come to the job as a child and he will like you. Of course, if he likes you too much I will want to kill him."

"You don't have to go *that* far," Kay said, smiling. God, she thought, this guy is only half kidding. She flashed fleetingly on Grandma's house in the Valley, thinking what a long way from home she was.

Ricardo was ordering another round. "Tell me about your father," Kay said.

As a young man, Roberto Alvarez worked with his younger brother Carlos in their father's furniture store, crafting bulky pieces in the Spanish Colonial tradition. Bogotá society attached great prestige to pure Castilian blood, and he was proud of his Spanish-born grandparents and his family name. It rankled him that he was making the furniture when he knew he should be the one ordering it.

In the 1950s, the brothers went into the black-market car business. Almost immediately, they began to make the serious money and the wide-ranging contacts that were to satisfy Roberto's ambition, and later, to form the base of his cocaine operation.

To protect domestic manufacturers and a fragile domestic economy, the Colombian government had levied a prohibitively high tax, from seventy to one hundred thirty percent of value, on such foreign "luxury" imports as cars and boats. Further restrictions and legal requirements kept car imports firmly in bureaucratic hands: the necessary import license required an advance deposit on the tax and registration fee, as well as special registration and discretionary review with the Exchange Registry of the Bank of the Republic and the Department of Foreign Commerce.

These conditions were tailor-made to promote a thriving black market in foreign cars in which "your local dealer" was also "your local smuggler," a man to be respected and honored for his skill and resourcefulness and the necessary service he performed.

Roberto Alvarez, expert in the time-honored South American custom of the bribe, soon had many influential friends in government, finance, tax collection, and border control to aid him in his chosen field.

Through family connections in Mexico, Roberto and Carlos began smuggling cars into the Colombian market. The vehicles came from a broadly based supply, including cars stolen in the United States and shipped to a central holding point in East Los Angeles.

Money flowed and the Alvarez boys invested profits back into the furniture shop, expanding the business, bringing prominence to the family name, and drawing on family members for an ever-widening circle of employees whose trustworthiness was assured.

Early in the 1960s, Roberto spotted opportunity in a new trend. Yankee demand for cocaine was on the rise, his Mexican cohorts told him. If he would supply the product, they would market it from their East L.A. stronghold.

By 1968, he had dropped the car business and shot from making $150,000 a year to $1 million annually in cocaine revenue. And that was only the beginning. By then, his bribes alone totaled $100,000 a year. His picture appeared often in *El Tiempo* endowing hospitals and schools, attending soccer matches, and sitting on civic committees. His children attended the best schools and he was training his oldest son to become his partner.

"My father wants to send me to Europe next year. He wants me to learn the international side of the business from my Uncle Reynaldo," Ricardo said, "the blond man you met at lunch."

Kay nodded, remembering the languid pose and the drooping eyelids. "Could we have another drink?" she asked, looking around. "This place is very empty for a downtown lunch spot, isn't it?"

"True," Ricardo said. He signaled to the waiter, who was standing in discreet attendance a few feet away. "Usually it's very popular here, but my father knows the owner. He told him he needed quiet for an important meeting. So, for most people"—he smiled—"El Fuego was closed today."

• • •

The next evening at twilight, Ricardo picked her up at Schneider's in one of his father's cars, a black 1965 Mercedes. She was going to work the night shift, he had told her, because newcomers were always given the worst shifts. They headed to the Carretera de Circunvalación, a ribbon of road right beneath the Andes heading north out of Bogotá. Embassies and private mansions lined the terraced mountains, bougainvillea spilling over their walled gardens in Bogotá's eternal spring.

Higher up on the slopes, sharing the same view across the orange roofs and sweeping savannah, were the patched tin shacks of Indians living three families to a room. Kay and Ricardo passed a woman carrying a basket on her back and three barefoot children shouting to them as they went by. The wind coming through the window was spicy with the smell of eucalyptus.

Ricardo turned back toward the town and drove slowly through La Candelaria, the old quarter where green wooden balconies bright with peonies and orchids jutted over narrow cobblestone streets. Passing the dark, dolorous doors of the churches, they entered the downtown section with its rows of bargain stores, book stalls, and blaring music shops. He stopped to pick up a wrapped package at a cloth shop and then drove along the Avenida Caracas to the Chapinero district.

Here, Ricardo turned into an alley of low, crumbling buildings just wide enough to permit a trick to pass. He parked the Mercedes behind a furniture van at the end of the alley. The van's doors were open, and as they got out of the car and skirted it, Kay could see that it was half packed with large wooden shipping crates.

"This is the fabrication warehouse, the furniture showroom is in the front," Ricardo said. He put a key into a low, peeling door on the side of the last building. "Remember, Carlos is my father's brother. Don't let him—" Before he could finish unlocking the door it opened, and Carlos himself was standing there in a small empty room, with a bottle of Costena beer in one hand.

"¿Qué tal, Ricardo?" he said, giving him a playful punch on the shoulder. "I am glad to see you have brought me my new man." He turned to Kay and laughed a deep, rattling laugh from down in his chest, which was wide but soft with the rounded swell of male breasts. He was wearing a polyester shirt with a pattern of small blue whales against a white background.

"So?" he said, obviously waiting for Ricardo to leave.

"Bye-bye, *Tío Carlos*," Ricardo said, and pulling Kay to him he kissed her on the mouth—mostly for his uncle's benefit, she knew.

The moment he was gone, Carlos turned to her, instantly serious. "Let me tell you how I work. In here I am the boss, I make the rules. If you have questions, if you find problems, you ask me. If anything goes wrong you come and tell me. Okay?"

From the other side of the door Kay could hear a soccer game broadcast, the excited voice of the announcer, the ebb and flow of the crowd roar. She nodded, and he opened the door into a windowless room the size of a basketball court. The original wooden walls were reinforced with a second wall of concrete blocks to a height of eight feet. Fluorescent lights buzzed overhead.

The contents of an entire household were arranged along the walls—tables, lamps, desks, boxes of kitchenware, Louis XVI chairs, rare European antiques mixed with fancy Bogotá design shop chrome-and-silk couches.

Some of the chairs and couches had been torn down, the fabric removed and the stuffing exposed. Suitcases stood in a corner, linings stripped, waiting for false bottoms. Others were already partially filled with plastic bags of coke perfectly contoured, with Plexiglas shields popped on top to keep the coke from shifting.

In the center of the room were three long tables arranged in a row. One of them held glue pots, scales, stacks of cotton padding and welt cord, staple machines, and a variety of tools.

The other two were used as a packaging assembly line: at one end were piles of paper upholstery patterns, next, large rolls of plastic sheeting, then several three-foot-by-three-foot bags of white cocaine. Here the powder was scooped onto the plastic and formed into packages of upholstery sections of the desired shape. At the end of the last table was the heat-sealing machine used to seal the packages off, and the layers of cotton padding that were applied as a final step before the sections were fitted into the furniture piece.

"*Malparidos*, what are you staring at," Carlos said to the

two men and a boy who stood by the tables. Kay recognized the men as her inquisitors from the day before. "Get to work. Nobody seems to care that we have exactly seven days left to load this shit." He turned to Kay.

"For tonight I want you to disassemble those chairs." He pointed to a row of bow-legged Louis XVI side chairs. "Do it just like you would for reupholstery, only be very careful. We use the covers again and they cannot show a single tear."

The boy came over to Kay and said, "You can use the tools on the table." He was about fourteen, with wavy black shoulder-length hair, large hands and feet, and a voice beginning to crack.

"Roddy, leave that to me. You're more useful if you go and buy us some beer now." Carlos reached into his pocket for his wallet. "My son Roddy is supposed to be learning something here," he said to Kay. "It is more that he is learning to listen to the soccer games and drink beer."

"I know what he'd like to learn, he'd like some lessons from our new *gringa*," the taller man said in Spanish. He was around twenty-five and had collar-length hair and a short beard, the cool thing for a lot of Colombian men. He grinned and rolled his eyes.

The other man laughed, but didn't say anything. He was built low, with short legs and a heavy torso, like an Indian clay figure, and he was a few years older.

"Eh, Franco?" the bearded one continued. "Do you think your wife will let you come to work when she hears about this woman?"

The situation reminded Kay of her first day operating a forklift in the fruit-packing sheds back home. She was sixteen, and the Mexican workers, too, had taunted her in Spanish . . . at first.

"By the way," she said, her voice very pleasant, "*entiendo español.*"

The men stared. The tall one started to say something, but Carlos cut him off.

"I'm sorry about that," he said to Kay, and then, raising his voice, to the men, "Señorita Kay is my new worker and you will show her some respect. We need her here, and if you keep that up, Miguel, I'm not so sure we need *you.*"

It was suddenly quiet as everyone looked at each other. Kay

opened her canvas carpenter's bag and laid her tools out on the table beside those already there. Each tool had an identifying mark, a dot of pink fingernail polish: jewelry-quality needle-nose pliers, a ripping tool, precision C-clamps, miter clamp, and divider. The men examined them in silence. Kay could tell they were impressed.

The bullish-looking man named Franco picked up the needle-nose. "If it would not be too much of a molestation," he said, "could you get me a tool like this?"

"Sure," Kay said.

"Let's get to work—this stuff won't pack itself," Carlos said dryly.

Kay walked away toward the chairs, uncomfortably aware they were all watching her ass.

Through the next seven days Kay found out that she didn't need to pretend to learn from Carlos—he was a true master, meticulous and imaginative. He was one of those fat men who surprised people by being a good dancer and having an unexpectedly delicate touch.

Under his stern yet almost maternal eye, working an average of twelve hours each day, she packed six chairs and four suitcases in seven days. Her experience with furniture stood her in good stead but the hardest thing was learning to gauge the exact amount of coke needed for each piece of upholstery and then shaping it properly.

Carlos had a light, humorous side and Kay could tell the men liked him. But now he was exhausted and moody with the responsibility of meeting his deadline. When he stamped furiously out of the room, angry at some small thing, Kay would exchange glances with the men.

Sometimes, he would stand close to her explaining some technicality, like how to wipe the glue away without leaving a trace, and he would "accidentally" brush against her. But she just smiled at him quietly. No encouragement, but no big deal either.

On the fourth day, Kay found out that she was not the only American that Roberto Alvarez had involved in his business. Looking at the crates that now stood packed and waiting to be loaded into the van, she saw that they were being sent to a name and address in Alexandria, Virginia. Prominently displayed under the address on each crate was the diplomatic seal of the United States, conferring immunity from customs search. This particular diplomat was going home from his post in Bogotá with more than his embassy pay, that was for sure.

It was dawn when the loaded van backed down the alley. "Come," Carlos said. "I want to give you what you have earned." He took Kay into the small room off the warehouse and handed her an envelope with five thousand dollars in it. When she began to thank him he held up his hand.

"We are very pleased," he said, "even more pleased than five thousand dollars. Here is a little something for your personal use. It's for your apprenticeship. You can be looking forward to a raise if you keep this up."

The packet he gave her contained a large piece of crystal cocaine. It sparkled in her hand, a jumbo chunk of rock candy. Kay knew immediately the crystal weighed no less than three ounces, and was worth at least fifteen hundred dollars.

Back at Schneider's she put in a call to Maggie to code their next run.

"How're ya doin'?" Maggie asked.

"Not too bad for an Okie kid," Kay said, laughing, and did a little dance step that Ricardo had taught her. But she hung up feeling a little off balance.

Maggie had received her letter, she had told Kay, and the schedule looked fine, but she was worried about things. It bothered her that Kay knew very little about Ricardo and his family. She felt, as she put it, that Kay was getting "sucked into it all a little too fast for comfort."

"I know," Kay had said, "but you know me—if you don't play you can't win."

And Maggie had said, "Okay, puss, but be careful."

The next day Ricardo appeared at Schneider's, but this time Kay couldn't be angry with him. He stood in front of her door and hid his face behind a big box.

"I bring you an invitation to meet the family at a party tomorrow night," he said, "and I have also brought you a surprise to show everyone how beautiful is my woman."

He watched anxiously as she unwrapped a pale pink silk dress, with an ultra-feminine full skirt and ruffles at the neck.

"I hope you like it," he said.

Kay couldn't imagine actually wearing it. "I'm not so sure it's really me," she said.

Ricardo either missed the English or pretended to misunderstand. "Oh no. It's yours. It is for you," he assured her.

Okay, Kay thought. I'll play along. He's certainly eager to get me into this family.

"Why don't I try the dress on?" Kay suggested. "Then we can practice what I should say and what I shouldn't say at the party."

"Yes, yes. Try it on." He was being overly enthusiastic. Kay knew he was trying to cover up the awkwardness of the situation, worrying whether he had insulted her.

She went into the bathroom. The dress fit but it made her feel terribly overdone and silly, like a twelve-year-old in party clothes. Would she be the only one dressed like this? But no, why would he have bought it for her if it wasn't absolutely correct?

She came out of the bathroom reconciled to the dress. "*Linda, muy linda,*" Ricardo said, beaming, "*perfecto.*"

"Do you really like it?" Kay said. Only half unconsciously, with the dress, she had put on the flirtatious vivacity of a Colombian woman.

The morning of the party she went to the beauty parlor, bringing the pink belt with her so she could have her fingernails done to match the dress. Most of the colors on the manicurist's table ran to reds and oranges but the girl found the right shade of pink. She was excited by this *señorita norteamericana* and wanted Kay to describe the dress to her in glowing detail.

The shop was full of chattering women of all ages. All kinds of beauty treatments were being performed: hot wax to remove facial hair, the chair tilted back, its occupant grimacing in pain; feet pedicured; hair cut, permed, and rolled in tin-foil wraps.

Señora Mimi, the owner, was over fifty, with peroxide-white hair and fingernails so long she had to use a pencil to ring up sales on the cash register. She oversaw everything, yelling at the servants when they didn't move fast enough with the little cups of *tinto* and plates of *dulces* for the señoras, or when her workers didn't sweep up the hair cuttings on the floor immediately.

Over her desk hung several large color photographs of various beauty queens: "Señorita Bogotá, 1967," "Reina de la

Pilsen, 1968," "Señorita Colombia 1969," "Reina de Azúcar, 1966." They were all credited "Hair by la Salón Francés," and some of them were autographed. Beauty pageants played a major role in Colombian life.

Beauty was more than a national ideal for womanhood. It was a major tradeable commodity in a world where women could come to power in only two primary roles, as wives of important men or as mothers.

Waiting for her turn under the dryer, Kay watched a señora and her three daughters. They were being groomed for an important Saturday-night function, Kay thought, judging from the fuss being made over the older daughter's hair. The mother, her own head crowned in a mass of tight rollers, stood over her daughter's stylist with a frown. "Not so much height," she said, "it must look naturally full." While the other daughters giggled and paged obsessively through American and European fashion magazines, the owner fawned over her rich customer, agreeing with her suggestions.

The beauty shop was a place where women could finally throw their weight around, and they did it by playing the games of family status and family money. It was a competitive little world and, after a while, feeling tight-lipped and melancholy, Kay retreated into an American movie magazine.

She flipped past "Burton, Taylor Arrive in London," with photos of Liz overweight, overtanned, wearing the Krupp Diamond, and photos of Barbra Streisand cozying up with Omar Sharif under the headline ELLIOTT GOULD ALONE IN NEW YORK? Turning the pages, she looked down at her hands. With their shiny pink fingernails, they seemed to belong to someone else.

The Padrino, as Roberto Alvarez was respectfully called by the clan members, lived in the Norte. Of course—where else? Kay thought, as Ricardo braked in front of a forbidding wall with gates and a sentry on duty.

The man nodded to Ricardo and opened the gates. In the landscaped entrance yard, a statue of the Vírgen de Guadalupe stood in a stone shrine, a cascade of ferns at her feet. The late-afternoon sun shone on the massed pink clouds of blossoming hydrangea bushes tall as trees. Ricardo led the way up a stone path to a heavy wooden door. He lifted a carved knocker in the shape of a ram's head, and almost immediately, the door was opened by a square-faced elderly woman in a black-and-white uniform.

"Buenas tardes, Señor Ricardo."

Ricardo turned to Kay. "Luisa has been with us since I was a baby."

"I'm glad to meet you, Luisa," Kay said. Ricardo gave her a reproachful look and shook his head. "Don't be familiar with the servants," he hissed.

The entrance hall was cold. Kay had an impression of Spanish formality: tiled floor, standing candelabra, pots of blooming orchids, ancient, dark oil paintings. They emerged into a blue-and-white tiled patio with a fountain in the center. Many layers of protection here, Kay thought. Laughter and music floated through the windows opening out onto a second-floor veranda.

At last they penetrated the house itself. The main room was filled with massive dark furniture made of leather and wood, and the walls glowed with paintings and drawings, each lit from above with its own small lamp. Treasures, Kay saw with excitement. Just walking through the room, she recognized a Goya drawing, an early painting by Fernando Botero, a Braque, a study by Rodin for one of his sculptures.

Ricardo took Kay's arm and stepped with her through the French doors onto a lawn surrounded by a high brick wall covered with bougainvillea. Embedded at the top of the wall were pointed shards of glass from old bottles and a string of barbed wire.

About thirty-five people were gathered under the trees. Long tables loaded with food had been set out: hams, barbecued chickens, sausages, all kinds of exotic fruits that Kay had never seen before. Children ran past grandmothers gossiping in the shade, men stood in little groups, teen-agers hung around the food tables. Servants with festive red neckerchiefs circulated with trays among the crowd.

Suddenly, as though a little fanfare had announced them, all eyes were on Kay and Ricardo standing at the French doors. The Padrino was coming across the lawn, smiling. With him was a thin, reddish-haired woman. "That's my mother," Ricardo said. She was wearing a frilly dress almost exactly like Kay's.

"You are most welcome," she said to Kay formally. Her eyes, cool and appraising, reminded Kay of two dark, hard cherries. "My son has told me about you."

"Please excuse me, Flora," Roberto said. "I want to introduce Señorita Wolff to a few of our friends."

"Of course." Her reserve was perfectly controlled; she gave not one iota more than was necessary to be polite. Ricardo didn't look as if he wanted to be left alone with her.

Roberto steered Kay through the crowd to an angular man with prominent features, a bizarre cross between Abraham Lincoln and Don Quixote. Beside him was a plump sparrow of a woman, with a sweet face and hair in a chignon at the nape of her neck.

"*Kay, permítame presentarle al Señor y a la Señora Gutiérrez, Clarita y Don César.* Don César is the head of our Medellín base. He is our chief of processing."

Don César held out his large hand to Kay. "Like they do in the USA," he said.

Carlos had talked about Don César. He was a good "cook"—a processor—Carlos had said, but he was arrogant, and too secretive. "Thinks he is above everyone because he is a professor of chemistry and biology," Carlos had ranted. "People from Medellín—Antioquians—always think they are superior."

"Señorita Wolff is our new designer from the United States," Roberto was saying. Kay was amused. We might as well be at an advertising company party, she thought.

"We are happy to have Kay in our family, Clarita"— Roberto looked at Señora Gutiérrez—"and I know you will do everything to make her feel at home. You know how hard it can be for a woman to make friends in Bogotá."

Kay thought she picked up a subtext in his remark.

"Such a lovely dress," Clarita launched in. "It is American, no?"

Kay laughed and said, "Thank you, but no. These days I'm happy to do my shopping in Bogotá."

After introducing her to several old aunts and his youngest son, Tomaso, a boy of ten with weak eyes and thick glasses, the Padrino suggested he take Kay upstairs to his study for a private chat.

"What do you drink?" he asked.

"Scotch," Kay said quickly. What she would have liked more than anything right then was a line of Roberto's *puro* cocaine, but casual snorting was out. That was for *gringos*. Not until the early 1980s would such complacency be shattered by the recognition that Colombia's own youth had been quietly becoming major drug abusers themselves.

At one end of Roberto's study was a long meeting table and chairs, at the other a desk, several easy chairs, and a bar. The room was carpeted with a rosy Sarouk Persian rug, and the walls were covered with awards and plaques commending Roberto for his many charitable works. Over his desk hung a large blueprint of the hospital wing he had built.

But Roberto Alvarez was building more than hospitals. He had begun to invest heavily in real estate and construction. Later, as the cocaine profits of the early seventies boomed, a new skyline would emerge for downtown Bogotá, the direct creation of cocaine lords like Roberto Alvarez.

After motioning Kay to sit down, he busied himself at the bar to give her time to look around.

"How do you find time for all this activity?" Kay asked.

"I hire reliable help," he said. "Mostly they remain reliable. Or"—he shrugged and laughed pleasantly—"they learn." Kay had been relaxing back into the chair, feeling very civilized. Now, hearing his words, she sat up and lit a cigarette.

"Please," he said, as he put her drink on a small table beside her chair and sat down opposite her. There was a small pause and then he said, "The women are really very nice. It is hard to get to know them at first, but I could see you are going to win them with no trouble at all."

"Thank you. I hope so."

"To speak sincerely, I am impressed with you. With your work. I think you can have a good future with us. You can become a wealthy woman under the protection of this family. But of course, that is all up to you."

Kay smiled, polite, attentive, waiting.

"However, there is one thing I think you should know. It's about my son, Ricardo." She folded her hands in her lap. "Flora and I have definite marriage plans for him, you see, and it's important that nothing happens to disturb these plans. You are a sophisticated woman, Kay. I am sure you can understand my position. I appreciate that."

"Of course I understand," Kay said, nodding. There was a short pause as their eyes met. Don't worry, your boy couldn't be safer, she thought.

He stood up. "I am glad I can talk to you with such honesty," he said. "Come." He took her arm. "I am told the children have prepared a special concert for us." When they reached the door, he turned to her. "You understand this was a confidential conversation, no? And you will say nothing to Ricardo."

"Of course," Kay murmured.

When they came down, Flora was standing at the bottom of the stairs. "Come, Roberto," she said, "the children have been waiting with their little performance."

Children are central in upper-class Colombian family life, sons to take over and hold the family together, daughters to marry and extend the influence, like jewels in a necklace each bound to the other. Babies have their own doting servants, but as soon as they begin to grow up, they are expected to succeed at everything they do and to obey their parents unquestioningly.

In Colombia, large families are almost a duty. Roberto and Flora had five children: Elisa, a daughter of twenty-two, married with a four-year-old daughter herself; Ricardo, the oldest son; seventeen-year-old Eva; fourteen-year-old Eduardo; and ten-year-old Tomaso.

The children's piano recitals were a tradition at the Padrino's parties. Kay slipped away to find an upstairs bathroom. Two teenage girls were primping in one of the bedrooms and as Kay passed them, they stopped combing their hair and looked at her. As soon as she closed the bathroom door she could hear them whispering and giggling. Suddenly they stopped.

"I think Ricardo is so handsome, don't you, Isabella," one of them said loudly. It was obvious to Kay that they wanted her to hear them.

"Yes. Much more even than Paul Newman."

"Anyway," the first one said, still loudly, "you're going to marry him, aren't you. *Es tu destino.*"

They both fell into another fit of giggles.

Everyone has plans for Ricardo. I wonder what plans he has for himself, Kay thought wryly. She opened the bathroom window to have a smoke. Down below, orange-tiled roofs plush with moss slanted into a windowless patio. Big clay pots of begonias and daisies stood around a stone washbasin, and a young girl in a white apron held a crying baby. "Don't cry, my little king," she said in a singsong voice, "don't cry my most darling one."

Kay went back downstairs to find that the chairs had been pushed back and a band was playing Colombian dances. In a corner, the Padrino was speaking seriously to his wife. A few minutes later, Flora came over and took Kay's arm.

"Perhaps you would like to learn some of our dances?" she said. As she showed Kay the accented step and glide of the *cumbia*, more and more men began to disappear upstairs. Soon it was only the women and children who were left to dance. The Padrino's family party was, in fact, a cover for a full-scale business meeting. And Kay had been invited, but only to remain with the women.

It was the end of October, Halloween time back at home. In California, the weather would be crisper, the shadows of the trees longer. But here the sky was always full of rainbows, the sudden fierce sun and cold misty mornings of Bogotá remained unchanging.

"There are no seasonal fruits here," Kay wrote Maggie. "Everything is always in season. We have mangoes and avocados and bananas and pineapples, and a green something called *coruba* that has wonderful juice. But no pumpkins."

She wrote letters to Maggie, but actually they were as much for herself. She needed to write them:

Nov. 3, 1969

Halloween was devastating. I came home to my little cell crying. I had spent most of the morning in my room because it was my day off. Ricardo called. He wanted to come over with the car to go shopping with me.

It was about 4:00 in the afternoon when we went out. There were children everywhere. They were roaming the streets with blackened faces and dirty rags, crying and screaming. Bizarre to the extreme. Like something out of the dark ages. Some of them were costumed like cripples and hunchbacks. It was difficult to tell who was and who wasn't real.

The sweet shops were all open and doing a good business to patrons with money, while outside the beggar children clustered around pleading. But the shops had hired armed guards who were chasing them and beating them with sticks. When some of them tried to come back, they beat them down to the ground. The smaller ones were squatting along the walls, scared.

I said to Ricardo—my God, what is it? It really hadn't dawned on me. Halloween, of course. He asked me if we didn't have such a day in the U.S. and I could only answer . . . yes . . . and no.

I tried to continue shopping. I've been in S.A. long enough now so I'm used to street boys shining shoes, selling papers, little beggars everywhere. Yet I really hadn't put it together. Ricardo saw I was miserable and he tried to explain. I could see he was embarrassed, feeling that I didn't understand. I understood all right. This was the night they all came out of their holes and ran through the streets like the little starving rats they really are.

So we go on buying stuff, expensive sardines in mustard sauce from Norway, crackers from England, American Scotch. I buy an enormous bag of candies. As we leave the store I begin to give the candies to the closest children. The guard objects. I pretend not to speak Spanish and smile at him.

I keep walking and all the little hands are grabbing, *dulce, por favor, dulce*. A large band is now following us toward the car, pushing and begging. Finally, the hysterical children tear the bag and it falls to the street and what seems like a hundred children pile on, all desperate to get a piece.

Ricardo pushes me into the car. He's furious and he yells at me how we could have been hurt and how can he take care of me if I won't listen to him.

I apologize immediately for upsetting him. I apologize several times, but he's still mad. I start to cry. So he explains again: these are not really children, they are thieves, they are *pobre de pobres*, less than poor, they are the thieves of the night, they kill people in vicious little packs, they have no real families.

I can only think to ask him . . . what about the Church? Are there no orphanages?

So he tries to be patient with me, having no idea who he's talking to. Orphanages are for the children of the Church, children whose parents married each other, children whose parents die and who have no godparents to turn to or family to take care of them. He goes on to say that many of these kids would rather live in the streets and, anyway, the Church could never take care of all the abandoned and homeless children.

I don't even need to ask him about the government and, besides, I think I've gone too far already, so I apologize again and say I'm just homesick and sentimental and he takes my hand and squeezes it.

When I get home I try to forget. I pour myself a Scotch and do a line, and feel like a pampered poodle.

Kay never completed the letter. She simply put down her pen and stuffed the paper into an envelope to mail in the morning. It was late, 3:00 A.M. She turned off the lights and sat at the window staring out at the mountains. The church on Monserrate was almost covered in clouds. Farther off, the illuminated statue of the Virgin stretched out her arms—like a plastic dashboard figure, Kay couldn't help thinking.

Chapter Four

Lola pointed out Altogrande, the president's edge-of-town [Bogotá] weekend retreat, a glimpse of white walls and red tiles surrounded by eucalyptus. . . . Here the big landowners had their dairy herds, stud farms and *haciendas*. Black and white Holsteins grazed on the brilliant green savannah. On either side of the flat valley floor rose bottle-green, black-ridged mountains. Clouds were banking over the range to our left, but when we came to a fork in the road—left to Zipaquira, right to Tunja—we took the right. Both these towns were once seats of the Chibcha kings, or zipas, who ruled these high tablelands before the Spaniards came. The Chibchas were farmers, traders and sun worshippers. They traded with lowland and coastal Indians: salt emeralds and woven blankets in exchange for gold, cotton, parrots and sea shells. The typical *campesinos* of this area, small, brown, trilbied and bow-legged, are remnants of the Chibcha. Some still use the old name for their country, Cundur-cunca, the land of the condor.

—Charles Nicholl,
The Fruit Palace

By early December Kay had been working for Carlos for nearly two months. She was earning ten thousand dollars a month, and her business with Maggie was bringing in fifty thousand dollars with each pass. Maggie set up the passes from Los Angeles, sending carriers to Kay in Bogotá and then meeting them herself in the Caribbean.

After a four-kilo pass made on a cruise ship, Maggie had enough coke in reserve to slow the business down, keeping the stash divided in various safety-deposit boxes around L.A.

There was no need to push, there were connoisseurs in town who understood real quality and were willing to pay top dollar for it.

With Maggie in control back in the States, Kay could now turn her attention to her new job. Except for rush jobs like the round-the-clock panic of her first week, Kay's average day was noon to 9:00 P.M., five days a week. She liked the hours—Kay had always been a night owl.

As soon as she arrived at the warehouse, letting herself in with the key Carlos had given her, the banter would begin. Only now, it had become friendly.

She often arrived twenty or thirty minutes late, always with every hair in place, and dressed in soft sweaters and slacks, her makeup fashion-model perfect.

"So the Princess has decided to join us," Carlos would say, starting in.

Kay just smiled. "Sorry I'm late."

"What kept the Princess?"

"Traffic." Miguel gave a hoot, which Kay ignored. "No, it's true, Carlos—traffic. It's worse than rush hour in L.A.— everyone honking and running the signals."

"It used to be no problem until they started letting women drive," Miguel said. "That was the big mistake." He had left the car door he was disassembling to come over to the table and drink coffee.

"Never mind traffic," Franco said in his serious way, "do you want to bet on the soccer match? Winning team and score?"

"*Seguro,*" Kay said. "I want to bet on Brazil."

Carlos laughed. "Good, Princess. Brazil is not playing. This is the Intercontinental Club Championship, Argentina and Italy."

"The match is going to be a surprise this year," Franco said.

Miguel said, "I wish I could be in Buenos Aires. I would love to be there when South America kicks those idiot Italians right back across the Atlantic."

"They play ball like a bunch of girls," Carlos said.

"It's going to be a surprise," Franco repeated, as though no one had said anything.

Carlos and Miguel began arguing with him and Kay said, "I want to bet on Brazil." The men groaned.

"*A trabajar, a trabajar,* let's go, there's work to do," Carlos said. "Kay, I have errands for you."

The Alvarez organization operated as a definite hierarchy, with the Jefe, or Boss, Roberto Alvarez, at the top. Directly beneath him, responsible to him yet each controlling his own domain, were Roberto's brother Carlos, "El Oso" (the Bear); Alvarez, chief of fabrication; and Roberto's brother-in-law, Reynaldo Quintero, director of international sales. The "cook," César Gutiérrez, though head of his own organization and family, was also allied to the Alvarez clan both through family connections and as director of their processing division.

These men were served in turn by a staff almost all of whom were related by blood, and whose duties, such as running errands, chauffeuring, bodyguarding, loading suitcases, carrying messages, and so forth, were considered interchangeable.

Carlos liked to send Kay on errands he thought were best done by a woman. Most afternoons she would spend several hours wandering around town buying presents for the Padrino's friends and important contacts; leather goods and handwoven articles for the German and French buyers, handbags for the wives. Then, too, there were always the incidental supplies for the shop: plastic, staples, fabric, glue.

Kay was a passionate shopper and didn't mind this form of male chauvinism at all. She had spent the lean Okie years of her childhood in hand-me-down clothes and too-tight shoes, and she viewed the hippie rebellion against materialism, the torn jeans and work shirts of middle-class American kids, with an amused cynicism. While shopping for Carlos she would also buy with abandon for herself: emeralds and jewelry, boots and hand-tooled shoes, imported wool suits, silk blouses, and fur coats. Shopping was like a search for perfection, and she spent her money as though driven by the fear that in the morning it would be gone.

Sometimes Carlos would ask her to make special deliveries, boxes of papers to the Alvarez accountant, envelopes to offices in the Avianca building, envelopes to government offices, airline offices, foreign consultants, and banks. Carlos never volunteered any information on the contents of the envelopes and Kay knew better than to ask, but she was fairly certain they contained bribe money.

When she got back, mostly in the late afternoon, Carlos

would usually assign her to suitcase work. Each suitcase took four days to process and there were always five or six of them waiting at different stages of readiness. Kay could load the cocaine in three hours. It was the drying that took time, and it depended on the weather. Occasionally, Carlos would use artificial heat, but it was risky. Too much heat applied too fast could completely ruin the coke or cause the seals to turn up at the edges. The final touches were also time-consuming—adding the ruffled band around the top of the lining, and adding the pockets, for instance.

Though the Padrino's suitcases were Colombian, on some days Kay would find a pile of alien bags leaning against the wall waiting for service, four or five matching cases in white or pale blue. These were special jobs for the Padrino's friends or for Colombian government officials whom he had bribed.

These officials not only traveled on nonrestrictive government visas; they were also allowed to bring cars home, duty-free, for their "personal use." Roberto did business with them coming and going. Outward-bound, protected by their visas, they were safe carriers for the coke; returning, they were an excellent source for Roberto's still-thriving car dealership.

At that time, the Padrino worked mainly with suitcase concealment, but his operation was diversified and he reaped large profits from special orders, such as sculptures or religious statues. The man who had introduced Kay to Ricardo, Professor Hector Guzmán, chairman of the Art Department of one of the universities in Bogotá, was the Padrino's "curator," procuring the artworks to be used as smuggling containers and arranging the exhibitions that served as their cover for export.

The Padrino was also involved with a group of Mexican smugglers who would contract with him for both cocaine supply and fabrication, mostly using cars and furniture.

By Kay's second month, the number of these special jobs had begun to multiply, and Carlos was increasingly relying on her for the suitcase work. It was a period of rain, bone-penetrating chill, and endlessly damp clothes, of constant gray skies and the *morro nublado,* a creeping fog that wrapped the city in a thick mist.

Outside the shop, the alley streamed with water like a small brook. Electric heaters hummed, creating islands of warmth in the echoing cold of the warehouse. Most days, the atmosphere was easy, the radio on, the crew talking and laughing and blowing coke as they worked. Carlos kept a sharp eye on his problem son, Roddy, making sure he didn't snort a secret line while no one was looking. The men used him for errands, sending him out into the rain to the Cocorico food chain to bring back beer and *pollo asado,* chicken and potatoes.

They had been working on a rush job for a week when Kay's relationship with Roddy changed dramatically. Tired after long hours of meticulous labor, she had accidentally overloaded a plastic bag of coke, rendering it too big to fit the sleek arm of a chair. Leaving the bag open by the sealing machine, she stood looking down at the chair's dismantled arm, trying to gauge how much coke she would need to remove.

Roddy had come in from the rain. She glanced up to see him at a side table taking bottles of beer from a brown paper bag, his hair plastered wetly to his head. He smiled at her.

"Let me help," he said, leaving the table to get her the bag of coke she had left behind.

"No wait, it's not sealed," she cried, but he was already standing there holding the pouring bag, his face dumb with shock. Cocaine cascaded down his front, covering his shoes and the littered floor around him in a coat of precious white powder, as Carlos came at him, roaring curses. Kay jumped up and pulled the boy behind her.

"That's right, hide behind a woman," Carlos shouted, menacing and bull-like. At last, still breathing hard, he turned away in disgust. "That's exactly what his mother would have done," he said. "Well, you can have him. He's your assistant now. He's not fit to work as a man. But I can tell you one thing, if anything like this happens again, it will come out of your pay."

Carlos put on his raincoat and stormed out. Without a word Roddy knelt on the floor and began to scoop up the cocaine with a spoon, depositing it carefully in a fresh plastic bag. No one spoke. The men went back to work, the radio jangling in the quiet room.

After a while Roddy had scraped up all the cocaine that was clean enough to salvage. Bending over her work, Kay watched him out of the corner of her eye. He was still kneeling there. With a hasty movement he lowered his face directly to the floor and tried to snort up the fine sprinkling of white that remained among the sawdust and the cigarette butts.

"Roddy, don't be an asshole. What do you think you're doing?" She ran over to where he was kneeling and kicked sawdust over the dregs of the spill. "Jesus. You've got to grow up or things will only get worse around here."

"Things could not get worse," he mumbled, his face flushed.

"You're wrong. Things can always get worse." She put an arm around his shoulders. "Come on. Help me clean the brushes."

"Roddy has the luck," Miguel said. "She doesn't put her arm around me." Kay wasn't feeling too lucky herself. Ricardo had warned her not to question Carlos, to remember her place.

Most nights after work, Ricardo would pick her up in the VW. "Has Carlos been saying things to you?" he asked one night.

"No. We're friendly. But that's it. Why?"

"He is too friendly, sometimes, I think." He sounded tense.

All right, Kay thought. Enough Alvarez machismo. She took several afternoons off looking for a car and bought a butter-yellow Renault she found advertised in *El Tiempo*. She paid cash. Ricardo told her she had paid more for it than it was worth, but she didn't care. He was probably just angry now that she had a car and wouldn't be dependent on him to drive her around.

In 1969, a woman driver was still a novelty in Colombia and Kay found she enjoyed road-jockeying with the men, returning their shouted insults with her brightest smile. A demon behind the wheel, she had learned to drive when she was fourteen, operating a water truck in the orchards of California's San Joaquin valley. Driving Colombia's roads reminded her of the bumper-car rinks in tent carnivals back home; it was every man for himself and make sure to keep your arms inside the car.

Ricardo teased Kay about her driving and boasted about her to his friends, calling her his American cowgirl. One Sunday morning, he called and woke her with a special request.

"My father would like to ask you to do a very great favor for him today," he said. "The men are all busy and I have to take my sisters to a wedding, so there is no one else. He asks you to drive a good friend of his to the cemetery and afterward to lunch.''

Kay was confused. "Has someone close died?" she asked carefully.

"No, no." Ricardo laughed. "People often visit their family graves on Sunday. It is a custom. They bring flowers, pay respect. It's a remembrance."

The address Ricardo gave her was of a modest four-story apartment building in the Chapinero district, not far from the Alvarez shop.

Kay parked the car and before she had time to switch off the engine, a street boy was leaning against the hood. Instead of waiting for the pitch, Kay just gave him a smile and a handful of change and said, *"Guárdatelo."* Astonished, the kid said, *"Sí, sí, me lo guardo, seguro."* She shaded her eyes, checking the building number, and saw a red-haired woman duck quickly away from one of the windows into the shadows inside.

A shy servant opened the door and showed her into the living room. It was furnished in fake white-and-gold French Provincial. Lamp bases shaped like ladies in eighteenth-century costume held up frilly lampshades. From the depths of the apartment, Kay heard the hysterical cadences of a radio preacher, a South American Oral Roberts.

After a moment, a tiny woman came clicking into the room on three-inch heels. She was dressed in navy blue for her trip to the cemetery, but to Kay everything about her was flaming, her hair, her nails, her lipstick—red, red, red.

She was petite and beautiful in a way that was delicate and hard at the same time, with thin, penciled eyebrows and fake lashes that made her small face look operatic. None of it was right, Kay thought, yet the overall effect was somehow very sexy.

She came across the room toward Kay, hand outstretched, smiling a practiced smile, making Kay feel like a giantess.

"I am Olivia," she trilled. "How nice of you to come to my rescue. Poor me, with no man to take me to the cemetery. Usually Roberto drives me there. I'm mad at him today, the *chico malo,* for not taking better care of me. But never mind, now I have a chance to meet you, the American *señorita* that he has been taking around town. A handsome family, no? And fascinating."

Kay said, "Yes very," mirroring Olivia's smile. This is odd, she thought.

A little girl came in and perched on the very edge of one of the French chairs, staring at Kay. The child was about seven and looked exactly like Roberto Alvarez, with the same high forehead, thin, long nose, and clear, gray gaze.

Odder and odder, Kay thought.

"Estrella, *mi corazoncito*, say *buenos días* to Señorita Wolff."

The child got up and executed a perfunctory curtsy. *"Buenos días, Señorita Wolff.* Do you know my father?"

"Yes, I am a friend of your father's and I'm going to drive you to the cemetery today." The kid was looking at her with a cool sort of appraisal.

"You drive?" she said.

"Yes," Kay said. "Look out the window, you'll see my car, a little yellow one."

"Mamá, why do we not have a car?" Estrella said from the window.

"Because your *mamá* does not want to drive, she wants to be driven. Come, *linda*, let's not keep the *señorita* waiting."

So the three of them set off for the cemetery, the Jardines de la Paz, in the northeast part of the city, stopping first at a flower stall down one of the side streets. Olivia didn't get out but seemed to be waiting for something. "He didn't give you money for flowers?" she said, hurt.

Kay dug into her purse. *"Gracias,"* Olivia said, taking the money. "I know he meant to send money. You will see. It is just an oversight, he will pay for all the little expenses, total *gastos* for today."

She bought gladiolas and daisies dyed blue, haggling with the old woman flower seller and calling her a thief, yet she must have known the price perfectly, Kay thought, or she would have moved on to another stall.

At the main cemetery entrance, Kay drove through heavy, wrought-iron gates, past knots of women dressed in black. They stood immobile, as though in silent vigil, black shawls over their heads. A ragged El Greco sky flared overhead, sheets of gray clouds moving swiftly behind the crosses and the mausoleums. Kay's skin prickled.

"Who are those women?" she asked.

"They are mourners," Olivia said evasively. She reached into her purse for a black lace scarf, which she put over her head.

"Come, Estrella," she said testily, "where is your handkerchief? Put it on your head."

The cemetery was dotted with women sitting beside flower-laden gravesites. Olivia's plot was quite far in. The graves of her father and brother were marked with stone crosses and photographs protected under Plexiglas shields. Her brother's photograph showed a young man dressed in an army uniform. Kay went back to the car to give Olivia and Estrella some privacy.

She turned the radio on low and watched them through the window. They were kneeling in prayer. Kay thought of the little vial in her purse and then dismissed the idea. No, she thought, wildly inappropriate.

They were back in the car faster than Kay had expected, Olivia wiping away tears and powdering her face, looking into the little mirror of her compact. "Do you know where to go for lunch?" she asked.

"No," Kay said. "Where would you like to go?"

"Good," Olivia said, smiling at Kay. "We'll go to El Barco." She was fishing around in her makeup bag and Kay was amazed to see her push her pinky finger into the neck of a little bottle of cocaine. The extra-long fingernail shoveled in and came out loaded with a neat pile. Daintily, she looked in the mirror and scooped a perfect shot into her nose without leaving a trace of white powder on her nostrils. She offered the vial to Kay, who took it silently.

The Restaurante El Barco was in the suburbs and they sped out of the Norte, feeling very high, Olivia giving vague directions and talking about her life and dreams.

Olivia's sister had managed to marry a tradesman and looked down at Olivia for her "situation." Her mother was ashamed of her. It was terrible, not being married to Roberto, but now she had the child and there was no turning back. She had to try and get as much as she could from him while she was still young and desirable. She wanted to be an actress. With all of his connections, why didn't he try to get her a part on one of the soap operas?

But her biggest worry was Estrella's Holy Communion. She

had a phony birth certificate that Roberto had arranged, with the father and mother listed as married, but he didn't send Estrella to the best Catholic school. Not like his other children. It really wasn't fair, she said.

Olivia talked about Estrella as though she weren't there, and the child sat quietly in the back seat, knees tight together under her pleated plaid skirt, looking out of the window.

They drove through patches of flowering countryside and endless little *barrios* where the not-quite desperate lived. Men sat on cheap chairs in front of the *tiendas*, chickens and pigs scattering as the car came through.

Sunday traffic was heavy, the roads jammed with families bringing flowers to their dead. The buses, crowded with people and animals and Indians in their Sunday best, looked like celebrations—every inch painted with bright designs, pictures of the Holy Virgin and Roy Rogers–style rearing silver horses.

After about twenty minutes, they arrived at El Barco. The place, filled with a happy holiday crowd, families, dating couples, children underfoot, had been designed to look like an imitation Spanish galleon. Kay had to duck to get in through the low door. The windows were all portholes and the tables were set on different levels, built to resemble wooden decks.

Immediately, Estrella began running up and down the ladderlike steps between the decks, excitedly talking to the waiters and ignoring her mother's pleas to calm down.

"I like this place," Olivia said. "We go here often." Kay guessed "we" meant Olivia and Roberto. It was certainly sufficiently out of the way.

The headwaiter showed them to one of the best tables, joking familiarly with Olivia. "Antonio, this is one of my good friends, Señorita Wolff," Olivia said proudly.

After lunch, Olivia wanted to go to the bar. Estrella had joined a group of other children and Olivia's idea of a Sunday outing seemed to include a little drinking and dancing. Kay noticed that Olivia knew all the help and several people at the bar as well.

The three musicians were costumed in "Spanish traditional" to match the galleon mood, their plump bellies encased in tight black jackets and their trousers shiny with wear. They sang sad songs of love and loss, accompanying themselves on two guitarlike instruments called *tiples*, and a violin: *"Quiero saber la verdad de lo que dicen tus ojos* [I want to know the truth that your eyes speak]."

Olivia loved the songs and was soon dancing with men who came over and seemed to know her. Every little while she came back to duck her head under the table for refresher dips of her long red fingernail.

Kay was having fun. Olivia was a great dancer, and when there were no available men she asked Kay to dance, showing her the Colombian version of the tango. Olivia would have stayed on and on, but there was a phone call for her and she came back pouting. Roberto had been calling around, looking for her. It was time to go home.

The following Sunday, Ricardo called again. "Let me guess," Kay said. "Olivia wants to visit her father and brother again."

"No. I want to take you to Monserrate."

Kay looked out of the window at the rugged peaks of the Andes. Everywhere in the city, their haunting presence hovered over the people, their wild summits capped with the twin symbols of Spanish Colonial power, Mother Mary and Mother Church.

"You mean you want me to climb up *there?*" she said.

"No. There's a better way."

The "better way" turned out to be a tram that climbed to the ten-thousand-foot summit almost vertically, clinging to Monserrate's slopes at a precarious seventy-five-degree angle.

"You're sure we couldn't walk up?" Kay said.

Ricardo laughed. "Only two kinds of people do that anymore—religious fanatics and the bandits who wait to beat and rob them. Truly, Kay, you're much safer in the tram. Don't worry, it's been a long time, a few years anyway, since the last serious accident."

"I'm not going!"

"Only a joke," he said and grabbed her hands to pull her unwillingly into the cable car.

At the top, they stepped out into a place of ripping wind and vast space and light. Ricardo put his arm around her.

Sparsely green at this altitude, the mountains were overwhelming, while down below the plateau swept away to the horizon, the red-tiled roofs of Bogotá dwindling into the distance.

From below, the church had looked stark and white, but up here it was a mellow saffron, with crumbling bricks and wooden doors a weathered blue. It had been built in the middle of the seventeenth century, and the small, square windows were clear glass, some of them missing a few panes.

Beggars, their faces brown and leathery, sat on the steps of the church and Ricardo bought two candles from an Indian woman. "Specially blessed," she said, nodding.

He took an immaculate white handkerchief from his pocket and placed it carefully on Kay's head. As he opened the church door for her, she thought how beautiful his face was, in its unconscious solemnity.

The church was dark inside, except for the alcoves where candles glittered. Smoke-dimmed paintings hung high on the walls, and the air, thick with incense under the vaulted ceiling, echoed with murmured prayers and pleas for mercy. Kay noticed a dusty jumble of discarded crutches and canes in a corner by the altar, mute testimony of miracles, and on the floor beneath her feet, bronze plaques commemorating healings.

In the center of the church, enshrined in a glass case, was the famous miracle-working statue El Señor de Monserrate. One-third life-sized, the statue represented Jesus on the road to Calvary, and showed him fainting to the ground beneath the burden of the cross.

To Kay, the tortured realism of the statue was both barbaric and horrific. The head drooped, the face was contorted in a daze of pain, eyes rolling upward. Scourge wounds dripped red trickles down a torso bizarrely wrapped in a purple silk loincloth. A gold medallion hung around the tormented neck.

The low wooden fence around the icon was hung with amulets left there by the sick and the desperate: hundreds of tiny silver body parts, arms and legs, waxen hearts, hands, and feet. While Kay stood there, an Indian woman came and laid her baby's palm against the case. Kay saw that the whole lower portion of the glass case was smudged and misty with the imprints of hundreds of kisses.

Ricardo sat in a nearby pew, eyes closed. Beside him, Kay, too, bent her head. The familiar feeling of a pew against her back, the sense of someone in prayer beside her, brought a

flood of memory: the Holy Pentecostal church of her childhood, her grandfather singing ''The Old Rugged Cross,'' the
nasal Okie voices of the congregation, the map of South
America with the colored pins stuck in the spots where the
missionaries had gone.

Ricardo stood up and touched her arm. They added their
candles to the altar at the front of the church and turned to go.

Outside, a cold mist now obscured the view. They walked
with the pilgrims and tourists behind the church and down a
dirt alley lined with Indian vendors on either side. The
makeshift stalls were thickly hung with an occult blend of
Christian and pagan charms: little pins bearing the suffering
image of El Señor de Monserrate, silver hearts and doves,
golden fists clenched in menace and defense like the one
Ricardo wore.

They stopped at one of the stalls, where, partially hidden
behind strings of tiny legs and arms, an Indian woman sat
nursing her baby. Black smoke rose from a cooking brazier.
Ricardo picked a small silver heart on a silver chain off the
line. He held it in his palm and then took down a second one,
the same as the first except for a spray of silver droplets that
had been added to the point.

''Would you like this one better, Kay?'' he said.

''I think I would rather not be wearing a bleeding heart in
this town,'' she said.

''It means the Saviour's heart,'' he explained patiently.

''Yes. I know. Well, if you don't mind, I think I'll just take
my chances with yours.''

He pressed her hand to his lips, bought the simpler necklace,
and fastened it around her neck. ''So you will never forget
today and me,'' he said.

She pulled him against her. His mouth was warm on her cold
cheek and she laughed, finding his blend of adult sexuality
and macho Latin boyishness irresistible. He was so serious and
romantic, so open to her, and direct. Not like at home, where a
lot of dangerous emotional games were played under the guise
of ''loving friendship'' and ''sexual freedom.''

Of course, Kay told herself, it was shallow and politically
incorrect to be seduced by all this courtship thing, all this
opening of doors and giving of gifts and needing a _nale to keep
you safe in the streets, but it was wonderful to relax and enjoy

it. And why not, as long as you stayed objective. And too, she thought, it was like being new—even in bed.

In the car at the base of the mountain, he took her hand before they drove away. "Now you are doomed," he said, mock-serious.

"You have inside information?"

"Yes! You are doomed to be forever under the spell of Bogotá." He tightened his hold on her hand. "There is a legend that all who do not climb Monserrate by foot are doomed to return here over and over."

Kay felt a chill pass over her. "Why not just say you want me to stay?"

He looked startled. Ricardo could never get over how blunt Americans were.

"The legend is true," he said quickly, "but you're right—I want you never to leave Bogotá."

Again the chill, like entering a dark cave on a sunny day.

Ricardo drove back in a jubilant mood. At the corner of Avenida Jiménez de Quesada and Carrera 2, he turned the VW into the garage of one of Bogotá's first "high-rise" apartment houses. It was a new building, ten stories tall, white with gold trim around the balconies, a panoramic view of the Andes, a garage attendant, and the unheard-of twin luxuries of good plumbing and electrical wall unit heating.

"What are we doing here?" Kay asked, unfolding her long legs and stepping out of the car. The uniformed attendant tipped his hat and said, *"Buenos días, Señor Alvarez."*

"You will see," Ricardo said.

They got off the elevator on the eighth floor and went to the end of the hall, a corner apartment. Ricardo took out a key and handed it to Kay.

They entered a small hallway and then a living room with glass doors opening out onto a balcony that faced Monserrate. The wall-to-wall carpeting was beige. There were faint indentations on it, circles where something heavy had once rested. An enormous white couch faced a round glass table with a chrome base and two leather sling chairs.

"I did not put much furnishings. I thought *you* might like to do that," Ricardo said, grinning like a madman. "Go out on the balcony, *bonita,* I will join you in a moment."

Kay went out and stood looking down at the street eight floors below. This is just a narrow ledge up here, she thought. Inside, Ricardo was talking to someone. What was going on with this offer of an apartment? She felt exposed and vulnerable.

Ricardo came out and stood beside her.

"Come in. Look around. Is something wrong? You don't like this place?"

"I love it, Ricardo. I'm just wondering what it all means. . . ."

He waved his hand impatiently. "You don't understand what it means? It means my father is happy with you. He had begun to trust you. It means . . . *Dios, qué quiere decir*"—he drummed his fingers on the rail looking for the elusive English word, finally saying—*"promoción."* He stared at her, waiting.

"A promotion."

"Yes, yes. Exactly. There has been so much business in the shop lately, my father decided to make a separate department, here, just for you to live and to work the suitcases. He owns the building, so there is no problems." In his excitement Ricardo's English was beginning to slip.

He pulled her to him and kissed her cheek. "So, how do you like it now? A new home and a new job, both together."

"It's great," Kay said. "I am a lucky woman. What does Carlos think about losing me at the shop?"

His eyes flicked away. "Carlos thinks it is fine."

Still jealous, Kay thought briefly, but by now the apartment was starting to look good. She could already taste the solitude, the comfort, the pleasure of hot showers. With a rising sense of exhilaration, she realized, too, that her new position represented the end of her apprenticeship.

Living in the Padrino's building meant she had achieved a new status, she had been accepted into the family. Probably it also meant a raise, although Ricardo had not mentioned it. It was the Padrino's style to drop raises and favors like surprises from the sky, his way of demonstrating his total control.

The sun went behind a cloud and the air instantly turned cold. "Shall we go inside and make a tour?" Ricardo said, making a big thing out of offering her his arm.

The bedroom was large and it, too, had a view of Monserrate and the Andes. There was a double bed with a powder-blue quilted headboard. White Victorian bedside tables on either side held matching lamps. A roomy dressing alcove with a closet led to a bathroom equipped not only with a tub-shower, but most exotic of all for Bogotá, a bidet.

In the kitchen, a young Indian girl with a long black braid down her back was unloading dishes from a crate. Her hair was so black it was almost blue, and Kay thought she was around twelve years old. The kitchen was small and windowless, furnished with a brand-new electric stove and refrigerator, an unpainted wooden table, and a little stool. The walls were bare except for a clock and calendar. A bit of bright striped fabric had been hurriedly tacked up in a corner, a makeshift curtain, and in another corner a door stood open to a tiny half-bathroom.

"This is Rosa," Ricardo said. The girl was very nervous, covering her mouth with her hand, and ducking her head.

"A la orden, señorita," she said.

"Rosa is here to work for you," Ricardo said. "She is sixteen but already a good cook."

Kay shook Rosa's hand, it was surprisingly hot. "I hope we'll be friends, Rosa," she said.

Rosa looked down at the polished red tiles of the floor. *"Sí, señorita."*

Ricardo seemed embarrassed. He steered Kay firmly toward the doorway, but she paused at the curtained area. "What's back there?" she said.

"Rosa's bed." He was not pleased, but Kay said, "May I?" And when the girl nodded mutely, she pulled back the curtain to peer in.

A thin mattress and a blanket covered an iron bedstead. There was no pillow. On top of a cardboard box placed on its side, Rosa had arranged a red plastic comb and a little picture of the Madonna and Child. Underneath, inside the box, were a gray *ruana* and a few folded clothes. A tattered rag doll with button eyes leaned against the wall at the head of the bed. Kay let the curtain fall. *"Gracias, Rosa,"* she said quietly.

On the couch in the living room Ricardo looked worried. "Kay," he began, in what she thought of as his "formal" voice. "I must ask you not to become too familiar with Rosa. It will ruin her for future service to the family and she herself will not respect you." He looked toward the kitchen and lowered his voice.

"Rosa's mother has cooked in my father's house for twenty years. He is giving her to you as a special favor, so you must not displease him by making trouble. You are an outsider and it is hard for you to understand. Rosa is not unhappy. She is glad to have a job when most of her kind are starving and without work."

He went on to outline the common household rules that Rosa and other servants in Colombia were used to observing and told Kay he expected her to abide by them. "Her daily hours are from six in the morning to whenever she finishes after dinner. She has permission to attend Mass every morning. Every two weeks she is permitted time away, from two in the afternoon until ten in the evening. She will be paid one hundred pesos a month [about four dollars]. At night, she is to stay locked in the kitchen area."

"What?" Kay had been trying to keep a polite expression on her face. Now she leaned away from him. "Why do I have to lock her in?"

"Please, Kay, just believe me. There can be serious trouble from servants."

"Of course. How did I miss it? Rosa's obviously a revolutionary assassin."

Ricardo sighed. *"Por favor, bonita,* respect these rules, even if they are harsh for your way of thinking. Rosa herself is *used* to this way. You'll only make her uneasy if you treat her differently."

He took her hand and squeezed hard. She felt the pain of her turquoise ring biting into her finger. "Trust me. Don't make a big *molestia* for us all."

She was about to say she didn't want to make a *molestia* for anyone, when Rosa came in carrying a tray with a bottle of champagne, two glasses, and the toasted triangles of several daintily prepared club sandwiches.

"¿Qué más?" she asked Ricardo, after she had put the tray down.

"Nada más."

Kay swallowed the thank-you that rose to her lips. She felt ashamed. Her Aunt Charlene had been a maid before she had gotten her beautician's license. Kay remembered the stories she used to bring home about the people for whom she worked.

After Ricardo had poured the champagne, Taittinger Brut, he raised his glass in a toast, "To your new home."

Kay lifted her glass, too, and smiled, crossing her fingers behind her back like a child.

After Ricardo left, it suddenly occurred to Kay that the Padrino might have had more complex motives than kindness in placing his servant in her home. Was Rosa there as his spy?

The girl was standing at the stove stirring corn cobs in a large simmering pot.

"Rosa, what are you cooking?" Kay asked.

"Soup," she said shyly, *"ajiaco* soup—with chicken and corn and potatoes and, in the end, avocado."

"It smells good."

Rosa smiled a compressed sort of smile, keeping her lips closed tightly over her teeth. She could make many good dishes, she said: *piquete*, combining chicken, pork, and corn with all the many kinds of potatoes in Colombia; *locro*, made from potatoes and corn; and she was proud to be able to make *fiche*, very good, with blood, sheep tripe, and vegetables. When Kay didn't understand the Spanish word for tripe, Rosa kept pointing to her meager belly and repeating the word until finally Kay said, "Oh, I see . . . stomach . . . well . . ."

Kay sat down on the stool and made a mental note to bring in some chairs. "I hope you'll be happy here, and you won't miss your mother too much."

"Oh no, *señorita,* my mother wanted me to come here."

"She did? Why?"

Rosa looked embarrassed. "My mother says it's good to work for foreign *señoras.* They let you have meat to eat."

"When you cook meat, I hope you put enough in for both of us. Maybe you'll teach me how to cook some dishes. Where I come from, we don't put avocados in soup."

Rosa ducked her head over the pot and didn't say anything.

"What's *your* favorite food, Rosa?" Kay asked.

"Helado—ice cream." At last she smiled, a big broad grin, forgetting to cover her mouth with her hand. There was a dark space where two of her teeth were missing. One front tooth was a jagged stump. Kay wondered what had happened to her.

. . .

In the next weeks, Kay had a hard time getting Rosa to relax.
She would hear her singing in a bouncy, chirpy soprano:

Bombo, bombo,
dale al bombo
para tocar la cumbia
oi que todo el pueblo
se escucha la bulla
se ponga

(Bambo, bambo, bambo,
the cumbia is the dance
for the entire town to dance,
listen to the beat
and go with it.)

But as soon as Kay walked into the kitchen, she would stop.

"Are you afraid I will tell the Padrino things about you?"
Kay asked one day.

"*Señorita,* you are not satisfied with me?" Her eyes were
panicky.

"No, no. I am very satisfied. I just want you to know that I
myself don't tell things. Things like how you spend time
talking to the guard downstairs, and how he thinks you're
pretty. *Para mí,* I think that's okay. And you don't have to
be afraid to take time to talk and visit in the market either,
because I don't mind." Rosa was twisting the cleaning rag she
was holding.

"I know Señora and Señor Alvarez would think badly of
this," Kay continued, "but they don't need to find out about it.
Would you be surprised if I tell you that sometimes I am afraid
of the Padrino myself?"

Now Rosa looked up from the cleaning rag.

"I worry that you will tell everything I do here. He knows
most things anyway, but I do have some secrets. So we will
keep our secrets, both of us, right, Rosa?"

"Oh, Señorita Wolff, I would never say anything that would
make a disturbance." She looked at Kay anxiously. "*Nunca.*"

Kay put her hand on Rosa's shoulder. "I know you
wouldn't."

• • •

On her days off, Rose went to see her mother. One day, making his usual morning appearance in Kay's apartment, Ricardo laughingly reported overhearing Rosa bragging to the other Alvarez servants.

She had boasted about the emeralds that Kay had just bought, her movie-star clothes, the electric things for the kitchen. The *señorita* had brought a machine that cut and stirred food from the Estados Unidos, and a tiny red radio just for her. But, he had heard her add, the *señorita* was a little strange, maybe because she was a foreigner.

"Yes," Kay said, taking him by the hand and leading him, laughing, into the bedroom. "I have strange foreign habits. I like to go to bed with handsome young Colombian men at noon. Worse, I like to leave the curtains open."

In her letters to Maggie, Kay left unanswered Maggie's sardonic questions about the "nonbusiness" side of Ricardo. She didn't want to talk about him. Increasingly, there were times when she didn't even know herself what she felt about him. It was a chink of vulnerability that worried her. She knew that she couldn't afford to take anything but a businesslike attitude toward the relationship. There was no room in the situation for her to lose her edge and become soft, she told herself. But Ricardo was hard to resist. No man had ever treated her with such devotion.

He came over to the apartment every day, always bearing gifts: baskets overflowing with hard-to-find items like good French wines and canned salmon; potted orchids and begonias for the balcony; and, of course, long-stemmed red roses, perfume, and chocolates, the traditional Colombian language of love and seduction. He escorted her on all her errands, no longer commenting when she gave change and candy to the *gamines,* but watching her with calm eyes.

"Are you here to protect me or to keep an eye on me?" she asked one day.

"It is a case of truly loving my work," he said, and they both laughed.

Ricardo had been made the coordinator of his father's Bogotá interests, and it was now his responsibility to keep Kay supplied with "product," which he brought wrapped in newspaper and packed in boxes tied with twine.

On these occasions he was always armed, a Smith & Wesson .357 Magnum concealed in a shoulder holster. One day he brought her a gun, too, a little snub-nosed purse job, an Astra Cadix .38, with a box of bullets to go with it.

"You're safe here," he said, "but I want you to have this because you never know. You must have protection."

She loaded the gun, and for a private joke, stashed it in the dresser drawer with her birth-control pills.

Roddy was coming over mornings, too, to help Kay and to bring messages, suitcases, and orders from Carlos. He liked to stay on and hang around, even when he wasn't needed, until sometimes, irritated, Ricardo threw him out.

Roddy never seemed to change out of his favorite T-shirt wheedled from Kay. It was a red one with a Grateful Dead skull with roses, and SAN FRANCISCO printed underneath. Mostly he would arrive late and hungry, and eager to hear her Marvin Gaye tapes.

"My father worries I'm never going to be a man," he told Kay. "He's always telling me how my brothers were fabricating and working for the family at my age, and how they were already shaving and women thought they were eighteen."

He shrugged. "*Mierda,* I don't care. I'd rather go to London and play drums anyway. Ringo Starr is short like me, and I'm at least that good-looking. Don't you think so, Kay? Wouldn't you rather have me than Ringo Starr?"

He loved the hippie culture, and in some ways he reminded Kay more of the kids she knew back home than a Colombian boy. He lived an intense inner life separate from the family, studying Rosicrucian books about reincarnation, locking himself into his room to listen to heavy-metal rock bands or to stare out toward the mountains in meditation.

Kay began showing him how to glue, teaching him the English words as they went along. Away from the constant scrutiny of the men, he lost his clumsiness and learned eagerly and fast. In the late afternoons, they would sit at the kitchen table while Rosa prepared pink *curuba* fruit juice and *canastos de coco.*

Kay told them things, stories about her pet wolf, Teddy, who was so smart he used to open the refrigerator door to see what he could steal. Sitting at the table, laughing together, she felt them becoming a special little team—the servant, the poor little rich boy, and the foreign woman, she thought with a touch of irony.

Sometimes Roddy would arrive dreamy and sleepy-eyed. It could have been that he stayed up late doing homework for his heavy school schedule. If Kay questioned him, though, he would tease her and say he had been doing street dope. She wasn't sure if he was or if he only wanted to impress her. "Go ahead. Take chances with your father," she would say. "Very smart." And he would grin.

They worked in a room off the bedroom and in the bedroom as well, with the door locked. The floor in the dressing room area was the assembly line and often a tarp was thrown over the bed and used for a work surface. Drying suitcases overflowed into the living room.

In the confined space, the smell of glue could become over-powering, so Kay kept the window open to the frigid Andean night air. It was like driving when you're falling asleep, she thought. You put down the window to stay awake, but then you have to turn up the heater full blast because you're freezing.

Maggie had sent her an electric blanket, which she had nervously hooked up to a converter, often waking up terrified of being electrocuted in her sleep. Many nights she and Roddy worked till 2:00 or 3:00 A.M., and sometimes the smell in the bedroom was so strong that she would have to make her bed on the living-room couch. While Roddy cleaned up, she would drag her electric blanket past the silent accusation of the locked kitchen door. That was always a bad moment, worse still if she could hear Rosa moving around on the other side.

As soon as Roddy left, she would unlock the door. Sometimes Rosa would still be awake, lying in bed listening to her little radio, and Kay would go to the fridge for a yogurt and some Maalox, yawning, yet strung tight, hoping to settle her tense stomach.

Rosa would ask her if she wanted anything and Kay would reply with *"Sí, quiero la luna.* [I want the moon]." And then Kay would ask if Rosa wanted anything. Rosa got used to the joke, but she never would tell Kay anything she wanted. The most she ever ventured was *"Buenas noches"* or, being comfortable with Kay now, she would giggle and say, *"La señorita es loca."*

"Probably so," Kay would say.

Chapter
Five

Camilo [Torres] was a rare man: priest, professor, agitator and organizer and, for an all-too-brief moment in his life, guerrilla fighter. In the space of not more than three years of practical political activity, drawn as he was into the vortex of the social struggle from his position as chaplain and professor of sociology at the National University of Bogotá, he forged an alliance of new political forces in Colombia that promised to develop an overwhelming mass following. It was a movement calling for profound changes, which . . . took religious dogma, in the most Catholic of countries, and made it a philosophical force that undermined and subverted the status quo rather than upholding it, that legitimized, nay compelled, revolutionary action.

—Maurice Zeitlin,
The New York Times,
May 9, 1971

THE CLOSET WAS always loaded with plastic bags of coke. The white powder seemed to be everywhere, free, pure, accessible. These days Kay was casually helping herself to lines whenever she felt her energy flag.

The cloudless blue sky of cocaine energy was there for whatever she needed—if she was down, it brought her up; if she was up, it kept her there; if she was tired, it made her sparkle. It cured her doubts and filled her with radiant confidence. She soothed her swollen nasal passages and stuffy sinuses with distilled water and liquid vitamin E, washing her nose out with a syringe and shrinking the irritated membranes with the cooling magic of camphor and eucalyptus cold-remedy inhalers.

Kay was not alone in discovering the magic of the coca plant. From 1969 to 1970, world cocaine consumption had risen four hundred percent (according to Drug Enforcement Administration figures). Business was booming for Roberto Alvarez. Kay was kept very busy producing suitcases for the twenty or so mules that the Padrino was running on a staggered basis to Europe and the United States.

As she learned more about the business from Ricardo, Kay realized that his father was a man who loved covering all the angles. It was a very Colombian trait, this pleasure in the game of seeing just how many times you could turn a profit from a single move.

Through his government connections, the Padrino would obtain visas for his mules. Some mules he recruited through newspaper ads: "Furniture salesperson, no experience necessary." These were carefully screened. Others were established businessmen—a jewelry salesman, a honey salesman, whose work already took them to Europe frequently.

For his European routes, Roberto preferred men to women. Out of his twenty mules, only about six were female. The women were often young, student age, but the men he liked to hire had to be old enough to pose as business types, even if they were not legitimately so. Sometimes he would team employees up, sending the women along as "wives."

The businessmen were pleased to work with the Padrino because of the neat little scams he offered them. Counterfeit United States money and bogus United States credit cards were cheap and readily available in Columbia, but hard to pass in Bogotá, a city teeming with con men. It was easier in Europe. The runners would take care of their own business in West Germany or France, collect on delivery of the cocaine suitcases to Reynaldo, who coordinated all European traffic, and afterward make an extra two thousand dollars passing Roberto's fake money. The hard-to-get goods bought with the phony cash or cards could then be resold for a profit in Bogotá—minus the Padrino's cut, of course. Working these angles turned every trip into a triple payoff for all concerned.

For a majority of Columbians and for Colombian cocaine *coqueros* like Roberto, smuggling was not preceived as a shameful occupation. There is a centuries-long tradition in Colombia that views smuggling and related practices simply as "smart business." In 1970, cocaine was merely the most recent commodity in a long line of contraband goods and services.

Partly, this time-honored outlaw mentality is the result of Colombia's position at the crossroads of South America. Bordered by Peru, Ecuador, Brazil, Venezuela, and Panama, with both Pacific and Caribbean coastlines, Colombia could scarcely help but become a smuggler's paradise. The addition of airline service and the Pan American Highway only served to modernize the trade.

Kay was to learn, later and at first hand, of the reign of terror and counterterror that accompanies this tradition. But in February of 1970 in the apartment at Avenida Jiménez de Quesada, she felt optimistic and grounded enough to leave Bogotá for a run on her own business. Her plan was to make the carry herself, taking a loaded suitcase to Los Angeles. The visit home would be the first in five months.

Carlos had taken to dropping over to visit Kay once a week or so, not only to inspect her work, but because he liked to sit on her balcony. He would prop his feet, encased in white socks and brown sandals, up against one of Kay's large pots of begonias, yawn, and drink a Costena before going home. He had begun to confide little bits of business gossip to her, airing his long-standing grievance against Gutiérrez, the cook.

"Don César is trying to grab more and more power for himself. He sniffs out new sources without our authority. He thinks his deals are secret, but I know his game. He's trying to set up a little separate business from which he thinks he can exclude me." Carlos shook his head. "No, no. Gutiérrez is a brilliant man, but he isn't using the sense God gave to him. That arrogant *hijo de puta* thinks I am stupid, he thinks I don't know that he slips in a little cut sometimes. When we get complaints from Europe, he plays the innocent one. He acts the hurt one. They are lying, he says. So now I have to test every ounce. But let him beware. If I catch him there will be consequences of the most serious kind."

He stopped to look at Kay, who had been listening intently. "So you see? . . . He is as bad as stealing from us. The man wants to be a boss but he doesn't even play on the team."

"What does your brother say?" Kay asked.

"*Pues* . . . my brother . . . and it has always been hard to make my brother listen to what he doesn't want to hear."

He sighed and lowered his feet. "Sometimes I think he's angry because you're so close with my crew now. He says nothing but I feel it. *Bueno*, he hired you and now he worries about your influence with his son. I like to have such a worry for my son—it doesn't seem so bad to me. *Bueno . . . pues . . .* " He shrugged, put the empty Costena bottle on the balcony ledge, and lifted himself grunting from the wrought-iron chair. "Time to go home, *niña*."

Kay had been preparing a Samsonite for the run back to L.A., and it was standing in the bedroom beside the others that Carlos had come to collect.

"When are you leaving with that little beauty?" Carlos asked.

"Next Friday. I'll be in L.A. for a week."

"My brother would like you to bring back as many of those as you can for us." The Samonsites were well-crafted to standard sizes and therefore easy to work on, unlike the Colombian suitcases, which were irregular and poorly made. "He would also like you to look around the stores and bring back tools and supplies."

Suddenly he took her by the upper arm, his hand closing gently above the elbow, like a soft retriever's mouth recovering a bird. "Are you all right, Kay?" he asked. There was something different in his eyes, and for a fleeting moment she glimpsed a private Carlos, sensual and delicate.

"Sure," she said, surprised. "Never better."

"Well, please, just make sure you come back from L.A. The world is a very small place when a Colombian is looking for you." Kay could see his massive walrus back and his balding head in the bureau mirror behind him.

As they passed the kitchen on the way out, laughter pealed from behind the closed door.

"Is Roddy in there?" Carlos said.

"Yes." Kay expected a flash of anger, but he simply smiled.

"He likes Rosa," he said, and winked, pursing his mouth. So there were ways, after all, in which a servant was not off limits—provided of course that she was female and young and you were a male and "family." It was understood.

Kay entered the United States at San Francisco, a less dangerous entry than LAX, the notoriously strict Los Angeles airport. She caught the connecting flight between the two cities to the L.A. United terminal, where Maggie was waiting to pick her up.

The Santa Monica freeway was jammed, but Maggie cheerfully navigated the creeping traffic, full of enthusiasm and talk. Kay tried to listen, but she felt sick and cocaine-irritable, her head aching and her nasal passages dry and sore.

Maggie went on, oblivious, describing the new house they had decided to invest in jointly. She had negotiated the closing and signed in both their names using Kay's power of attorney. Kay was really going to like it, Maggie said, it was a true bargain, a great investment in a coming neighborhood—and such a relief for her after sharing the three-room apartment with Teddy.

Teddy even had a back yard now. Maggie laughed. She had hoped that the high fence would keep him out of trouble but . . . and she embarked on the story of his latest misdeed.

The back yard had been lovingly landscaped for the previous tenants by a Japanese gardener. There was a pond with a little wooden bridge and a number of flower beds. Bored by the end of the first week, Teddy first dug up most of the flowers and then went on to eat all the fish in the pond, daintily leaving just their tails.

The Japanese gardener had quit. Maggie mimicked him perfectly: "Carp live to be very old. Very valuable, very sacred. This great disgrace, dog like wild animal. I go, I no work such a house."

Maggie turned onto a shady street lined with neat suburban homes and two-car garages. To Kay's jet-lagged, Colombian vision everything seemed strangely open and unprotected.

"That's ours, the one with the weeds in the front yard."

"Oh," Kay said.

"Are you okay, hon?" Maggie asked.

"I have a really bad toothache. It's been going on for weeks and I've been pouring coke on it, waiting till I could see an American dentist. But now the damn thing really hurts." Kay didn't know that accelerated tooth decay was a side effect of habitual cocaine use, a fact that even most dentists would not understand until several years later.

Maggie turned off the ignition. "You look like you could use a Valium," she said.

As soon as they opened the front door, Teddy hurled himself at Kay like a hurricane, leaping and barking and bringing her his chewed-up tennis ball. But when she ordered him to sit he obeyed instantly, as though he had been waiting months for her command, and she put her arms around him, sinking her face gratefully into the familiar comfort of his fur.

In the bedroom, Maggie put the loaded Samsonite next to Kay's bed, knowing it would be the first thing she would want to see when she awoke from her nap.

Kay got up in the middle of the afternoon and found a strange girl in the kitchen. Another woman she didn't know was using the phone, and a third was sitting at the dining-room table reading *Variety*.

Who were these women, Kay thought irritably. Was Maggie running a hotel here or what?

The skinny blonde in the kitchen looked up from the wheat germ and bananas she was mixing with a fork. "Hi," she said, "who're you?"

"It's more like who're you, isn't it? Where's Maggie?" Kay said.

"She's out." The blonde was eyeing her with undisguised curiosity.

Kay turned on her heel and went into the living room where the girl at the desk quickly hung up the phone.

"You must be Kay," she said with a sunshiny grin. "I'm Crystal and my friends are Sage and Frankie? Maggie's so great, she's letting us stay in the room over the garage until we get a place here in L.A.? We're starting a women's record company?"

Kay couldn't stand the way she ended every sentence as though it was a question. "Are you asking me or telling me?" she said. She returned to the kitchen and began washing out the Italian coffeepot.

"I'm sorry, you're out of coffee," the blonde girl said carefully. "Want some Chinese herbal tea?"

"No," Kay said. "I want some fucking coffee. And by the way, this is my house."

The woman reading the newspaper glanced up as Kay passed on her way back to her bedroom. "Have you unpacked the suitcase yet?" she asked eagerly.

The bedroom was cool behind drawn shades. Kay's paintings were stacked against one bare wall and the still unopened suitcase stood in front of another. An overturned packing crate served as a nightstand beside a double bed-sized box spring and mattress.

This is supposed to be home, Kay thought, looking at the wadded tissues and pill bottles that lay under a Tensor light on the crate. She popped a codeine into her mouth and stretched out to wait for sleep in the unfamiliar room.

When she awoke, Maggie was alone in the kitchen. In the quiet house, the throbbing of Kay's tooth was like a sound.

"How are you, puss?" Maggie asked, handing Kay a cup of coffee with a steaming head of milk, *café con leche* Bogotá style.

"Sour puss," Kay said.

The root canal surgery and recovery took several days, during which Maggie's business phone rang night and day. On the third evening, Kay felt well enough to unload the suitcase. She dismembered it deftly and meticulously, taking it apart stitch by stitch with a pair of surgical scissors and a knife. She and Maggie celebrated the safe completion of the run by opening a bottle of champagne and inaugurating the first lines. Nothing could match the high.

In the following days of inevitable business flurry for Maggie, Kay was left to herself. After five months with the strong contrasts and colors of Bogotá, the washed-out pastels and wide, innocent sky of L.A. depressed her. Nothing was the way she remembered it, yet she knew that nothing had changed. The city seemed familiar yet alien, like the face of an ex-lover.

She anesthetized herself shopping and tooting, driving around town in a rented Lincoln Continental. One day, in a leather shop on Rodeo Drive that smelled like the interior of a new Jaguar, Kay found a line of luggage by a company called French that she thought was the wave of the Alvarezes' future: fancy three-hundred-dollar garment bags of a sturdy, tapestry-like material in a muted floral print. They were well made with thick side panels and tops that would allow as much packaging as a Samsonite, but being garment bags, were less likely to attract suspicion. She bought several in different sizes to bring back as samples.

Arrests for false-bottomed suitcases were more and more frequent. Although Carlos's fabrication technique flattened the cocaine in a layer so thin it was not detectable to the eye, Kay knew that the days of the Samsonite were numbered. The secret of success in the smuggling game was constant innovation and the ability always to remain one step ahead of customs.

She stashed the bags in her bedroom and began thinking increasingly of going home to Bogotá. She was not in the mood for socializing, although Maggie pressed her to see friends, and wanted to throw a housewarming party. Finally, feeling pressured, Kay agreed to join some of the old gang at the Clam Digger.

Reluctantly, she got into character, a silk blouse and tight knit pants with high-heeled boots and a short fur jacket. She ratted her hair wildly and shook her blond mane back over her shoulders, L.A. expensive don't-give-a-damn chic.

Maggie was at the door as Kay snorted a line off the rim of the sink. "Ready?" Maggie said.

They drove the ocean route toward Malibu with Kay tooting and changing radio stations till Art Garfunkel's achingly clear voice stopped her: "Bridge over Troubled Waters." Her mood sank. *When you're in the street*, she heard him sing. She thought of the *gamines* in the rain, small cardboard-covered lumps huddling against the walls of buildings.

The Clam Digger was an old wooden boathouse converted into a waterside show place with a large dining room. It was jumping with a Saturday night "in" crowd, eager to see and be seen.

Kay and Maggie pushed up to the bar to order a beer. "Very uptown," Kay said. "This place has changed." The bartender rushed by and Maggie shouted, "Two Heinekens."

"Darling Kay, my pet"—it was Alex, tall and thin and bubbling—"give your hairdresser a kiss. You look great, so super thin. You'll have to turn me on to your diet." He giggled meaningfully.

There were three men and four women when Kay's group finally sat down. They were all in their twenties and all working in jobs related to the movie, music, or TV industries except for Alex the hairdresser and Joanie, who was in real estate.

Talk ran from new houses to new cars, to why the Smothers

Brothers TV show was canceled. The waiter brought fries, lobsters, steaks, more wine. Kay drank steadily and with purpose. She was lost, drifting in and out of the conversation. Joanie said she couldn't get tickets to something, what a bummer; Alex said he never watched the news anymore because it was all the same and too, too depressing.

Kay felt as though a tight metal band was encircling her head. "Forget it," someone was saying, "Nixon's on cruise control anyway."

Joanie asked her something about Colombia and when Kay tried to explain, to tell her about the *gamines*, about the time she had been driving and had seen the dead bodies of two children lying abandoned by the side of the road, Joanie gave her a quizzical look. "Oh, come on, Kay," she said, "it probably was something else, you're exaggerating."

"No," Kay said, flinging out her hand. A glass went over and she saw the spreading stain on the tablecloth in front of her and all the faces gaping around the table. "You make me sick," she spat out. "So smug, 'Oh, look at Kay, she must have gotten a little too high.' You're so sensitive, you see a dead dog in the road you turn your heads—'Oh I just can't take it'—but little kids rotting in a ditch like some kind of roadside kill . . . well, Kay's just exaggerating, she's just drunk or stoned. So good for you—stay comfortable . . . stay fat . . . stay blind. . . ."

Maggie had pushed her chair back and was coming around the table.

"Crazy Kay's making a scene, that's all it is, right?" Kay said, but Maggie had her by the arm. "Come to the bathroom with me, Kay."

"At least in Bogotá they don't lie to themselves." Kay was shouting now. She knew how bad it was but it didn't matter, even when she saw the manager coming toward them.

The next day, Kay was filled with remorse and self-disgust, but she knew for sure that Los Angeles was over for her, for a long time to come. Maggie tried to get her to talk some more about Colombia, but Kay shut her out. Anything she could say would sound forced to her now, and Maggie's prompting was vaguely embarrassing, like a therapist trying to "open" her up. Kay remained withdrawn, knowing guiltily that she was hurting Maggie, that Maggie was only trying to help.

"Shit, Kay," Maggie said, finally angry, "I've had it with your moods." They were in the bedroom and Kay was packing.

As always, as soon as Maggie gave up and pulled back, Kay felt a wave of intense relief, and then after a while, anxiety. She went over to the bed where Maggie was sitting and laid her head in her friend's lap.

"Please, Kay, I can't stand this," Maggie said.

Kay tightened her arms around Maggie's waist.

"We always end up fighting," Maggie said, keeping herself rigid against Kay's embrace. They sat like that for a moment and then Maggie lowered her hand to Kay's hair. "I don't know . . . " Maggie said.

Finally the day came to go home to Bogotá. Maggie drove Kay to LAX on a Monday morning with five new suitcases of varying sizes crammed with American goodies impossible to obtain in Colombia: designer sunglasses and clothes, expensive watches, tape recorders, new Hendrix tapes as well as James Brown and girl groups like The Supremes. The Colombians were not big on protest music like Country Joe and the Fish, The Mamas and the Papas, or Bob Dylan.

For Ricardo, she had bought American sports clothes and tennis shoes as well as the tapes, and for Rosa she had special American sweatshirts with pictures of Hollywood and Disneyland.

She had filled a separate suitcase for the Padrino with needle-nose pliers, C-clamps, leather-cutting shears, long tweezers, scissors, fabric pullers, glues, upholstery tacks and needles, fancy braiding, high-quality thread, and designer fabrics.

Maggie's car was a battle-scarred 1964 VW notchback. On the freeway, with the sun beating down through the windshield, they talked of future plans, finally promising to meet each other for a pass in the Caribbean.

Maggie had laughed and drawled, "Hey, like far out, man," in her best imitation hippie voice. But in the end, they had not been able to settle on which island.

"Okay, then, close your eyes and just say the name of the first island you can think of," Maggie urged, but Kay's mind had already shifted gears as soon as she saw they were approaching the first low airport buildings.

She opened her roomy carpetbag purse to check the papers again—ticket, money, passport. In her purse, too, was a beige shawl in case she needed a last-minute change of image, but she decided to stick to the three-piece suit she was wearing. Under the off-white armor of its linen elegance, Kay was a walking bank, carrying ten thousand dollars, Maggie's investment money.

Kay didn't want anyone to see her get out in front of the Avianca entrance with Maggie, so she made Maggie drive two airlines down, planning to get a porter and walk back inside the terminal.

"This isn't necessary," Maggie said, maneuvering the car irritably through the clogged traffic of the entrance ramps.

"Look, I don't know if I'm hot here or not. I'd rather be too paranoid than have you recognized and tailed. I'm probably going to end up dead or in a jail cell anyway."

Maggie sighed, parked at the curb, and got out to help Kay with the bags. "Good-bye, toots, stay well," she said, and pulled away without a good-bye kiss or a backward glance, just as Kay had told her to do.

"What have you got in here, bricks?" The porter was grouchy as he wrestled the suitcases onto his hand truck.

Kay stood and watched Maggie's car merging into traffic, one taillight taped and the trunk bouncing slightly. With all the money they were making, why didn't Maggie buy herself a car? Then the VW disappeared, and for a moment all Kay wanted was for Maggie to turn around and come back.

At the Avianca counter, Kay and her fortress of luggage blended in perfectly among the returning Colombians burdened like carpenter ants with precious American appliances. Her seatmate on the plane was buried under so many boxes and bags that he couldn't put his food tray down and sat enviously eyeing Kay's dinner.

It was too hazardous to fly into Bogotá's El Dorado airport after dark, so Avianca passengers were routinely checked in for an overnight stop at the Continental Hotel in Panama City. Kay hated the stopover. She was nervous about holding so much money and strung out over the next day's border control.

The hotel was understaffed and full of CIA and American military men. Kay had no problem playing the weary traveler and holing up in her room. She pushed the dresser in front of the door, checked to see that the windows were locked, switched the TV to Johnny Carson, and got into bed with her ten-thousand-dollar bra under her pillow.

Yet even after Carson, sleep evaded her and she lay listening to the muffled sounds of doors slamming and people returning to their rooms. She kept thinking about Bogotá, wondering what had happened while she was gone.

Coming into El Dorado, Kay knew immediately that things had changed. The airport bristled with many more armed soldiers than usual. Customs had been rearranged by the military into three separate areas, one for inspection of papers, one for interrogation, and a last for baggage search.

Standing in line, she kept fear at bay by concentrating on the details of her cover story, which was that she owned a small boutique in Bogotá and had been away on business. It wasn't so much that she feared being caught with the money, they would simply confiscate that, it was that she was traveling under false identification papers, a serious crime in Colombia. When her turn finally came, they passed her without a single question, barely glancing at her. She wondered whom they were after.

The porters stood pressed against the gates, waiting. Kay wanted to find the youngest, the one she had used when Maggie came down that first time. She looked around but saw only one of them, the boy with two missing fingers. She divided her baggage claim tickets between him and a smaller boy.

"Where is your friend Condorlito?" she asked as she helped them drag the bags to the customs line.

"I don't know," said the missing-fingers boy evasively. The littler one put his bag down to rest for a moment and swiped at his forehead with a grimy sleeve. "He's gone," he said and picked up the bag again.

"Where did he go?" she asked, but either they didn't know or didn't want to tell her.

As soon as they came out to the taxi rank she saw the black Mercedes. Carlos's assistant, Miguel, was at the wheel wearing a brand-new suede jacket. He got out to open the trunk, making a thumbs-up sign to Kay and saying "¿Qué tal?"

Then the back doors opened on each side and Ricardo and

his father got out. Kay hid her surprise and everyone embraced, touching cheeks the Colombian way in an *abrazo* embrace. "*Bienvenida,*" the Padrino said. He was dressed in gray flannel sports slacks, a navy blue cardigan, and a maroon silk foulard. As usual, he emanated a faint trace of musky perfume and a starchy cleanliness, as though, Kay thought, he had just changed and showered.

Miguel paid off the two boys and Kay slipped them each the small fortune of a folded American dollar bill. Instantly they became desperate not to lose her. Kay could see they were afraid of Miguel, but they hung on doggedly anyway, trying to look useful, holding the doors, making sure the trunk was securely closed. When the Mercedes finally pulled away, she looked out of the rear window. They remained standing where the car had left them; then the smaller one sat down on the curb.

"You must have done well in the States, no?" Miguel teased. "Throwing your money away like that."

"Sure, Miguel," she said. "You're just jealous. You want me to throw it away on you."

"*Seguro*, Kay. I would like that."

She sat in the back beside Roberto. Ricado twisted around in the front seat to join the conversation.

"You saw the changes in the airport?" Roberto said.

"Yes. What's going on? Are they looking for someone?"

"They are looking for Carmilo Torres," Roberto said, and Ricardo gave a short, mirthless laugh.

"Who is he?"

"He was. He is dead. But I said that because like Che, for some people he is still very much alive. He was a priest who joined the guerrillas. Four years ago on February 15, the military ambushed him in the mountains and killed him and this week they are nervous because it is the anniversary of his death. You see, Kay, anniversaries are used in many different ways here, depending on your politics." He smiled humorlessly.

"Anyway, since then, many more priests have followed him . . . there must be fifty the army would like to get. They preach unrest to the poor in the *barrios* of the cities, especially now, because of the election."

Kay could find no chink of passion or opinion in his quiet voice.

"The election is coming in April and though they are saying it will be a peaceful democratic process"—he smiled his dry smile again—"nobody knows what's going to happen."

Roberto Alvarez's father had been a Liberal, a passionate believer in the cause of a decentralized, democratic government, but Roberto himself was a pragmatist. He had grown up observing the simmering, often violent battle between the fanatically pro-government, pro-Church Conservatives and his father's populist Liberal party. When, at last, the struggle had exploded into a devastating civil war, he had witnessed years of seemingly endless and sickening atrocities committed by both sides.

The war had been precipitated in 1948 by the mysterious assassination of the shining hope of the Liberal party, a dynamic, Kennedy-like figure and mayor of Bogotá, whose murder, many felt, had struck a death blow to the progressive popular movement, driving it underground and creating the precursors of the Colombian guerrilla movement.

Though the country had been governed by a system of alternating Conservative and Liberal presidents since 1958, Roberto Alvarez had concluded, with a touch of stoic cynicism, that there was very little difference anymore between the two parties. What interested him about Colombian politics was how he could best use the system to further his dreams of wealth and power for himself and his family. He backed the traditional, landowning aristocracy, among whom he had many friends.

The attendant at Kay's underground garage recognized the Mercedes and tipped his visored hat. Upstairs, Rosa opened the door to an apartment full of flowers and wine. "Señor Ricardo's orders," she whispered to Kay. Fruit and cheese rounds, white and smelly, sweets, *tungo* buns, and the fried chicken legs and *arepas* that Ricardo loved were already set out on the glass coffee table. Miguel began to open bottles and Roberto poured himself exactly two fingers of aguardiente.

Kay left the men examining the new Stanley tools and other implements she had brought back and went to strip off her money corset and take a shower. She came back in a blue velour lounging gown, her hair pulled up on top of her head, in her hand a Baume & Mercier watch for Ricardo.

"*Fantástico! Muchas gracias, bonita mía,*" he said enthusiastically and kissed her on the mouth. Kay was intensely aware of Roberto's gaze, taking them in. She excused herself to get napkins from the kitchen.

Roberto put a restraining hand on her arm. "*You* don't go to the kitchen to get napkins," he said sternly. "That is Rosa's work. She should be reprimanded."

"*Rosa, servilletas*," he called out imperiously. He continued shaking his head, "*Malo, muy malo, no tiene sentido*—she has no sense."

Kay sat down, careful to place herself opposite the men, on the other side of the coffee table from Ricardo. The Padrino leaned his head against the back of the couch, closed his eyes for a moment, and then opened them very wide, a habit he had. "Yes," he said.

They began talking about the upcoming election again, and about the explosive feelings running between the bosses in Bogotá. The Padrino feared that some of them would take advantage of the political violence and chaos to settle old grudges.

He felt that some of the families in the cocaine business would use the unstable times to make power grabs: the suppliers and dealers who transported the paste to the processing kitchens; the cooks who ran the kitchens, turning the raw cocaine into white powder; the bosses who sold and held control over the finished product.

After Rosa timidly cleared the dishes and food, the Padrino brought out a small packet. "You have not yet tested the new product, how about a sample, a *muestra*," he said, like someone offering a round of afterdinner brandy.

He spread generous lines on the glass tabletop and worked the cocaine skillfully with the blunt end of a single-edged blade. He then made a fist and poured a small pile of cocaine from the paper directly onto the flat back to his hand. Bending his head, he snorted, with loud gusto, straight into each nostril.

Kay had never seen the Padrino do even one line and the crude, macho gesture looked like something from his younger days. Glancing up quickly, he caught Kay's amazed stare. His laugh was another total surprise, high and gleeful, *hee-hee-hee*.

"No, I don't like straws," he said. "I am a purist. For me, things are best taken straight and strong—just as they are."

"What is this 'Krazy Glue'?" Miguel said, picking up the tube Kay had brought home.

And they all started joking about what could be done with this magic stuff.

"Entonces, jóvenes," the Padrino said after a while. He stood up, signaling the end of the evening.

The next day he called Kay. "Very nice, very clever, the things you have bought for us. The new French luggage is a timely idea. You did well. How would you like to go to Europe on a buying trip for the company?" Kay knew she wasn't really being asked her opinion. Questions like this from the Padrino were just his polite way of issuing a command. He had decided that—even though she was a woman—the *norteamericana* had proven herself smart enough for a place on his A team.

Carlos had liked the tapestry garment bags; the concept interested him. The Padrino, ahead of the game as usual, wanted Kay to go to Paris, research the luggage there, and bring home a variety of samples for Carlos to judge. On the way she would carry a loaded Samsonite to West Germany and afterward do some banking for him in the Grand Cayman Islands. She would be paid four thousand dollars for the run, one thousand dollars to fabricate the bags, and an additional four thousand dollars for the banking.

"When you are in the Caymans," he told her, "take a few days, have a holiday, do as you please." Kay understood the unspoken message. She had the Padrino's blessing to go ahead with a little private business of her own. The decision on which Caribbean island to meet Maggie had made itself.

Chapter
Six

The four-way presidential election campaign in Colombia has entered the final stretch, and the question "Will it come off peacefully?" is receiving nearly as much attention as "Who will win?"

. . . "I have noted a lack of communication between the ruling class and the people in my country," said Misael Pastrana Borrero, the 46-year-old candidate of the majority of the ruling coalition known as the National Front—in a recent interview. According to most Colombian observers, Mr. Pastrana and two competing splinter candidates of the coalition between Liberals and Conservatives represent portions of the ruling class.

The fourth candidate is Gen. Gustavo Rojas Pinilla, who ruled the country as a military dictator from 1953 to 1957 and now heads the opposition to his democratic successors.

The former dictator, who will be 70 next month, is running on a populist platform that includes promises to reduce taxes while increasing government spending on education, and providing free medical and dental care for the poor.

"The National Front has made our campaign for us in 12 years of government," the General's daughter and political mentor, Mrs. María Eugenia Moreno Diaz, said in an interview.

—Joseph Novitski,
Special to *The New York Times*,
February 23, 1970

KAY HAD ALWAYS planned on building up her own business once her position with the Alvarez family was secure. She had been busy preparing for that moment by collecting false documents through Maggie's underground antidraft connections in the States and by perfecting a number of disguises. Behind the safety of different identities she would be able to cross and recross the same border numerous times without arousing suspicion.

During the months working for Carlos, she had stocked her closet with wigs, hats, body padding, suits for dowager ladies and conservative pants-suit ensembles. Her makeup case held dozens of different bases, rouges, eye pencils, shadows, and mascara.

For Kay, there was no security in a disguise unless every detail rang true. Nothing was too small to warrant attention, from the correct choice of jewelry to the right shade of nail polish. To create the look of a true redhead, the makeup base had to be burnt sienna, an older woman was darker complected, a blonde was rosy.

Kay had learned the tricks of this craft from an old UCLA classmate who had gone from studying physics to studying the beauty secrets of the Hollywood stars. He had become a famous drag queen as well as one of the best beauticians in L.A.

For her move to Bogotá, he had presented her with a gift-wrapped box and a card that said, "To darling Madame X from Alexandria the Queen." Inside was a set of the latest quick-rinse hair dyes and a box of disposable plastic gloves for applying the dye. She promised that on her return she would bring him a vial of the finest cocaine he had ever had.

Now that the Padrino had bestowed his unofficial blessings on her enterprises, she was glad she had done her homework. She planned her wardrobe for her upcoming trip, giving herself a well-to-do yet sporty Scandinavian image. She bleached and straightened her normally dark-blond, wavy hair, and redyed it to a pale, almost white, Nordic blond. She wore it swinging long and silky and accented her high cheekbones with a pale base makeup and darker blush.

Feeling confident and ready to move, she phoned Maggie to tell her that her boss had just given her a vacation and to meet her for a few days of sun and fun at Grand Cayman Island.

A few weeks later, in mid-March of 1970, Kay boarded an Avianca flight for Rio, carrying two suitcases loaded with concealed cocaine, one for Reynaldo in West Germany and one for Maggie in the Caymans. Without leaving the airport in Rio, she changed planes from Avianca to TAP for Lisbon.

The plane was half-empty. A few businessmen sat with their attaché cases open and their jackets off. The weather was bad and the sudden stomach-lurching bounces made it hard for Kay to sleep. Most of the airports on the Continent would be closed, but she knew that Lisbon's Portela would be open. It almost always was, no matter what the weather.

It was open, but it was also a nasty shock. Lisbon had always been a good beachhead into Europe. Closely allied with Brazil, customs checks on arrivals from Brazilian cities were notoriously lax. This time, however, the unforeseeable x factor, the dangerously unpredictable variable that haunted Kay's fears, had become a reality.

Waiting for her was a customs and security check as tight as anything she'd seen in Berlin, London, or Mexico City, if not tighter.

Marcello Caetano had just recently taken over a Portugal that had been suppressed for forty years under the extreme right-wing dictatorship of António Salazar. With much of the populace demanding change, Caetano, himself a reactionary Conservative, was attempting to maintain tight control over an inflammatory period of transition.

Colonial Africa was wrenching away from Portuguese rule in an increasing climate of terror and bloodshed, and the cream of Portugal's youth had joined their American counterparts in the Pacifist Movement. The good old days of a relaxed and jocular bureaucracy were gone.

The two stone-faced men waiting to examine Kay and her baggage were intent on doing their jobs. There had been a recent terrorist bombing in downtown Lisbon and they gave the Samsonites a complete and agonizingly slow inspection, dumping the contents of the bags on a table.

One of the men tore the wrappings off all the presents Kay had brought along for the Padrino's European contacts, while the other ran his hands carefully around the insides of the suitcases. Kay could hardly breathe as she watched his fingers probing, sensitive as a heat-seeking device. Finally, they threw all the things back into the suitcases and snapped them shut.

But it was not over.

The one who seemed to be the senior official asked to look

at the camera she wore slung over her shoulder and examined it carefully.

"You say you are going to Paris for make the shopping," he said in broken English, "but maybe you are *journalista?*" His eyes, boring into hers, were cold.

At last, after examining her ticket to prove to themselves that she was in transit and was leaving the next day, they stamped her into the country.

"Welcome to Portugal," Kay later wrote Maggie. "I thought it was all over for me."

Lisbon was only a few miles from the airport. Through the taxi window, Kay got a brief glimpse of citrus-shaded Moorish arches and ancient pastel houses colored pink, yellow, and green. The air was heady with a briny-sweet mix of sea breezes and garden courtyards.

She liked the giant palms in the lobby of the Ritz, their shaggy heads high above huge terracotta planters, fronds stirring slightly in the air-conditioned breeze. Once up in her room, everything was suddenly very quiet. The bureau mirror reflected a king-sized bed with one side turned down and a bedside table with lamplight illuminating a black phone. There was a trace of stale pipe smoke in the air.

She stood in the middle of the room wanting desperately to do a couple of lines. It would be so good, make a new woman of her. She could just taste the slight bitterness, feel the magical sensation of clearing in her head, as though a misted window-pane had been wiped brilliantly clean.

Instead, she sank her exhausted body into a hot bath. One of Kay's unbreakable rules was never to do cocaine while on a run. On these trips, even the slightest distortion in viewpoint could result in a fatal error. When she got out of the tub, she sat in her bathrobe and wrote her grandmother a letter. She told her she had a nice teaching job and was in Europe on a vacation. "I hope your arthritis isn't bothering you. Write soon and tell me how you're doing and all about everyone."

In the early morning, she took a taxi back to the airport. They drove through a leafy park and down the empty highway lined with spicy rose-laurel bushes. The driver never turned around and never spoke to her. She felt taut as a winch wire. Yesterday's scare was still with her and Frankfurt was ahead, not quite as dicey as Berlin, but not a place to take for granted, either.

Portela didn't have a duty-free shop, but she bought a bottle of port, which was good here. Kay knew that the Padrino's wife, Flora, really liked it, and she had them send a case of it to her from the airport post office. The post office was open twenty-four hours a day and was the most efficient one in Europe. She went there herself and posted the letter to her grandmother and one to Maggie, knowing they would arrive in forty-eight hours.

It was cold in Frankfurt. Kay wore a high-style sheepskin-lined coat with matching high-heeled boots—sporty-rich. The speedy knocking of her heart seemed to have taken over her whole rib cage, but as soon as her turn came and she pushed her luggage cart up to the customs official, she was dead calm. Everything fell away. There was nothing left but the instantaneous present and the man in front of her who had a double chin and a small, moist mouth. "Destination?" he asked.

"Paris. Shopping." She smiled.

He looked her over, nodded, and began chalking the suitcases. As she pushed her cart away, she gave him a friendly wave with her gloved hand. He nodded.

Gotcha, she thought with an almost violent sense of triumph.

Then the high came on, as though a tourniquet had suddenly been removed, releasing a rush of stemmed blood to her veins and head, the adrenal hit that came from marrying the terror of risk with the elation of victory. No other feeling, not even coke, compared with it. It was addictive.

She saw Reynaldo waiting for her through the glass doors. Tall and blond, he was one of those fair Castilian Colombians who could easily pass as a German. It was hard to believe he was Flora's brother.

"*Ciao, bella,*" he said. He embraced her, taking advantage of the situation to hold her just a little too long. She maneuvered with a cheek kiss and an arm between them, catching a whiff of alcohol on his breath. Whiskey, she thought.

He picked up the two Samsonites and headed toward an airport bar. "No, I'm starving. Let's eat," Kay said, taking his arm firmly.

The airport café was done up like a miniature beer garden and the waitresses were all hefty blondes in Tyrolean outfits.

Kay slipped into a booth and put her big purse on the bench beside her, forcing Reynaldo to sit across the table.

This was her first time alone with him. On the few occasions when she had met him in Bogotá, he had made a point of ignoring her. Ricardo didn't like him, said he was always trying to prove himself. He was the youngest in Flora's family by a gap of ten years and had been spoiled from the time he was five when his father had died mysteriously in a car explosion. The Padrino thought he was bright. Reynaldo had gone to a Swiss boarding school, spoke four languages, and had a degree in business administration.

He ordered an Irish coffee. Kay glanced up at him and frowned slightly. He changed to a Loewenbräu and bratwurst.

"My girl friend is afraid I'll get drunk," he said to the waitress in English.

"I sure am," Kay said brightly. "Just black coffee and a ham *Stulle* for me." She was angry at him for drawing attention to them.

At a nearby table a man sat carefully perusing the *Frank-furter Allgemeine Zeitung*. Kay could feel her abdomen cramping, and excused herself.

In the ladies'-room mirror, her face was tired and pale. Automatically, she began to repair it. Suddenly, a little girl materialized at her elbow, a pasty kid of four or five, with wispy braids and pale blue eyes highly magnified behind steel-rimmed glasses.

"Oh! I didn't see you. You scared me," Kay said. From behind one of the closed stall doors a querulous voice said, "Trudi?"

"*Ja, Mutti,*" the little girl said, staring fixedly at Kay. Kay put her makeup away and left, flustered.

Their food had come, but she wasn't hungry anymore. She knew she was just jumpy about this pass, but Reynaldo had set the wrong tone from the beginning.

She sipped her coffee. "Here's a special envelope direct from the Jefe himself, and I brought all the items you wanted for the members of the firm. They're in the gray bag, so you can just take that with you." Kay had packed the presents she had chosen on her Bogotá shopping errands into the loaded Samsonite.

"Fine." He glanced at the suitcase, then leaned back

languidly and looked at her from under slightly drooping lids. "Do you have a place to stay here in Frankfurt?"

"I thought you knew, Reynaldo," she said, coolly, "I'm going on to Paris." It seemed to her the man with the newspaper had not turned a page in a long time.

"Yes, I know." He stared directly into her eyes now. "Stay an extra day . . . with me."

She held her coffee cup to her mouth, looking at him over the rim. Why was he doing this? It was such a surprisingly stupid move. How could he be sure that she wouldn't tell Ricardo or the Padrino or even Reynaldo's wife, although his wife would probably blame *her*.

"Not a very good idea," she said finally. "I'm new in the family, no? I think it's best for me to play by the rules."

He pushed his plate away with sudden violence. "I've been watching you," he said, breaking into Spanish. "You think you're really something, don't you? You *gringos* all think you're better than the rest of the world! Well, now the yellow men are wiping you out in Vietnam and the Russians will soon get into the act and really bring your high ass down to where it belongs."

Even knowing he was slightly drunk, she was still stunned by the intensity of his anger. He waved for the check and looked at her challengingly, his face red.

"Thank you for the world analysis," she said, getting up and putting her coat on, "but let's forget it. Anyway, who knows, you're probably right." She leaned over and kissed his cheek. The man with the newspaper had gone, but she didn't feel any better about anything. "You're a lucky man, Reynaldo. You've got a nice wife and baby." She picked up her bag, leaving the other for him, and turned to smile at him. *"Ciao,"* she said.

She walked away briskly, wanting to run. Reynaldo had behaved very badly, which only made it harder to shake the feeling that something was off center, not right. Vibes, she thought. She hated that word. How could anyone base a judgment on a word like that? "Okie sense, woman's intuition," her grandmother had always called it. Whatever it was . . . in her heart she had always trusted it and now it was telling her to stay as far away from Reynaldo as she possibly could.

At Orly, the French agents searched her luggage, dipping

their hands in among the underwear and sweaters, but found nothing to set off any alarms. She left the airport for a free twenty-four hours in Paris, elated to be released, even temporarily, from constant paranoia, a necessary side effect of any smuggling trip.

At the Meurice, in a fin-de-siècle room with plaster garlands on the ceiling, she had fresh-squeezed orange juice and croissants for breakfast. The concierge told her where *Madame* could find the best luggage shops on the rue St. Honoré, the addresses of the fashionable boutiques, and the perfume shops on the second floors of the old buildings on the Place Vendôme.

Business first. She found several luggage styles and garment bags that she thought might inspire innovations from Carlos. Some of them, sturdy canvas bags in fall colors manufactured by a famous French company, Hermès, she had shipped to an address in the United States, where Maggie had paid a woman to accept packages. The rest she carried off inside one large suitcase: garment bags of various types folded into each other, and a selection of suitcase samples and hatboxes nested smaller and smaller.

Then pleasure. In three days she bought two Chanel suits and a suitcase full of Courrèges resort clothes and Yves Saint-Laurent vests, tunics, knits, and evening dresses. She spent a few hours in the echoing halls of the Louvre and a crazy night, in a black satin tuxedo, sampling the champagne and high life of the trendy Paris clubs. On the fourth afternoon, she boarded a Royal Dutch Airlines flight for Jamaica.

The way to the Caymans led through Kingston, Jamaica, with a one-night stop at Morgan's Harbor near the airport. The evening air was soft and sweet, and the lights of Kingston across the water were inviting, but Kay stayed in her room to baby-sit the suitcase. There wasn't enough security in the hotel to leave it unguarded.

She called room service and got a bottle of rum and a cheese sandwich. The handsome black waiter suggested she take a ferry ride to Kingston. They talked a while, but they both knew he was just being friendly.

After he left, Kay brought the tray outside on the balcony and sat looking at the finger piers along the shoreline and the boats of the local yachtsmen rocking at anchor. Later, she went in and read *The Andromeda Strain*, sitting in the middle of her bed, cross-legged and barefoot like a kid, the fruits of her Parisian shopping binge piled on all the chairs. Music drifted up and she began to feel really good as the breeze ruffled her hair and the rum hit home.

She felt safe and peaceful, the way she did when she was fourteen and would hide away in her room, reading and listening to the radio turned low, out of range of her father's simmering blue eyes and the possible outbreak of a violence that was always as sudden as it was inexplicable. That year, 1956, when she was fourteen, was the year she started to make money.

At first it promised to be just another year in the fields and orchards for her, picking up after the prune shaker and then, later in the season, picking freestone peaches. Then her older cousin Ray heard of a job packing in the plum shed.

The most money Kay could make behind the shaker or in the peach orchard was twenty-five cents a bucket, and all she would have to show after ten hours of hard labor would be ten dollars. But the shed packers were paid an incredible forty dollars a day. Kay was tall and strong for her age, and the foreman believed her when she said she was sixteen. He signed her up for the job on the spot.

In the dusty shed, a crew of women picked the fruit off a rapidly moving conveyor belt and packed it into boxes as fast as they could. Every box, complete with its neat rows of plums folded into purple paper, was numbered so the management could measure each packer's speed.

The completed boxes racketed down another moving belt to the Mexican men who nailed the lids on and sent them to wait on the tracks beside the shed. In the evening, when the noisy belts had been turned off, Kay could hear the railroad cars moving away from the siding with their cargo of "fancy-packed" plums. She wished fiercely she was on one of the cars herself, speeding toward towns where city slickers didn't know that a prune was really a plum and that certain kinds of plums were prunes.

At least she wasn't just an Okie kid anymore. She was passing for a woman now. She wore a red bandanna over her long blond ponytail and had another kerchief tied around her neck. The second one was for pulling over her nose and mouth when she was working, to keep out the choking clouds of dust and dirt. At lunchtime, she would take off her blue work shirt and tie both bandannas together in a bikini top and parade around in her jeans, drinking Dr Pepper and flirting with the forklift drivers.

The son of the rancher, who owned the two-hundred-acre place, drove a forklift, too, because his father wanted him to work and learn the business from the inside. Kay knew him from high school. His real name was Frank Wallace, but everyone called him "Sonny" and he had a prissy-assed girl friend who went to St. Mary's, the Catholic girls' school across the river. He had attached a portable radio to the roll bar of his forklift and he played music all day long.

At lunch break, Kay would take her sandwich over and sit on the seat of his lift, listening to the teeny-bop station while pretending to drive with the engine off. She didn't think Sonny was too sharp, but she didn't hate him. She hated his sister, who ignored Kay at school and sat painting her toenails beside the family pool while Kay trudged by on her way home from work.

The Wallaces had one of the biggest prune dryers in the county, big racks for drying the fruit. In the summer, Mr. Wallace increased his crews to one hundred people and took in drying and packing work from other smaller farms all over the Valley. Kay was glad for the job on the belt, but her secret ambition was to drive a forklift. If you worked ten hours a day, you could earn as much as seventy dollars.

Then one day after she had been on the belt for a month, something miraculous happened. She and Grandma were relaxing in the back yard after supper and chores, watching the pink glow in the sky over the orchard. Suddenly her cousin Curtis and her cousin Lee rocketed into the yard in Uncle Avril's pickup and leaped out full of big news. Sonny Wallace had broken his arm and collarbone in football practice. His father had come down to the field to follow the ambulance in his big yellow Caddy.

Kay jumped off the porch swing and ran into the house. She studied herself carefully in Grandma's cloudy full-length mirror, trying to see what Mr. Wallace would see, and what he would want to see. The first thing to do, she decided, was to set her hair.

At 5:30 A.M., she was at the Wallaces' kitchen door, dressed in clean jeans, her old cowboy boots polished as shiny as she could make them. Through the screen, she could see the Mexican maid making pancakes and Mr. Wallace sitting at the table, his gray hair freshly locked in place with Brylcreem. He was wearing glasses and was busy looking over some papers on the table in front of him. Kay knocked softly. Mr. Wallace, coffee cup in hand, motioned for her to come in.

"You're up early, aren't you," he said, as she opened the door. He was eyeing her curiously over his glasses.

"I heard about Sonny," she said, "how is he?"

"He's doing fine. Would you like some coffee?"

"No, thanks, Mr. Wallace. I came because I know you need someone to operate the forklift till Sonny gets better, and I'd like to do it."

She could see he was about to say something, so she hurried on. "I know I can do it, Mr. Wallace. I've driven the water tank and I know gears."

He just sat there grinning, and she didn't know what to do next, so she threw in, "Mr. Wallace, my family could sure use the help." Oh no, she thought, Grandpa would hate that, and she crossed her fingers behind her back.

Mr. Wallace took off his glasses and had a sip of his coffee. "How tall are you anyway, honey?" he said. Kay had never noticed before how nasal his voice was.

"I'm five foot eight," she said.

"Well, you sure are tall and pretty. You sixteen? What're you gonna do, go to college or is there some lucky guy?"

Kay smiled. She knew she was in. "I don't know yet," she said, "right now I just want to drive the lift."

"Oho," Mr. Wallace said, "so you just want to drive the lift. Well, let's just try you for a week, see how you make out."

Kay said, "Thank you, Mr. Wallace," and tried not to show how excited she was. It was a cinch that Sonny was out for the summer, so all she had to do was get through the week.

When she came in her first morning and climbed up on Sonny's forklift, the drivers were a shocked crew. The Mexicans leered and talked among themselves in Spanish. The Okie guys were pissed and ignored her. The local teen-aged boys, whose fathers had arranged their jobs with Mr. Wallace, thought it was a joke. Kay didn't care what anyone thought.

She knew how to drive a stick shift, and the fork was just a little bit tougher. She rammed a couple of pallets before she got the hang of it, but after a while it was easy. Every day she was early to work, careful, tireless, and happy.

At the end of the week, Mr. Wallace hired her for the summer. It was a great day. With her first week's pay, she bought a pair of fancy red cowboy boots and a little red transistor radio, and there was still money left to put in the bank. She polished the boots every day and took the transistor everywhere, listening to the local Spanish programs as well as the teeny-bop station and learning words like *corazón* for heart and *alma* for soul.

Sometimes she could even understand a few words of what the Mexican drivers were saying and she learned their dirty words and curses in self-defense, words like *puta* for "bitch" and *chiches* for "tits."

They were local Mexicans, and they were proud to be drivers and not like the *braceros* who came across the border to work in the fields as migrant labor. The first time she called one of them a son of a bitch in Spanish they all broke up. *"Jesús, esta puta es un hombre* [This bitch is a man]," shouted one of them. He had cut her off, driving his load in front of her so she had to slam on her brakes. They called out "Ee ha" whenever they saw her coming, but she knew their shrill teasing was laughing and friendly.

As Kay became expert at operating the lift she began to think she was hot, almost like she really *was* sixteen. She began wearing makeup and smoking with the Mexicans during the short breaks they took. They'd ask if she would go to drive-in movies with them and pull down their pants. She'd laugh and tell them to go to hell. She pretended she had a boyfriend, and if he didn't keep his pants *on*, she told them defiantly, she'd get herself another man.

She liked joking with the guys at work, but mostly she saw the boys she knew as part of a conspiracy that would trap her in the weary cycle of hick Valley life forever. All of the older girls she knew fell in love with some guy in school, got married, and next thing they were stuck in a tiny trailer by the

levee, pregnant and surrounded by washing lines and screaming kids.

Kay had other plans. She had begun to draw and paint. And
she was going to travel to all the places she had read about.

Maggie had already been in the Caymans for two days and
waiting for Kay at the Georgetown airport, which was nothing
more than a glorified shed. Kay spotted her from her seat in the
little twin-engine Cessna as they taxied in. There was Maggie,
leaning against the chicken-wire fence, looking easy in tennis
whites and a visored hat. What was it, Kay wondered, that set
people like Maggie apart, that gave them away as coming from
privilege no matter what they chose to wear.

After the usual calm greeting for form's sake, they pulled out
of the airport in the Corvair Maggie had rented. It had no
muffler and she gunned the engine exuberantly. "I know the
road now, and we don't even have to go through Georgetown,"
she said. At the sign marked BODDEN TOWN she turned onto a
narrow, dusty road.

"Mags, you're the best thing I've seen in months." Kay
leaned over and kissed her friend's sunburned cheek. She took
off her jacket, sighed, and relaxed against the seat, looking
forward to the four days of R and R they had decided on.

"I can't wait to get out of these clothes." Kay rolled her
window down all the way. The strong sea breeze filled her
nostrils and she held her blowing hair away from her face with
one hand and closed her eyes. "It's so good to know I can talk
and not have to check every word that comes out of my
mouth."

They passed a sign that said FRANK SOUND, and Maggie said in
her best Irish brogue, "Now what could they be meanin' by
that I wonder, 'Frank Sound'?"

Kay laughed. "You were always good at frank sounds.
Where are you taking me?" she asked.

"I rented us a modest little domicile at Rum Point across the
island from the banks, the hotel, and the fishermen. Fins and
finance—that's what happens here. Nothing much else. The
developers haven't smelled blood yet, thank God."

They were on a road that snaked across the island, barren
and desolate in some parts, with minimal vegetation and queen
palms standing tall against puffy clouds. The traffic signs were

all British and so were the rules of the road. Driving on the left side was making Kay nervous.

Maggie glanced over at her. "So tell me about your recent adventures, Kayleen," she said, and Kay told her about Reynaldo and the tense situation in Lisbon.

The turquoise Caribbean came into view as they drove north along the shore. Maggie told swashbuckling tales of the island's history she had learned from the brochure of the sole motel—stories of pirates and buccaneers and shipwrecks.

The house was in a cove just off a sandy road marked PRIVATE, a three-room wooden bungalow with a screened porch and a dock jutting out over shallow, perfectly clear water. Kay left the door of the car hanging open and ran naked down to the dock and into the sea.

For the first twenty-four hours, the lazy, tropical pace of life on the island made Kay crazy. Her thoughts returned often to Bogotá and she missed the town, missed Ricardo, and missed her coke stash. The first two nights, she had insomnia, her nervous system unbalanced by two weeks of abstinence from what was now a heavy though unacknowledged cocaine habit. While Maggie slept, Kay prowled the house, taking repeated trips to the refrigerator, staring into its lit, white interior, and closing the door again without choosing anything.

Gradually, however, she relaxed. The two women read and sunbathed and went snorkeling in the shallow, reef-protected water of their front yard. In the evenings, they walked down to Rum Point for cold beer and fried conch. Maggie even scored some Jamaican weed from a local character named "Conchy," who had fallen in love with her red hair.

The day before Maggie was scheduled to leave, Kay took the car into Georgetown to do the Padrino's banking. The bank president spoke with the sort of strangled British stammer that Kay recognized as upper class, and had a receding hairline freckled by constant exposure to the sun.

Kay told him the Padrino's name and a false name for herself that Ricardo had given her, and was immediately shown into a small side room that smelled of mold and furniture polish.

The man sat her at an oak library table and turned on a bronze lamp. It was getting cloudy outside and the room was dark. "Here are a few papers for you to sign, Miss Peters," he said, handing them to her fussily. As she penned her name, she could hear the fitful buzzing and bumping of a fly against the windowpane. And then the first large drops of tropical rain.

"Where were you born?" the man asked.

"Toledo, Ohio."

"Yes. Fine. Mother's maiden name?"

"Martin."

"Yes, very good. And now, the birthmark please?" The man looked away from her and coughed.

The Padrino had prepared her for this ritual of ID precautions. She faced the wall with her back to the man, unbuttoned her green cotton blouse, took it off, and held it against her naked chest. Just below her left shoulder blade was a dim, reddish-brown mark the size of a nickel. The room felt chilly to her bare back and behind her she could hear the man breathing through his nose. What was he doing, something creepy? He was taking too damn long. "All right?" she asked.

"Yes, certainly, very good, very well then," he said gruffly and left the room.

He knocked when he came back, murmuring discreetly, "May I come in now, Miss Peters?"

The man had one hundred thousand dollars in one-hundred-dollar bills in a gray canvas sack, like a mailbag. He began counting the money out onto the table in one-thousand-dollar bundles. The rain was drumming at the window now; she could no longer hear the fly. He finished counting, looked up at Kay, who nodded, and then put the money very carefully back into the bag and handed it to her.

"Righty-o, then, good luck, Miss Peters," he said.

Kay stashed the canvas bag into her deep-bottomed purse and said, "Thank you. Where is the powder room, please?"

She went into the bathroom, locked the door, and took the money and the long-line bra out of her purse.

"You're very quiet," Maggie said when Kay got back to the house. "Was something wrong?"

"Nothing," she said. "Let's just take a swim and forget it."

That night, sitting in the dark on the porch, Kay speculated on the Padrino's financial dealings. "The way I see it, he's probably evading income taxes by setting up offshore, 'paper' companies. Taxes in Colombia are so high now, everyone's doing it. Plus it would be a good way for him to launder his money—put the cash in a British bank, invest it in real estate, and then take it out again in 'profits.' ''

She passed Maggie the spliff they were smoking, got up, and looked out into the darkness. It was always hard to figure what the Boss was really up to, all you could do was theorize. Kay's rangy body was relaxed and tan, her feet bare, but her mind had already left the island. The night insects, chirring loudly from the trees and long grasses, accompanied her thoughts.

"I wonder what I'll find when I get back," she said to Maggie.

Although her position with the family was outwardly secure, she knew that the threat of a shift was ever present, like the threat of a quake in the earth beneath Bogotá. Her usefulness and her relationship with Ricardo bound her close and offered a modicum of protection, but if for any reason push came to shove, Ricardo, like any other good Colombian son, would do exactly as his father dictated. And reasons in Colombia, Kay had found, were seldom either reasonable or predictable.

In recent months, she had learned a great deal about the volatile Colombian character in which devotion to etiquette masked a nature as quick to burst into joy and warmth as into rage and violence. The newspapers she read every day were full of reports of crimes committed for the most trivial of incidents, the slimmest of motives: a mischievous hint, the suspicion of a wife's infidelity, a heated word in a card game, a professional competition. The Padrino himself was a perfect example. Ricardo had told her a number of stories of his father's uncontrolled fits of rage. Once, when Ricardo had come home a few hours past his curfew, his father had thrown him off the second-floor balcony. Ricardo had shown her, with what to Kay was a strange pride, the thickening in his shin where the broken leg had mended.

Kay was fascinated to find that Colombian history had an equally dark side, stretching across centuries in an unending saga of bloodletting and oppression, from the Conquistadores to the War of Independence to the civil war, which began in 1948 and ended ten years later with three hundred thousand dead. It was a war of such brutality that Kay still heard people speak fearfully of the time as "La Violencia."

"We are riding a wildly spinning wheel where today's victims become tomorrow's executioners and these in turn, the future victims. Each victim feeds on the idea of retaliation, so that there will be enough hatred in Colombia for the next one hundred fifty years,'' Kay had read in an old issue of *El Colombiano* newspaper. And though the writer was referring to La Violencia, Kay thought it was a chilling metaphor for what she was beginning to believe was the permanent condition of her adopted homeland.

Even now, with Colombia on the eve of a national election scheduled for April 19, the question that had been on everyone's lips before Kay left was whether it would be a peaceful process. She sighed in the soft Caribbean night breeze, wondering yet again about the powerful magnetism between beauty and violence and the raw attraction it had for her.

''I wish I could just stay on this island and never leave,'' Maggie murmured. Her chair creaked as she stretched her legs out in front of her. Kay could hear the weariness in Maggie's voice.

For the last month she had been working night and day for the Peace Movement. Her phone rang continuously, she shuttled around in her beat-up car, immersed in a tangle of arrangements from anti-Vietnam protest marches to arranging false passports for conscientious objectors who needed to leave the country.

''I don't think you should do another pass for a while,'' Kay said. ''No question your movements are a subject of interest to the Feds. We need to go slow and careful.''

''Too bad,'' Maggie said. ''I wanted to come to Bogotá, stay for a few days, be a tourist-type smuggler.''

''It's bad timing for a lot of reasons,'' Kay said. She sat down in a rocking chair and told Maggie about what had been passing through her mind, guiltily leaving out any mention of Ricardo.

Around three in the morning, after they had their last cigarette, Kay came and stood behind Maggie's chair. She put her hands on Maggie's shoulders in a gentle massage, gradually shifting upward onto the warm neck beneath the tangled mass of curly bronze hair.

Kay returned to find that nothing had changed in Bogotá and three weeks later, in early April, she was back in the Caribbean to meet June Stoltz, a friend whom Maggie had set up in the

Curaçao Plaza Hotel in Curaçao. June had body-carried cash and was also transporting the bags and suitcases that Kay had sent to the States from France. Kay was to meet her with one of the first of Carlos's new French garment bags.

He had designed the bags to hold one kilo of cocaine each, building it into the hard paneling along the top, sides, and bottom, the cardboard stiffener of the snap-on lingerie case, and the plush padding of the coat hangers.

The women acted as if they didn't know each other and stayed on different floors. Late on the second night, when the elevators tended to be empty, June arrived in Kay's room. They lost no time exchanging the suitcases. While June had already spent four days in the hotel to establish herself, the actual pass took only five minutes.

"It's all yours," Kay said, relieved to be handing over the Frenchie.

To maintain her cover, Kay stayed on for three more days of "sun and fun." She haunted the casino every night in evening clothes and Bogotá emeralds. Playing blackjack and roulette, she felt as though she had cast herself in her favorite movie. It was like being both the audience and the star.

Men and women—tourists and gamblers—approached her, but she politely put off even those who intrigued her. Only the handsome young croupier, expressionless, tuxedoed, lord of the blackjack table, tempted her. She sat in front of him watching his supple hands manipulate the cards, while his well-bred Yankee face remained utterly aloof. Interesting, she thought. What was *his* story?

She would have liked to find out. But strangers did not mix well with smuggling, and she resisted the challenge. She limited her gambling, too, never allowing herself to lose more than one thousand dollars. It was a shock to realize that what she now thought of as a modest loss, a year earlier would have left her stranded and unable to pay her rent. Right, she thought smiling to herself, everything *is* relative.

There was a little tourist shop in the lobby just off the exit to the pool, the kind that sold suntan lotion, tampons, sweatshirts, postcards, and international magazines and newspapers. Among copies of *Time, Newsweek,* and the *International Herald Tribune*, Kay found a beat-up *New York Times*. Three days old, it was dated April 12, 1970. She pounced on it, and took it poolside to read it.

"General Turns Colombian Presidential Campaign into a Class Struggle with Undertones of Violence," she read. There it was, it was beginning.

Kay arrived home in Bogotá from Curaçao on April 17. The twilight was clear and cold and the first stars over the Andes shone with a radiance so intense she thought of UFOs. Ricardo was waiting at the airport with his VW. She felt his arms around her, and was surprised at how glad she was to see him.

But he was subdued, and didn't pick up on her banter as he usually did. He smoked as he drove, changing gears with a gloved hand, the cigarette stuck in the corner of his mouth.

"Listen, Kay," he said, "things are serious here in Bogotá. Whichever way the election goes, it will be bad—there will be death and violence."

Kay nodded. "I know." She felt a tremor of fear.

"My father is calling a meeting for tomorrow to discuss this. I will come for you."

Safety-conscious and a Colombian gentleman as always, Ricardo escorted her upstairs to her apartment. But this time he kissed her at the door and didn't come in. "Don't worry about it, *bonita*," he said. "You are with us."

The drive to the Padrino's house was much faster than usual in the light traffic. The downtown streets, normally alive with shoppers, beggars, and strolling couples looking for something to do after work, were silent and empty. Armed soldiers and jeeps full of white-helmeted military patrolled every corner.

At the house, Kay was surprised to see about thirty-five people, many of whom she had never met before. The Padrino had assembled his network from all over Colombia: César Gutiérrez from Medellín with several of his men; the paste sources from the mountains; investment and business interests from the industrial town of Cali; transport connections from the coast—Santa Marta, Cartagena, Barranquilla.

Many of the men were related by blood or intermarriage and had brought their families along. Flora linked her arm through Kay's and brought her into the kitchen to see the younger children, all eating around the wooden table. Rosa's mother,

Luisa, was serving them. She smiled at Kay and said, *"Buenas tardes, Señorita Wolff."*

Before dinner, Kay found a moment between the samba dancing and formal chatting to take Flora aside and give her a gift of a pair of Christian Dior sunglasses from Paris. Clarita Gutiérrez looked on wistfully. "Next time I'll bring you a pair," Kay said, after Flora had moved off with her prize.

Kay liked this quiet, round-faced woman, Clarita. She knew Flora thought Clarita was provincial but was nice to her anyway because of Don César's importance—and because she wanted Ricardo to marry their daughter, Isabella. In private, Ricardo had laughed at the idea. "Isabella is a baby, she's only seventeen," he had said to Kay, giving her one of his melting looks. "As you know, I prefer someone a little older."

It amused Kay to be an "older woman" at twenty-seven. "You won't always think that way," she had said. Now, Kay remembered Isabella's words at the last party. Ricardo's *destino*, the girl had called herself.

After an elaborate six-course meal, the living-room furniture was cleared away and the dancing began, the music lively, but not too loud. As at the last gathering Kay had attended, the men slowly began disappearing upstairs, but this time Carlos lumbered over and took her by the elbow.

"Come," he said. "You belong to the business upstairs now, *hermana mía.*" Kay suddenly felt cold and excused herself to get her jacket and check her makeup.

When she came back, Carlos was waiting. "Ladies first," he said. As she climbed the stairs, she knew that behind her, in true Colombian tradition, he was admiring her ass.

The room was already full of smoke. Roberto was sitting at the head of the conference table, an ashtray, a pad, and several short, sharpened pencils neatly lined up before him. To his right was an empty chair, and to his left Don César was busily unwrapping a small box of sugared candy drops. He crumpled the wrapping with his long grayish fingers, popped a sweet into his mouth, and put the box on the table in front of him.

Ricardo sat at the foot of the table, his back toward Kay. The men from Cali and from the coast filled the remaining seats. They talked quietly among themselves. Kay noticed that Reynaldo was absent from the meeting. He had not flown in from Europe.

The less important men had been placed in wooden ladder-back chairs along the wall. Across the room, Miguel sat nonchalantly balancing on the two back legs of his chair, and Franco gazed blankly, his hands folded patiently in his lap. Carlos nodded Kay to a seat near the door.

As soon as Carlos took the empty chair to the Padrino's right, the meeting quieted down.

"We are here," the Padrino began, "to discuss these troubled times and what we are to do to remain in a favorable position. Many of the friends we have may be shifted from power or may find themselves tempted to take advantage of these times to ask for larger donations. That of course, is unfortunate for them, but . . ." He trailed off, then began again in a slightly louder voice.

"Each of you, therefore, needs to reinforce an unassailable cover and anything concerning the trade must be buried or expertly hidden: tools, scales, etcetera, as I'm sure you are aware."

Don César nodded, leaned back, and popped another candy into his mouth. "Certainly, Don Roberto, exactly what must be done?"

Roberto ignored him and opened the meeting to an exchange of information on specific situations that were already reflecting the unstable times. He began with the disclosure that his inside man with Avianca security at the airport had been put on suspension. Getting him back in whatever new administration was coming would take finesse, as the position was a crucial one and other families would instantly start trying to push their own men for it.

"However," he said, smiling, "yesterday I had a fruitful lunch with a man of influence at the airport, a man I have reason to believe will not be replaced by the election. Which brings me to the question," the Padrino continued, picking up one of the short pencils, "of who our friends and enemies are at this moment and what sides they seem to be taking." Kay listened, fascinated, to a discussion of what names could be counted on to accept bribes or gifts of airline tickets and special privileges, names she had frequently seen in the newspapers and magazines, featured in headlines and society columns.

She had begun to understand that politics in Colombia functioned not only through bribes but through an intricate network of familial relationships, loyalties, and favors, a system that formed the warp and woof of Colombian social life at its higher levels.

The Padrino had left for last the touchiest issue—the question of power struggles and violence within the trade. While not looking directly at Don César or any of the men the cook had brought with him, Roberto addressed the dangerous problem of the growing hostility between different processing cooks.

"It seems there has been trouble lately," he said, tapping his pencil on the table, "trouble over prices, rumors of chemists making synthetic cocaine or even putting on secret cuts. I have heard of cooks invading each other's territories, working for more than one boss. These things create"—he paused—"certain 'risks.' I know, of course, that no one here is involved, but I thought it was an important thing to mention."

César Gutiérrez lowered his eyes and smiled down at the table in his melancholy Lincolnesque way. "Certainly. You were quite correct to mention it. Fortunately, no one here stoops to listen to rumormongers." He lifted his eyes again to look at Carlos.

"*Pero seguro, seguro querido amigo* [But of course, my dear friend]," the Padrino said pleasantly. "*Bueno. Entonces*"—he got up from his chair—"now it is time to forget business and to enjoy yourselves, please. Flora has dessert and coffee waiting for you downstairs." He motioned to Ricardo and Kay to stay.

"Ricardo, *mi hijo*, please, go downstairs and tell them to send us up a tray."

Roberto placed Kay in the armchair opposite him. "You should be very proud," he said, opening and holding out to Kay an old-fashioned silver cigarette case.

Kay said, "*Muchas gracias,*" and took one of the Marlboros.

"*De nada*. Your 'Frenchie' is a great success." He leaned forward to light her cigarette, briefly revealing a powerful square-boned wrist. "Business is good, better and better, money to throw to the air, *gracias a Dios*.

"Kay, permit me to say to you without offending"—his light gray eyes seemed full of genuine kindness—"I can see you are disturbed."

Disturbed? Kay thought. How about terrified? She nodded politely. "Oh yes, thank you. I'm concerned . . . of course."

"There is no need. Here in Colombia we have had La Violencia, or 'political unrest,' as our government chooses to call it, since 1948." He stopped and corrected himself. "Officially speaking, since 1948. To my way of thinking, it has been going on forever. Today's victims are tomorrow's executioners, but nothing changes. *Así es la vida. . . .*

"In any case, I want you to remain tranquil. You must know for certain that no harm will come to you and you must trust that we know very well how to take care of things." He paused, and after a moment he said, "Ricardo has told me that you love our beautiful country . . . even with all its trouble. Trouble dies down, but the land you love remains. I hope you understand that you are at home here in Colombia. And that you will always find a home here with us."

He looked at Kay questioningly. "Okay?" he said, in English. His sudden smile had the stuff of true charm, and Kay realized for the first time that, the hustle he was giving her aside, he actually liked her.

"Okay," she said, and smiled back. Strangely, he was right. Colombia was totally alien to her, but at the same time she had, from the first moment, recognized its fierce colors as her own. She was at home in this place of rainbows, terror, and elation. Besides, as Roberto had so delicately implied, she was in too deep to leave now.

"*Con permiso.*" A young mestiza girl of around fourteen stood at the door with a tray. "*¿Con dulces y café?*" she asked timidly.

"*Aquí,*" Roberta said and pointed to the desk. He waited until the girl was gone. "So," he said, "we have a little problem. I heard through my sources that the police and secret service may be searching apartments in your district, looking for someone. They are questioning everyone and, of course, they would be happy to take along anyone else whose answers they do not like. Since you are an American and not familiar with how to handle such a situation, I think it best that Ricardo stay with you. For this occasion only, of course," he added, giving her a quick little glance.

"We have secured papers for you that identify you as a teacher of art at the university in Bogotá." Kay flashed on stubby little Professor Guzmán with his crinkly hair and Rolex watch at the gallery opening so long ago. And now, here he was, being useful again.

"However," the Padrino was saying, "it will be much safer for you if, in addition, they believe you are the mistress of a Colombian man. And it will allow Ricardo to interfere if they begin to get complicated in their questioning. You just play at being the stupid blonde. How do you feel about that?" He laughed.

"Sometimes it's harder to act like a dumb blonde than to be a dumb blonde. I'll be glad to have Ricardo there. Soldiers make me very nervous because you never know what they're going to do."

"Well, yes, they are unpredictable. It is good that you understand that, but please don't worry. Ricardo will discuss the details with you. Would you like some dessert . . . coffee? No?" Carefully, he filled two small crystal glasses to the brim with the clear fire of aguardiente. They raised their glasses. "*Salud,*" he said. "*Pesetas y amor y el tiempo para gustarlos* [Money and love and the time to enjoy them]."

He took a milky glass cutting block from the little bar and laid out some coke for Kay, handing her a silver straw. He didn't take any himself, and when she had finished and she was smiling with the fresh breeze of the hit, he presented her with the silver straw as a gift.

"Now go downstairs," he said. "Have fun, dance, find a Colombian man you like and fall in love. They are all looking at you. Who can blame them?" As she left the room, he was already sitting down at his desk and opening a file drawer. Working late, she thought. Just another busy executive.

The next morning, Kay got up early and even Roddy arrived yawning, but on time. Carlos had left a rush job to be done on her return from Curaçao. By noon she was finished and Ricardo arrived to load up the tools, glue pots, and all the rest of the concealment paraphernalia. He took them away and returned with a basket of food.

Kay could see Rosa was hurt. Ricardo had brought food precooked in his father's kitchen. Behind Ricardo's back, Kay shrugged her shoulders and winked at her.

It took an hour for Ricardo and Kay to transform the bedroom from coke fabrication shop to boudoir. The curtained dressing room, normally Kay's workspace, was now ultra-feminine, stuffed with clothes, a manicure table, and a small flouncy chair with a ruffled skirting. Negligees and fluffy high-heeled slippers, black lace panties, and filmy scarves were flung around helter-skelter. Kay finished off the scene with a triumphant squirt of the perfume atomizer and turned to see Ricardo in the doorway, ill-at-ease, holding his toilet articles, suits, and shirts.

"Ay de mí, Ricardo." She put her hand to her mouth in mock horror. "My reputation is ruined. A man living in my apartment. What will my mother say?"

"What would she say?" he asked.

"Not much. We don't do too much talking." Kay took him by the arm. "Honey, now y'all tell me what I should wear for mah gentlemen callers. Somethin' frilly?"

He laughed, and said, "What is 'frilly'?"

Ricardo had brought fried meats and bread with cheese inside, which Rosa had arranged on trays. On plates she had arranged slices of avocado and a circle of *panela* squares, jellied and sweet. Kay could tell Rosa was still moody.

Bottles of wine and aguardiente were on the table. Ricardo stood back and looked around, cracking his knuckles nervously.

"What's wrong?" Kay asked.

"Nothing, but I just want it to be perfect. These people can make you disappear for no reason at all."

"Thanks," she said.

"I'll bet you the soldiers will eat all the meat and *panela*, and leave the fruit," he said, trying to regain a lighter mood.

"I don't care what they eat," Kay said, "as long as they leave me alone."

While she was putting on her makeup, the lobby guard phoned to say that the police were in the building. Sick with fear, she opened the window to look out.

The air was fresh after the rain. The usually busy street was desolate and filled with puddles. On the corner were a clutch of green army trucks and white police vehicles. Several armed soldiers leaned against the buildings, smoking. One of them seemed to look up in Kay's direction.

Loud voices were coming down the hallway outside. Her story was well rehearsed, yet her stomach cramped violently.

"Listen, *bonita*," Ricardo said. "Don't be frightened. You look perfect, a big, beautiful blonde. Just act dumb and I will do the talking. For once." She smiled wanly.

There were four of them—three soldiers, and a man in a brown suit and scuffed, pointed shoes—secret service? Kay wondered. The man came into the living room, while the soldiers hung back in the hall.

"We were just having lunch," Ricardo said, "would you care for some good food and drink?"

Certainly, the man said, they would be most delighted. Kay thought how slick this little ritual was and how good Ricardo was at it, how well they all played their parts.

The soldiers came in from the hall, grabbed hunks of meat, and took them back out on pieces of bread. At the coffee table, Kay sat with a frozen smile, afraid to open her mouth. The man in civilian clothes sat down beside her; she could smell his sweat. He opened his briefcase and took out some papers. While he was shuffling through them, pretending to look for something, Ricardo offered him a drink.

"No, no." He refused at first, then let Ricardo convince him. "Well yes, maybe an aguardiente with a lime on the side."

Ricardo served him and brought the bottle over on a tray with a plate of food. He poured Kay a drink, too, and said, "My girl friend loves our Colombian aguardiente also." Kay was happy to drink it down.

The soldiers had left the hall and gone into the bedroom. The time for questioning had come. Ricardo explained that he worked for his father, who owned a furniture business, a family business. He had met Kay in the States while vacationing in Los Angeles.

Suddenly the man turned to Kay.

"What do you like about Colombia, Señorita Wolff?"

She pointed to Ricardo for an answer. Ricardo grinned broadly and the man gave her a guarded smile.

Good, she thought, he liked that.

He went on: What is your work? What does your family do, any other teachers? Writers? Do you talk to them often by phone? What is your phone number?

She lied straightforwardly. From the bedroom she heard the whoosh of curtains, and after a pause, hoots and laughter. The soldiers had discovered the dressing room with its careful preparations.

"And the Colombian political system, what do you think of that?"

Kay looked around. She could still hear the sounds of the men opening and closing drawers and doors in the bedroom. The man had been conducting his investigation in Spanish but she replied in English. "Well," she said, "what I know is that you have two parties, elections, representatives, you are a democratic system, no?" She looked at his face to see how she was doing. His eyes remained impassive.

Finally he said, "Yes." He asked to see her papers, wanted to know how long before her visa expired. Then he turned to Ricardo and asked whether they had a car and what the plate number was.

One of the soldiers now stood at the bedroom door openly leering at Kay. Another soldier had arrived at the apartment door and signaled the questioner into the hall. They talked in low tones and then the man returned.

It was over: he was ready to leave. "Well, stay out of trouble, anyway," he said to Ricardo in a jocular, man-to-man way, looking at Kay. Ricardo managed a little chuckle. One of the soldiers picked up the last piece of meat on his way out, leaving the fruit, just as Ricardo had predicted.

Kay and Ricardo were drawn to the windows. They watched the men leave the building. Suddenly, from around the corner, came the sound of shots and screams. The uniformed men lounging on the corner hurled themselves into their vehicles. Then an open cattle lorry appeared. Silent men huddled against its slatted sides. Kay could see that one of them was slumping down splattered with blood. She kept staring even after the trucks had sped away.

Darkness had come. "*Pobrecita,*" Ricardo said, "you're not used to Colombian law and order." He put his arms around her. "Your teeth are chattering." He rubbed her back. Waves of cold radiated from the pit of her stomach.

"Let's have a Scotch and a couple of lines and go to bed," she said.

Afterward, they lay in the bed with the curtains drawn and the lights low, watching television. A man talking about ways to avoid earthquake damage suddenly went off the screen and was replaced with the image of President Lleras Restrepo urging the citizens to remain calm. The phone on Kay's night table gave its chirping, double ring-ring. It was the Padrino checking to see how they had made out.

The government had begun to issue radio warnings, he reported. Anyone participating in demonstrations would be arrested and sentenced to thirty days' imprisonment. Anyone organizing demonstrations would receive 180 days in jail. A bulletin listed four official deaths in disturbances, one that of a shoeshine boy.

From the south of the city, the malodorous shantytown section, came the sporadic pop of gunfire.

Chapter
Seven

In the latest ballot count of Sunday's presidential voting, General Rojas, . . . was trailing his major opponent, Misael Pastrana, by almost 50,000 votes.

General Rojas charged fraud in the election count. Last night about 5,000 of his supporters went on a window breaking rampage through Bogotá prompting President Carlos Lleras Restrepo to impose a state of siege and martial law.

. . . The government placed all offenses against state security and public order under military courts.

—Reuters, April 22, 1970

The General's strong showing was based on the frustrations of the urban poor, unemployed or underemployed and hungry, and on the resentment of the lower middle class—in the cities and on the small farms—against the use of taxes to finance social reforms.

—Joseph Novitski,
Special to *The New York Times*,
April 22, 1970

SUNDAY NIGHT KAY sat up alone, watching the election returns on TV. Rosa had gone to bed and Ricardo had phoned to say he wasn't coming over. His father wanted him at home. He didn't say anything more and Kay could tell he was angry. She suspected Flora was behind it.

Outside, Monserrate was dark. The floodlights of the church were out and the mountain rose, a massive hulk, against the starry sky. Kay wondered if the blackout had anything to do with the election.

When she went to bed, Betancur and Sourdis were out of the race. The ex-dictator General Gustavo Rojas Pinilla was in the lead against Misael Pastrana Borrero, the forty-six-year-old former ambassador to Washington and candidate of the incumbent coalition. But by morning, with ninety-three percent of the vote in, it was Pastrana who had inched ahead—1,447,000 to 1,442,000. An ugly mood was brewing and schools were closed. Carlos returned all of Kay's concealment tools and bought Roddy over to work with her.

"Turn on the television," Roddy said eagerly. "Maybe I won't have to go to school tomorrow either."

President Lleras Restrepo appeared on the set, his round face serious, black-frame glasses flashing in the TV lights. Because of the extreme narrowness of the plurality, he was saying, it would not be possible to announce the final election result until the following Sunday. He hoped for order and a peaceful acceptance of this necessity.

In the afternoon, Pastrana made a cautious victory statement, anyway.

"Oh, that's bad," Roddy said enthusiastically. "Rojas won't like that at all. Neither will his daughter, and she's *really* the important one."

Rojas took the president's announcement of delay as a declaration of war. "There is no explanation for delaying the vote count," he challenged, "except that the delay is an attempt to use fraud. I am sure that the people will not resign themselves to the bald robbery of their election victory." And then he added: "I must make it clear, that when the reaction comes, General Rojas Pinilla has no responsibility for it [*The New York Times,* April 20, 1970]."

"*Entonces,*" Roddy said, satisfied, "now there's going to be a lot of action. No school tomorrow, *seguro.*"

Ricardo called to say he was sorry, he would be late. Pastrana's house was under heavy military guard. Rojas was under house arrest. His followers had taken their frustration to the streets, smashing windows and looting stores. It was only a matter of hours before a state of siege would be declared.

Kay asked him what that would mean.

"It means everything will be closed down," he said shortly, "a real *dolor en el culo.*"

Amazing, Kay thought, the country is about to explode and this guy thinks it's just a pain in the ass.

"*Bonita,*" he said, "I am sorry about my language. I apologize, but there are complications here. The phones to Venezuela have been shut down. We can't get through. There are difficulties. I will explain later." Kay heard the Padrino's voice saying something in the background as Ricardo hung up.

Rosa was standing in the doorway, "Señorita Kay, I am afraid to go for the marketing," she said. Kay smiled at her.

"We'll go together," she said. "I want to go to the post office anyway. I want to get my mail before things close down."

"No, no. Please. Señor Ricardo will be angry with me."

"Don't worry, Rosa, he won't be angry. We won't tell him." But Rosa just kept standing there. "I promise you," Kay said. "What do you think, Rosa?"

"Señorita?"

"About the election?"

"*Nada.*"

"That's not true. I know you don't think nothing."

"I don't like the election. I wish it were over."

To Rosa, politics meant violence and death, or at best a distant shuffling of governmental arrangements that affected the aristocracy and had no bearing on her own life. She was not alone in her perceptions; in the election of 1964, seventy percent of the population had failed to cast ballots.

Rosa took along her string shopping bags and turned immediately for the small *tiendas* nearby, but Kay wanted to go to the post office first. She was hungry for the cozy normality of a letter from Maggie, and curious about the encoded business report it would also include.

There was a sense of urgency in the street. People were walking briskly, trying to get their business done before the city shut down.

When they turned the corner at Parque Santander they found the park dotted with little clusters of armed soldiers. Indian women sat under the acacia trees trying to watch over barefoot toddlers while selling packs of Marlboros and lottery tickets.

Kay opened her purse and gave Rosa a one-hundred-peso note to buy a pack for her.

"But Señorita Kay, cigarettes are *más barato* in the *tienda*," Rosa said, looking down at the money in her hand.

"*No me importa,* Rosa, I want to buy the cigarettes now, from them. And while you do that, I'll go get the mail. Wait here and I will be right back." She could see Rosa was upset. "Buy a *caramelo* for yourself," she said, "and I'll be back before you know it."

Kay always made a point of buying something from the Indians. She thought of it as a form of tithing that would bring good fortune back to her. Her grandfather had always given ten percent of his income to charity and the Pentecostal Church. Too, she wanted to buy from these women who were so proud, not begging or abandoning their children to the streets, making change out of apron pockets, faces unsmiling.

The post office was in the basement of the Avianca building. Kay passed the first-floor jewelry shop on her way in. She loved to look at the displays in the window, but today there were no green-fire emeralds and silky pearls to tempt her. Instead, the window had been boarded up against looters.

Kay had spent several thousand dollars in that store and the manager came out when he saw her. "Come again on another day and we will have a *tinto* and a talk," he said, smiling. She thought he was handsome and reassuring, standing outside his door as though nothing were wrong, as though the chaos threatening the city were a minor inconvenience.

The post office, always busy, was even more packed with people than usual. Its boxes were used not only by foreigners, but also by those on the run for political and other reasons, and the unstable conditions in Bogotá made them frantic with the fear of being trapped in the city when it closed down.

Narrow little dead-end corridors lined with numbered mail-boxes branched off the brightly lit main room with its green paint and exposed ceiling pipes. Kay shouldered her way among bodies in moist *ruanas* and damp raincoats, to her box. An envelope from Maggie was waiting. She opened it immediately, putting the rest of the mail on the floor at her feet.

The card showed a picture of Frodo from *The Lord of the Rings,* and Maggie had written "Grok this" and a line asking if she could come to Bogotá in July to spend her vacation with

Kay. There were some encoded business figures, a date for the next phone call, and a few xxxx's. That was all. Kay was disappointed.

She fished a card from her purse and wrote a short answer, leaning against the wall, using her purse for support.

She would have to let Maggie know about the vacation later, she wrote, things were too uncertain in Bogotá. More later. She sealed the envelope feeling ambivalent. Was she discouraging Maggie only because of the political insecurity, or was she dreading some kind of awkwardness between Maggie and Ricardo?

Among the rest of the mail were several envelopes that Maggie had forwarded: a pale blue invitation to a baby shower from a college friend, an IRS form, and a bill from the student loan office at UCLA. To Kay they seemed like mail for a dead person, strange messages that had nothing to do with her.

The lines for posting letters were long and almost all men. They shuffled slowly forward, seeming hardly to move, and as Kay waited with her note to Maggie, the man in front of her said to no one in particular, "What a mess. We will be lucky if our letters arrive within three weeks."

He was paunchy and small and wore a loose shirt with an ink stain from the many pens lined up in the pocket.

"Yes," said the man in front of him, "but the only ones who are surprised are the rich and the newspapers. They thought Rojas was just a ridiculous old man, a joke, but now they don't laugh anymore." His dark, mixed-breed face had a look of heavy disdain.

"You are a Rojista?" said a third man who had turned around to listen.

Kay stiffened, wondering if there was going to be trouble.

"Rojas was a dictator, but he was good for the really poor," the dark man said resolutely. "If you had any money you didn't make out under him, and that might be good again."

"Well and good," said the paunchy little man with the pens, "but I was a traveling salesman during his time and food may have been a little cheaper, but life was much more dangerous, that I can tell you. I remember what it was like in the taverns when the armed Rojistas were there. If you valued your skin you had to shout *'Viva el Excelentísimo Señor Presidente y*

Jefe Supremo General, Gustavo Rojas Pinilla.' Nothing less
would do.'' He shook his head.

The third man shifted the jacket of his suit from one arm to
the other and loosened his tie. ''Did you ever hear that old joke
about Rojas?'' he said. By now, Kay saw that several other
people in the line were listening with interest and the man
glanced around and lowered his voice. ''The Jefe Supremo had
gone to visit a struggling rancher. When he admired the
rancher's prize bull, the rancher—a careful man you see—
offered it to him as a gift. Well, then the Jefe said he couldn't
accept gifts but that he would pay the man a peso for the bull.
And he handed the rancher a five-peso note. 'I'm sorry, my
Presidente, but I have no change,' said the rancher. So the
General said, 'That's all right, give me four more bulls.' ''

The three men laughed gleefully and then the dark mestizo
said, ''Still . . .''

''Oh come now,'' the paunchy little man said, wiping his
eyes with the backs of his hands, ''you have seen yourself it
doesn't make any difference in the end who it is.'' The line had
moved up and they were almost to the postal window. ''They
are all members of the same club.''

''The Jockey Club,'' the third man said, chuckling. Kay had
heard of the Jockey Club. The Padrino belonged. It was an
exclusive organization composed of Colombia's wealthy business and social aristocracy.

Walking home with Rosa, Kay didn't have too much to say.
What could you say? That the little man was right—that the
whole thing was a farce and nothing that you tried to do about
it could matter? That back home with Nixon and Vietnam and
assassination and racial injustice things were different? In
Colombia, it was just more up front, she thought. And in the
end it was always about money.

In the late afternoon, Carlos came to get Roddy. Ricardo was
with him and they had brought along a carload of Frenchies.
Looking at the number of bags piled on the floor of her
bedroom, Kay said, ''Oh good. I can see this is another
promotion and you're planning to give me a second assistant.''

Carlos quirked an eyebrow and took a cigar from his shirt
pocket. ''As you may have noticed, Kay, some of our good
citizens are in a sour mood.''

He bit the cigar and lit it, narrowing his eyes against the smoke. He waved the cigar at the suitcases. "These should have been out of here yesterday."

"Of course," Kay said. She looked at Ricardo.

"I'm sorry." He shrugged and avoided her eyes. "Wait in the car for me," he told Carlos. "I'll be right down."

"Tiene huevos, Ricardo," Carlos said. "You've got balls. You are playing Jefe now? Giving me orders?" But he went anyway. At the door, he turned and said, "Be careful, Kay."

"I want to warn you what you must do, how you must behave in these times," Ricardo said. Kay saw that he looked tired. He sat down on the couch with her and held her by the wrist, willing her serious attention.

"When you go out, even just down the street, you must always carry your *cédula* [identification card] and your passport. The police or the soldiers can stop you for them any time and sometimes they may want a bribe to let you go. If that is what they want, they will find some little thing wrong with your papers. It doesn't matter that the papers are perfectly in order, they will say something like you have been too long in the country, your visa is bad.

"Then they will threaten you with jail and they will mean it, so you must always carry money with you for them. Always have at least three hundred dollars in cash and give it all to them. They use these times to take advantage of foreigners and Colombians who might have problems of some kind." He kissed her briefly. "I am sorry, *mi amor,* I must go."

Ricardo's warning put ice in Kay's veins. She had heard what happened to blond American women in Colombian jails. Death was preferable. She would gladly stay home permanently, she thought, or pay whatever ransom they wanted, rather than risk confrontation with the military. They were above the law, killers for amusement, the most dreaded force in Colombia.

The next days were twelve-hour marathons of tooting and packaging. In the heavy air, muffled by closed windows and drawn drapes, Kay could hear the constant rumble of trucks going by, and gunfire, sometimes a *"boom!"* very close by, at others, a distant series of pops.

A naked bulb burned all day in the small workspace, and

Janis Joplin wailed on the tape cassette. The outside world was reduced to the blue flicker of the TV screen and phone calls from Ricardo. At night, dreams came . . . of running along the top of the levee back home, terrified of slipping and falling down its sheer curve to the roiled water below. In the weedy place by the railroad tracks, her cousin Ray grinned and held out on his open palm a freshly killed, twitching frog. . . .

In the world outside her curtains, Rojas demonstrators were driven off the streets, and after a second night of rioting and looting, a state of siege was declared. A curfew and ban on the sale of alcohol went into effect, one hundred thousand troops were called to full alert and travel at airports and harbors was restricted. Anyone could be stopped and asked for identification papers at any time, and the military was empowered to arrest, try, and execute at will.

Kay's gut felt like a clenched fist. She kept a bottle of Maalox by her bed and ate little except half-pint cartons of Colombian yogurt called Alpina. Rosa tapped on the bedroom door shyly, trying to tempt the señorita with her favorite flan and *pan dulce*. Kay would force herself to eat a few bites so as not to hurt Rosa's feelings. It couldn't only be the cocaine, could it? She wondered if she had picked up a parasite, even though she had been careful with food and water, drinking only bottled Agua Cristal.

Halfway through her work on the last suitcase, she impulsively picked up the phone. She lay on the bed and watched television while the phone receiver rang in her ear, and rang and rang. Finally an operator came on.

"Tengo una emergencia en los Estados Unidos." Kay raised her voice to an urgent hysteria. "I must be put through immediately. I have just received the news that my grandmother is dying." She put a catch in her voice. "Please help me, señora, I want to talk to her for one last time." She put down the cigarette she was smoking and crossed her fingers.

"Oh, I am very sorry to hear that," the woman's immediate and genuine sympathy made Kay feel terrible. "I will try my best to put you through, but these are difficult times."

"Thank you so much, señora."

With eyes closed, Kay listened to the rushing hum of the wires and the clipped voices of the operators talking back and forth. She felt both sleepy and edgy.

Twenty minutes went by. Then, suddenly Grandma's voice. "Hello, who is this?"

There were faint voices in the hollow background of the open lines.

"Can you hear me, Grandma? It's me, Kayleen, your long-lost grandbaby."

There was a slight pause. "Well, Kayleen honey, I am just so *glad*. Where are you? Are you callin' me all the way from South America?"

"Yes, Grandma. You might have heard, we're having a little political trouble down here, but I'm doing just fine myself."

"No, we haven't heard anything. You sure you're all right?"

Kay held the receiver a little bit away from her ear. The old lady had begun to shout.

"Yes, I am. How's everyone?" Kay sat up now, her eyes on the half-finished suitcase on the floor and the big plastic bag of cocaine.

"Oh, about as usual, honey. It's been raining, so I've been down with my back and my arthritis is bad. And, of course, your mother changed her hair again. I can't imagine what she thinks is wrong with her own hair color."

Kay had a flash of her mother's heart-shaped face under pink rollers peering critically into the small bathroom mirror.

"Well anyway, this time it's not yeller, she's got it a kind of orangey color, and Darleen's expectin' again." Kay lay back down on the bed, listening to the familiar flow of her grandmother's voice. "I'm working on a quilt for her and one for you, too, with the money you sent me. I want to have it for when you come home. Just when *are* you coming home, darlin'?"

"I don't know exactly. I'll write and tell you." There was a crackle in the wire and the faint voices were replaced with dim music, like the sound of a tiny party light-years away.

"Haven't heard a word from your cousin Ray over there in Veet Nam. I see terrible things on the TV. Do you have a TV down there?"

"Yes, we do. I see terrible pictures of the war too."

"I pray for him every day. Don't know nothin' about Veet Nam, but President Nixon must know what he's doin' over there."

At the mention of Nixon, Kay rolled her eyes. "Grandma,

I've been thinking a lot about you. Are you taking care of yourself? I *know* you're taking care of everyone else.''

"Of course I'm taking care of old Grandma. Listen here, we can't go on talkin' like this, it must be costing you a pretty penny. You come on home and see me as soon as you can, ya hear? God bless you, darlin', and keep safe.''

"Good-bye, Grandma, I love you.''

"Bye, darlin'. Bye-bye.''

Kay put down the receiver and swung her feet to the floor, pressing the palms of her hands to her eyes. Her lie to the operator haunted her and she wished she could have thought of some other way to get through. It was unlucky.

She got up and washed her face and went into the kitchen. Rosa was sitting there at the table, braiding her hair. The little red radio Kay had bought her played a soulful song full of Colombian melancholy and a pot steamed away on the stove.

Rosa stopped braiding and half-rose from her chair. "Señorita Kay," she said. "*¿Qué pasa?* You look very sick.''

In late May, the state of siege, though still in effect, was less restrictive. In Miami, the exiled General Rojas issued accusations and veiled threats from a sickbed while his daughter organized the gathering resistance of her party, ANAPO, in preparation for the final vote tally.

"I don't like the way things are," Ricardo shouted suddenly one afternoon. They were in the VW heading downtown to see *The Good, the Bad, and the Ugly*, with Clint Eastwood.

Kay's mind went instantly cold and sharp. What was it? Politics? Family? Their affair? The business?

"You don't like . . . ?" she prompted cautiously.

He didn't answer, and Kay cringed at the sound of the gears grinding as he shifted angrily in the heavy traffic. At Carrera 14 he turned the car north again.

"We're not going to the movies? I thought you really wanted to see this." Most American movies were banned in Colombia, and Ricardo had been talking for days about this one.

"We will go to see a later show.''

"Do you want to tell me where we *are* going then?''

"We are going home, to my home.''

"Good." She smiled. After a pause she said, "Will your parents be there?"

"My father is out. My mother will be there and my sisters and brothers too." He continued to drive very fast, even by Colombian standards.

They entered the house by the garage and back door. Flora was yelling at a servant. "Are you stupid?" she was screaming. The servant listened, expressionless and calm, a young Indian woman wearing a blue-checked apron over a worn sweater and black wool skirt, her feet in socks and plastic sandals.

Seeing Kay and Ricardo at the door, Flora turned to them without skipping a beat. "How nice, what a fine surprise," she said brightly, then turning back to the girl, "Go ahead then, Mercedes, what are you waiting for?"

Ricardo went to kiss his mother's cheek. "*¿Hola, Mamá, qué tal?*" He was breezy. "I have brought Kay home for a game of billiards before we go to the movie."

"You are most welcome in my house," Flora said, "but Ricardo is a bad son." She shook her finger at him coyly, making the reprimand acceptable. "He should have told me so that I could have prepared something. But please, my house is your house."

"Thank you, señora, but you must not trouble yourself on my account," Kay said.

"Oh, but I must insist. You will take a little *jugo*, a sandwich, some ham and cheese perhaps? Some *dulces*?"

"Thank you so much, señora," Kay said and looked dutifully to Ricardo for a cue. She was doing well. She knew her behavior was impeccable by Colombian standards.

"Nothing, Mama, thank you. We will have a snack later, before the movie." He was at the fridge, getting out two bottles of Colombiana, his favorite *gaseosa*.

"But, Ricky, a snack? That is not a proper dinner. You must have a real dinner."

"We will have a real dinner—later—downtown."

Kay saw a combative look flash between mother and son, and busied herself with the vase of camellias and freesias on the kitchen table. "These are very beautiful, Señora Alvarez," she said. "Are they from your garden?" Going through customs is easier than this, she thought. Ricardo came up behind her and took her arm. "Come," he said.

He opened his bottles of *gaseosa* in the game room and poured the soda into a cut-crystal highball glass. There was a pool table of polished mahogany, with ornately carved legs. Ricardo took a cue from the wall rack, positioned it on the edge of the table, and sighted along it. "This is a good cue," he said, his voice elaborately casual, "my father brought it for me from Chicago." He pronounced it "Tchicago."

Kay took down a cue for herself and began chalking it. "Okay, then, Rick," she said, grinning. "Rack 'em up."

He gave her a funny glance, and she realized he didn't know what she meant.

Ricardo played a clean, precise game of straight pool. He bit his lower lip with each shot, his dark hair hanging over a face brooding with concentration. Kay loved occasions like this, when forgetting himself, Ricardo was most himself, full of young-dog energy.

She had learned to play pool in a bar in Santa Monica. After Ricardo won two games, she asked to switch to eight-ball. She was better at that. She began making hot shots and Ricardo got excited and loud, saying *"Bueno"* every time she sank a ball. When she finally won, he glanced at the open door and then ran around the table to hug and kiss her.

"What a woman," he said. "Colombian women never play pool."

In the middle of the third game, Ricardo's sister Eva came in and sat down at the card table. She was just seventeen and looked disturbingly like Ricardo. She watched politely and didn't say anything, but suddenly Kay was intensely aware of all the sounds of the house, the clock ticking on the wall, voices behind a closed door, the canned laughter from an upstairs TV. It was getting harder and harder to stay on top of the game.

Tomaso, Ricardo's ten-year-old brother, a thin boy in short pants, came to the door. His brown hair was neatly parted and he wore glasses firmly held in place with a rubber strap around the back of his head.

"Ricardo thinks he is Fast Eddie," he said and giggled. "And Tío Carlos thinks he is Minnesota Fats." He laughed even harder and threw himself into a chair. Ricardo pointedly ignored him. This kid knows about Minnesota Fats? Kay thought.

After a while, Tomaso slumped down in his chair and closed his eyes. "This is boring," he said. "Boring."

No one answered and he sat up again. "Ricardo, play Ping-Pong with me. Please, Ricardo. Please. Play Ping-Pong with me." Ricardo told him to shove off upstairs. "Don't you have homework today?" he asked.

"Oh, go ahead. Play with him," Eva said. She looked at Kay.

"I think this Ping-Pong is a good idea, Tomaso." Kay put down her cue. "Anyway, I need to be rescued from this game."

"Thank you." Tomaso was surprised, and ran to put the cue back on the rack for her.

The Ping-Pong table was in the garage, and as they left the room, Mercedes, the servant in the checked apron, materialized at the door. "*¿Usted quiere?*" she said.

Ricardo ordered soup and sandwiches for six o'clock at the card table in the game room. The dining room was too formal and he wanted to play music while they ate, he explained to Kay.

His tone to the servant was mechanical and brisk, like his mother's, Kay thought, only less shrill. She tried to make eye contact with the woman. Do you notice how he talks to you? she wanted to say. Doesn't it bother you? Are you really used to it, or would you like to kill him in his sleep one day?

As they passed the living room on the way to the garage, Flora called out, "Eva, come in here and look at the beautiful engagement picture of Francia in *El Tiempo*." Eva looked annoyed, but she went.

Playing Ping-Pong with his little brother, Ricardo forgot about having to be a man, and kept dancing around yelling "Move, move," and "Rally, rally," and calling him *"Raton-cito,"* and "Topo Gigio," the Latin mouse Ed Sullivan used to feature on his show.

After he played Tomaso, Ricardo challenged Kay to a game. "Look out," he said, his face flushed, "I'm a killer at this game."

"So am I," Kay said.

"Please excuse me for interrupting you, but Tomaso must go

upstairs now. He has things to do." Flora stood at the garage door. Tomaso started to say something, but Flora stared him down.

"Good-bye, Kay. Next time will you teach me to play pool? Ricardo is too good and he gets mad when he tries to teach me. And anyway, he always wants to practice alone."

"*Seguro.* Next time I will teach you how to beat him."

Ricardo laughed and Flora put her hand to the back of Tomaso's head and gave him a little push toward the door. "*Vámonos, Tomaso.*"

She's trying to keep her other children away from me, Kay thought. One son under the bad influence of the wild *norteamericana* is enough.

In the game room, two places had been set. Ricardo put on a Beatles record and took a bottle of Chiliano from his father's wine rack under the bar. He opened it grandly, savoring the moment, and poured them each a glass.

"*A mi vida, a mi corazón, a mi amor,*" he toasted, looking into her eyes.

Kay lifted her glass to him, but she was anxious, aware that the Padrino might appear at any moment and think she was taking her relationship with Ricardo a step too far.

Ricardo held her hand against his cheek. "What are you thinking?" he said. She forgot sometimes just how quick and tender he could be. "Are you disturbed about my mother? Don't mind it, *bonita.* She will get used to you in time."

"I don't know. Maybe," she said. "That would be nice. What time is the movie?" She felt the tired drag of melancholy, and his sweetness made her lonely. She would have liked to let down her guard and be easy and simple with him, a real lover.

Late May was the time of the rains again, and it seemed to Kay the chill came down from the mountains and settled into the very stones of the unheated houses. Cars splashed through the huge puddles in the street, honking and tying up traffic, and even clothes put away in closets and drawers were perpetually damp. The floor of the workshop flooded, and Kay, debilitated from coke use, fell prey to frequent colds.

On the surface, life in Bogotá seemed to resume its normal routines. Pastrana would not be installed as the new president until August 7, and the Rojistas were rethinking their strategies. The shattered shop windows were replaced, the curfew lifted.

The talk in the *tiendas* and cafés was all about the World Cup and whether Bobby Moore, the blond British soccer star, had been set up when he was arrested for stealing a bracelet from the lobby jewelry store of the Tequendama Hotel.

The beggars had reappeared on the church steps and the *gamines* worked the town once more, hanging on like fierce little ticks to the body of the city. Kay wondered how they had survived and down what alleys they had fled during the time when glass splintered and the soldiers swept through the streets.

Ricardo told her, with an ironic smile, that behind her back the Padrino made fun of her and called her "the Madonna of the *gamines*," but she just shrugged and continued to keep her large purse stuffed with change and *dulces*.

It was a hopeless gesture, she knew, but the more illegal money that poured into her bank account, the more she gave. "It's for good luck," she told Ricardo, "I just want to stay on the right side of God." Only half joking, she was horrified that like everyone else, she might become immune to the sight of them.

Although Bogotá waited in a state of suspended animation for the next act in the drama of the election, Roberto Alvarez had begun to think of moving his operation out of the capital. The election had simply been too close, he told Ricardo. Disruption and violence would not fade away with the new administration. Bogotá would remain a hotspot. The hills around Medellín offered a safer cover for clandestine operations, and the city itself, Colombia's fastest-growing industrial center, was becoming both geographically and economically a more practical choice for headquarters.

While Roberto was away from home increasingly, looking into Medellín real estate, Kay had begun spending more time at the Alvarez house in the Norte district. But she never felt at ease there. She felt lighter and freer in the shop, laughing and snorting with Carlos and the men, and staying out till morning with Ricardo dancing the merengue and bambuco. After breakfast, they would drive through intermittent sunshine into the moist, ferny countryside full of the whistles and calls of thrushes and blackbirds.

One night, as Kay and Carlos stood in the alley closing up shop, he struck his head with his hand as though remembering something. He looked embarrassed. "My brother has asked me to see if you would do a favor for him," he said. "You don't have to do it, you know, this is just a private favor which he would appreciate."

Kay knew instantly it was going to be about Olivia.

"*Bueno, pues* . . . there is going to be a school pageant tomorrow. At the school Estrella goes to. Estrella mentioned to my brother that you might like to come . . . she is in the choir. . . ."

"Of course I'll go," Kay said quickly.

"You don't mind! For myself, I find these kind of things"—he held out his hands and laughed—"very long sometimes," he finished.

"No. I'd really like to go." Kay was pleased, not only because doing a favor for the Padrino was smart business, but because she was curious about his private life.

"Will your brother be there too?" Kay asked.

"Perhaps." He laughed and shook his head. "I hope so, because otherwise Olivia will be like a crazy woman."

Kay drove Olivia and Estrella to the school at eight the next evening. Estrella sat in the back, carefully holding her white choir robe and begging her mother for the perfume that Kay had brought her, a gift left over from one of her free-port stops.

"No, *preciosa,* you will spill it. I am guarding it for you in my purse."

Estrella fell silent. She rolled the window up and down a few times. Kay saw her in the rearview mirror smoothing her wind-ruffled bangs with a little comb.

"So, Kay, tell me. You have been in the Alvarez home, no? What is it like? I understand you were there this week, no?"

"Yes, Olivia, not no." Kay glanced at her and saw the shiny red smile, perky and unfazed.

"How many rooms? Is it as luxurious as I hear?"

Kay sighed. "Olivia, I'm sorry, but I don't want to talk about it. Anyway, why do you want to torture yourself?"

"Oh, I understand now," Olivia spat out. "You are a friend of the señora."

"Flora?" Kay laughed and Estrella leaned forward, resting her chin on the back of her mother's seat to listen better.

"Flora would love to see me go home, disappear forever. Still, Olivia, think about it. I'm a friend of the family, they've been very nice to me, so you see I can't take sides . . . under the circumstances . . ." Kay was advancing carefully. She was in dangerous territory.

"I have the highest right to know what's in that house," Olivia said indignantly. "My mother showed me an article in the paper. There is a new law, and illegitimate children are now entitled to an equal share of everything the father owns." She turned to face Kay. "I'm not stupid," she said. "I'm going to see that my daughter gets her rights as much as his other children. Sit down, Estrella," she flared. "You are making me crazy leaning over like that."

"Have you said anything to Roberto?" Kay asked.

"No, but tonight I will tell him and we will settle this communion business. He must give Estrella a communion."

"I make a left turn here?" Kay asked. Olivia nodded, looking unhappy and ruffled. "Turn on the radio, find some good music for us," Kay said.

Olivia twiddled the knobs with her long fingernails, and Kay could see she was glad for the chance to cool herself down. She had probably revealed more than she had intended.

The school, abutting a church, was a buff-white, two-story building with a red-tiled roof. Before they got out, Olivia redid her lipstick and then pulled out her purse vial, a peace offering. They sat together companionably and got stoned while Estrella sang along to the music on the radio, *"Tengo, tengo, tengo ganas de bailar, bailar, bailar."* She beat the catchy rhythm on the back of the seats with her hand, her voice high and sweet.

The auditorium was crowded with parents dressed as though for a night at the opera. A nun in floor-length habit came out to stand on a small platform and ask for donations for the music program. Midway through the "Ave Maria" solo, Olivia nudged Kay. The Padrino was coming in through a side door. He sat down discreetly in the back. "I knew he would come," Olivia said.

Afterward, in the parking lot, the Padrino placed a formal kiss on each woman's cheek. They waited for Estrella to come out. The Padrino took out his silver case and lit a cigarette. Olivia talked animatedly about the performance.

Estrella and another little girl came running toward them. They were very excited and giggly and the Padrino seemed to relax a little with them, saying they had sung like little angels and giving them each a *dulce* he produced from his pocket.

"*Entonces,* where are we going?" Olivia asked brightly. Estrella began jumping around repeating, "Where are we going? Where are we going?"

Roberto looked at Kay. She felt like saying, "Who, me?" She had no idea what was appropriate for this strange social occasion. "Why don't you all come to my house for *helado* and a drink," she suggested. "Or I could just go home and you go out, or I don't know, whatever you like . . ." She looked at them, hoping she didn't sound as lame as she felt.

Roberto looked relieved. "Good," he said, "I think we would like some refreshment at your house, thank you. Olivia, why don't you ride with Kay?"

But Olivia had other ideas. "I'll come with you," she said quickly, taking his arm. "Estrella would so love to ride alone with Kay."

At the stoplight, Kay could see them in the Mercedes. Roberto was doing the driving himself tonight and he sat stiffly behind the wheel, holding it with both hands and looking straight ahead. Olivia was gesturing. She is giving him the communion pitch, Kay thought. She lost the Mercedes in traffic, or what was more likely, the Mercedes purposely lost her. She was glad; she wanted to get home first anyway.

At Avenida Jiménez Kay said, "Watch this," and took the downward dip into the garage a little too fast. Estrella screamed with delight. They got out into the musty underground air, and a few cars down, Kay saw the familiar baby blue of Ricardo's VW.

Damn, she thought. Ricardo had been dropping by unannounced lately, something which had begun to make her nervous. She found him lolling on her bed with his shirt and shoes off, reading American magazines. His face, foolish with surprise at the sight of Estrella, sent Kay into helpless laughter.

"Your father is on his way up here," Kay said, giggling, as Ricardo jumped awkwardly into his shoes and shirt like a lover about to be caught by a husband.

Roberto and Olivia didn't come up for another five minutes. They were probably sitting in the car, talking. Kay could imagine the scene, the tears, the Padrino staring in front of him and shaking his head and saying finally, *"¿Qué más? ¿Eh, Olivia? ¿Qué más?"* And finally, the Padrino noticing the blue Volkswagen.

Ricardo pulled her into the bathroom to do a toot. She wanted to save her nose. It had been stuffy lately and an ugly red, so she opened her mouth and had him blow the coke straight onto the delicate membrane at the back of her throat. Wedged between the sink and the bidet, they began laughing and kissing. This is idiotic, she thought, but she didn't care. Ricardo kissed her neck and said, *"Dios,* mother would turn green."

The doorbell rang and they looked at each other. *"Más tarde,"* Ricardo said. She opened the door and saw him glance furtively in the mirror, passing a hand over his already perfectly combed hair.

At the door, Estrella immediately grabbed her mother's hand and dragged her toward the balcony. "Look, Mama. Señorita Kay has everything. She has everything. You said she lives alone and has to work, but she has a car and you should see the other things she has. She's rich."

"Mi casa es tu casa," Kay said quickly. The Padrino sat down on the couch and poured himself a shot of aguardiente. "So, Ricardo," he said, "this is what you call going to see Carlos?"

Ricardo had his back to his father and was fixing gin and tonics. "I was waiting for Kay. I came by on my way, to talk to her about the German trip next week," he said without turning around.

Roberto made a noncommittal sound, a kind of blank bullet of a response that gave no clue to what he was thinking. Kay always found it unnerving.

Estrella had come to stand by her father. "Go and play, Estrellita," Roberto said. Kay could see how tense this was making him. Drinking with his mistress and his son was one thing, but to have the children of his legal marriage and his liaison together in one room was making him profoundly uneasy.

"Come. We will show your mama the apartment," Kay

said. Olivia had been looking around with the eyes of a hungry auction house appraiser. Kay took them into the bedroom, wondering what the two men would say to each other.

"Señorita Kay, how come you have no *esposo* but still you are so rich?" Estrella asked.

"Estrella," Olivia said, "be polite."

"It's because I'm so smart," Kay said, tapping the child playfully on the head.

Olivia frowned and turned away, and Kay thought oh, no, she thinks I'm putting her down.

Shortly after that, everyone left except Ricardo.

"Olivia is not as sly as she thinks," Ricardo said. "Too much coke, too much Valium. It gives her ideas." They were sitting on the couch. Absently, he stroked the inside of Kay's palm with his fingertips.

"She has been threatening my father with legal things because she wants him to give Estrella a communion. She thinks she can push him because he is crazy for her and gives in to things when she cries, and because he is afraid she will take another lover. But threats?" He laughed and sat up. "She's a silly little canary. If she goes too far, my father could snuff that bird in one minute." He made a chopping gesture with his hand.

Kay stared at him, a chill crawling over her body, and Ricardo stared back, his brown eyes questioning. He sat forward and began to tickle her.

"*Más tarde,*" she said. "I'm tired."

In the following weeks of June, Kay made several smuggling trips for the Padrino, going to West Germany by way of Brazil and Portugal, picking up several hundred thousand dollars in deutsche marks from Reynaldo and body-carrying the cash for laundering to the Caymans. She made use of the trips for her own passes, quick airport jobs at Portela with friends recruited by Maggie.

This time, Reynaldo was polite and somewhat reserved with her. He had started supplying a famous German film director and was hanging around with an avant-garde crowd. Kay thought his long, elegant face was going a little seedy, a little puffy around the eyes.

Because of the frequency of her travels, Kay had to change her identity completely with each trip. Armed with fresh papers and doctored passports supplied by Carlos, she slipped from one disguise to another, elusive as a shamanistic shape-changer.

By the end of June, the tension of these trips left Kay exhausted yet keyed up enough to need Valium to sleep. That was why, on her second night home from Germany, it took her a long time to answer the ringing phone.

She had been dreaming—hiding underwater in the tangled reeds at the edge of a lagoon, completely submerged except for her lips, her mouth filled with the brackish taste of rotting plants. She could see the soldier sloshing along the embankment and probing the reeds with the butt of his rifle. He was closing in now, his booted feet moving around in the muck directly above her. He pushed the rifle down into the small of her back while she tried desperately to mimic the feel of decaying leaves. He pressed her body down against the murky bottom.

The phone rang for several minutes before she could understand what it was.

"Maggie?" Her mind was a jumble of relief and anxiety as she tried to make sense of where she was.

"Kay, I woke you. I'm sorry. I just had to talk."

"What time is it?"

"Four where you are, one here."

"Did something happen?" Kay sat up, alarmed now, plunging her hand into her hair.

"No. I've just been sitting here with the cat and the dog." Her voice was strained, a little drunk.

"How are they?"

"They're adorable and spoiled and fat, like me. I read about Vaughn quitting Colombia. He's been letting it leak out that Washington more or less forced his resignation. Typical. He was the best damn ambassador we ever had down there."

"If Nixon doesn't like him," Kay said, "he must be a good man. I hope he had the sense to take home a nice nest egg." She reached across the night table for a pack of cigarettes and lit one. "Maggie, you didn't call to talk politics, did you?"

"I went out to the Palms Bar tonight," Maggie's voice sounded a little blurred, as though she had momentarily turned her head away from the mouthpiece, then she was back, "and they all kept asking me when you were coming home again, and if you were coming home at all"—she paused—"or had you decided to live down there."

"Oh, Mags."

"Yeah . . . well . . ."

"You know how much I need you," Kay said. She got out of bed and stood in the middle of the room, holding the phone on its long cord.

"Oh, I know you *need* me, but you still aren't going to come home."

They didn't say anything for a moment, and then Kay said, "Listen, Maggie, I know things are weird, but I haven't forgotten my friends and I haven't forgotten you. You have to know I love you."

Kay could hear the ice cubes clicking in Maggie's glass. "Never mind, Kay, I'm just a little bummed out lately. Still feeling shitty about Kent State. It was only a month ago. Things are—"

"I know." Kay could just see her sitting there, shoulders hunched, bare feet stuck out in front of her. Maggie never allowed herself anything, Kay thought suddenly, not even her own real feelings.

"So why don't you come to Bogotá for a few days," Kay said. "You know, have a good time, play the tourist like you always wanted to, pick up a suitcase full of nice things to take back."

"Well, if the mountain won't come to Mohammed, Mohammed will come to the mountain," Maggie said, but she sounded more cheerful.

They decided she would arrive on July 12, a little over two weeks away.

But the next day, Kay was on the phone trying to persuade her not to come.

"I must have been crazy," Kay said almost angrily. "It's explosive down here right now, it's not safe. There's a lot of reaction going on about the election results. You should know, you read the papers."

"I don't care, Kay, I'm not going to let you back out of it that easy—I'm coming."

"Well, don't say I didn't try to warn you, you stubborn Irish mick." After they hung up, Kay realized how much she wanted to see Maggie, how much she missed her, not only because she was Maggie, but because she was a piece of home.

Nevertheless, Kay was truly worried.

Chapter
Eight

Bogotá, Colombia—(UPI) July 17, 1970. The army occupied this Andean capital early Thursday to head off possible protest demonstrations by partisans of defeated Presidential candidate . . . Gustavo Rojas Pinilla.

The maneuver followed an announcement Wednesday night by Carlos Lleras Restrepo that the government had learned of a plot by members of Rojas' Alianza Popular Nacional . . . Party to foment "great internal commotion."

It followed the Supreme Electoral Court's proclamation of Misael Pastrana Borrero as Colombia's President-elect and official successor to Lleras, whose term expires August 7.

. . . Thousands of armed soldiers in battle fatigues patrolled the streets early in the day as the residents prepared to go to work under a persistent rain.

MAGGIE ARRIVED IN Bogotá as scheduled on July 12. They had planned for her to stay in Colombia for a week and then take a ship home from Cartagena. She'd be the perfect young tourist, very Ivy League, traveling to Bogotá, buying some emeralds, and then cruising home through the Caribbean for another week of sun and fun. "My family is so happy," she told Kay. "You can imagine: 'Finally Maggie is doing something normal.'"

Maggie had called the day before to tell Kay the flight had been delayed. "Are you okay? When was the last time you ate?" she had asked suddenly, and Kay wondered how she was always able to pick up on those things. Since Maggie had seen her last, Kay had dropped ten pounds.

Feeling edgy, Kay took *El Tiempo* and went down to wait for her in the lobby. The attendant in the small glass cage by the door nodded and smiled. One of his little kids was in the cage with him and waved at Kay.

The news was not good. There had been a midnight-to-dawn mobilization in the past week, amid reports that with Misael Pastrana now the declared winner of the election, the Rojistas planned to create major disturbances throughout the country.

Security measures in Bogotá were tight and the presidential palace, normally open to the public, was closed to all except those with special-entry permits.

The minister of defense, Major General Gerardo Ayerbe Chaux, had vowed that any disruptions by Rojas would be crushed: "For each of his plans there already is a solution. . . . Any attempts at violence will be suppressed with all energy," *The Miami Herald* quoted him as saying on July 9.

Finally, there was Maggie, stepping from a cab in a chino skirt and a navy blue blazer, her crazy-halo curls tamed to a shoulder-length bob of smooth copper.

Kay rushed out into the street and hugged her. "Your hair," she said, and Maggie said, "I know, and you think I shouldn't have come." And Kay said, "That's right, you shouldn't have."

Maggie squeezed her and said, "'All right, so call me another cab and I'll go back."

She whistled when Kay swung open the apartment door. "Nice place you have here, dearie," she said.

"I brought you protein powder, peanut butter, energy bars, and Tampax," Maggie called out from the bedroom. She was unpacking and stripping off the money bra. "I can't wait to see this town. I want to take pictures." Kay lay on the living-room couch drinking Argentine wine.

"We can't, Mags. Too dangerous."

She waited, but there was no answer except for the sound of the shower and the groaning whoosh of water through the pipes.

When Maggie came out, Kay was waiting on the balcony for her. The rain had stopped, and across the street a giant fir tree stood darkly silhouetted against the paler green of the mountain behind it. Rows of brightly colored buses churned down the street and the setting sun fired the sky over Monserrate.

"Ridiculous, overproduced," Maggie said, her face glowing with reflected light. She went back inside to get her camera and tripod. "What can we see tomorrow?" she asked happily. She bent her head over her favorite old Leica and focused a wide-angle lens.

"Maggie, I keep telling you, Bogotá is not a tourist spot right now. Maybe this will convince you, since I can't." Kay handed her a copy of *El Bogotano*.

She had opened the paper to a page of photos showing a stained and mutilated body lying on newspapers beside an open suitcase.

"This is what happened to a European visitor just last week," Kay said. "They found him in a locker in the bus depot."

Maggie looked at the photos and sighed. "Thanks," she said. She turned a few pages. The paper was full of beauty queens and stories about two-headed babies and movie stars. She put the paper down on the tiled floor.

"I know," Kay said. "The paper's a rag. But the story is true anyway. I just couldn't think of a better way to make you see."

She had Maggie now. "People get desperate when the military tighten up on the city," Kay said.

"What people?"

"People whose lives are on the line because they have no papers or they are guerrillas, for fugitives from some other South American country. There are people in Bogotá now who'll do anything for money."

There was a click as Maggie's time exposure went off. She shook her head, "And it's so beautiful," she said.

When it turned cold, they went inside and Kay rolled the sliding doors closed and pulled the drapes, shutting out the night.

Rosa had prepared a special dinner. "She keeps staring at me when she thinks I'm not looking," Maggie said.

"You don't have to whisper, Maggie, she doesn't know that much English yet." Kay picked nervously at the already ragged cuticle of her thumbnail.

Her thumb started bleeding and she put her hand in her lap. "Things may be bad at home, but at least someone like Rosa can get lucky and make it out of the kitchen and into the living room. Down here, if anyone tries to change the order of things they get killed.''

Maggie put her fork down. ''You're saying we're not killing people at home? Have you been watching the news lately?''

''I don't want to talk about it,'' Kay said. ''Let's have our coffee in the living room.'' She got up and went to ask Rosa for the *dulces* and coffee.

Sitting on the couch, Maggie leaned back and looked at Kay. ''You do four lines and you eat no dinner. You look like a clothes hanger and you nearly bite my head off. What does that tell me?''

Kay said, ''I'm handling it. Do you want to do a line?''

''No,'' Maggie said. ''These *dulces* are my poison for the moment.'' She rested her head against the back of the couch, chewing thoughtfully.

After a moment, she said to the ceiling, ''I've never seen you with this much furniture in your life, not to mention the spectacle of your bulging clothes closet. Did he buy them for you?''

Kay opened her mouth to speak, but Maggie held up her hand. ''All right, so I'm a jealous bitch, but that's not the whole thing. I mean these are scary people you're in with.'' She turned her head to look at Kay. ''I'm scared for you, puss. You're not serious about him, are you?''

''No, I'm not,'' Kay said flatly. She sipped her coffee. ''It's hard to explain.'' She looked down at the neutral beige carpet, away from Maggie's bent head and her pale bare feet inches away on the couch.

''I like him.'' She was trying for an impersonal tone, but instead her voice sounded strained. ''Oh shit, Maggie, I don't know how to tell you about it.''

Maggie didn't answer and she plowed on. ''We're friends. We laugh. He's curious about things.'' Maggie was silent. ''Anyway, one day soon it'll be over. Probably when his father thinks it's time to call it off.''

Kay felt adrift; the couch was like a boat, with herself at one end and Maggie with her knees hugged up to her chest at the other. Neither of them said anything for a moment.

Finally, Kay said, ''Anyway, Mags, I don't love him like *that*.''

Maggie put her hand out and touched Kay's arm. "Thin," she said. Kay took the hand and interlaced their fingers.

"Don't worry about it," she said, "I'm a big girl. It's just something I want to do right now." She pulled Maggie's feet into her lap and cradled them close. "Cold," she said, and she slipped them under her shirt and held them against her bare warm skin.

The next morning, Monserrate was gone behind a mist that dissolved periodically to let through bolts of sunlight. Kay had compromised about sight-seeing and called Ricardo. It would be safer with a man in the car, she explained to Maggie. Even in normal times, a woman was better off in the streets of Bogotá with a male escort.

Ricardo came to pick them up in the VW. He was courtly and apologetic, assuring Maggie she would have to come back again when things in his city were "less distressful." He turned on the radio and passed a joint around, joking easily and pointing out the sights. Maggie asked him to stop every now and then so she could take photos.

There were few people in the cramped lanes of the old quarter as they drove toward the house where Simón Bolívar had lived with his married mistress.

"Manuelita Saenz was a heroine," Ricardo said. "She rode with Bolívar at the head of his troops. When the government soldiers came to the house to arrest him, she opened the door in her nightgown and kept them talking while Bolívar escaped."

"I bet the other women didn't like her," Kay said.

The house was a national shrine, surrounded by a wooden veranda painted green and set in a studied wilderness of heavy-headed roses, daisies, and jasmine. Sunflowers big as dinner plates nodded against a wall. In the middle of the garden a sun-bleached wooden bench stood in the striped shadows of an ancient palm.

Kay bent down to look more closely at the worn mosaic pathway leading to the front steps. There was a peculiar uniformity about the shiny brown stones that made up its geometry. On their way to the Gold Museum she asked Ricardo about it. They weren't stones at all, he told her, embarrassed, they were the bones of Indians.

Kay repeated, "The bones of Indians?" and he hurried to

explain that the bone mosaics had been a custom in colonial times when people didn't know better, but of course now it was considered barbaric and most of those floors and garden paths had long been covered over. Sometimes, he added as an afterthought, bones were still used to make mosaic paths, but of course now they were the bones of cattle.

"Ah," Maggie said politely.

Ricardo parked the car around the corner from the Gold Museum in a lot of a few blocks away from the Plaza Bolívar. The lot was surrounded by walls topped with barbed wire and spiky shards of glass to keep the cars safe from the piranha-like attentions of thieves. They could strip a vehicle in seconds.

As they walked toward the museum, a small man suddenly appeared and shoved a knotted handkerchief under Maggie's nose. His head was too large for his body and he was wearing a dirty sweater and a plaid suit jacket. A gold tooth gleamed in his smile. *"¿Esmeraldas para la bonita señorita?"*

Ricardo laughed. "Blood could flow in the streets and these *muchachos* would still come out. They would sell emeralds to the devil."

"Are the emeralds any good?" Maggie asked after Ricardo had waved the man away.

"Street *esmeraldas? Seguro.* They can be very fine if you want small ones and if you know how to bargain. Or they can also be glass. You have to know."

The Gold Museum was empty. They walked through darkened rooms where the clatter of their footsteps echoed loudly. The vanished culture of Colombia's Indian nations glowed around them, a great treasure hoard etched in gold and encrusted with jewels.

The golden glory of the Sun God shone at Kay from behind glass, celebrated in objects both humble and sacred: human figures, masks, spoons, tweezers, necklaces, and *poporos,* the beautiful three-lobed vessels the Indians used to store the lime they mixed with the sacred coca leaves. Even the lesser gods, the spirits of lizard and owl, eagle and frog, were captured in a loving perfection of stylized gold.

On a black velvet base rested the pride of the museum, a tiny gold raft sailing away forever, bearing the spun-gold figures of a regal chieftain and several assistants.

"The Chibchas practiced the rite which became the single

most decisive motivation for the Spanish expeditions; the ceremony of El Dorado,'' Kay read.

"Beside the sacred lake, the chief, after anointing his body with aromatic oils, sprinkled himself with gold powder, thus transforming himself into a living golden statue. Magnificently adorned and accompanied by the principal men of his tribe, he embarked on a raft made of rushes. Just as the sun appeared on the horizon, the chief dove into the water while at the same time the priests threw religious offerings into the lake: golden objects, ceramics, weaving spindles, jewelry, and the fruits of the harvest. As the chief emerged from the water, the gold washed from his skin, and the silence was broken by the sound of music coming from flutes, drums, and clay whistles. Great clouds on incense rose from the shores of the lake.'' Kay could visualize the scene with perfect clarity.

"Although El Dorado was never found,'' she read on, "in the first one hundred years of the Conquest, one hundred eighty-one tons of gold and sixteen thousand tons of silver were produced for the royal coffers by melting down confiscated Indian artifacts.''

"Enough of a haul to help them forget El Dorado for a while,'' Kay said.

Maggie and Ricardo moved on, but she lingered, mesmerized, in front of the fragile raft and its golden riders.

When they emerged from the museum, the sudden fierce light hurt their eyes and Kay stared around at the little square park. It was empty but the Indians were there anyway with their wares spread out on the pavement: handmade leather chains, *ruanas* and blankets, newspapers, religious articles, lottery tickets, Marlboros.

"Look what happened to El Dorado,'' Kay said.

"I'll be right back,'' Maggie said, and moved away to find a discreet place from which to shoot some photographs.

Kay and Ricardo stood watching her walk away, suddenly awkward with each other. "I'll go and get the car,'' he said.

Kay waited until Maggie came back, and they crossed the street toward the Avianca building. At first, she didn't realize what was happening.

There were shouts and Kay saw several men gathered in front of the post office. Soldiers had herded three or four people off to one side against the wall. The next moment, the world exploded in a stuttering roar of gunfire and shattering glass. Screaming seemed to come from everywhere. Kay saw Maggie down on the pavement pressed against the wall of the building, yelling for her to get down, and then Kay was down and the pavement was there, hard and gray beneath her cheek.

The screaming and the gunfire continued. Kay wrapped her arms over her head. She opened her eyes and saw bodies scattered in the street. The snout of an old green tank was just poking its way around a corner into the square. She closed her eyes again. There was a strange panting sound. After a moment, she realized it was coming from her.

Up on her feet, she ran, crouching, along the wall, Maggie in front of her. Down the narrow side street they ran to where the blue VW waited, the driver's door open, Ricardo running toward them.

The whole area around the Avianca building had been cordoned off and traffic inched toward a roadblock checkpoint. It had begun to rain. Kay reached back between the seats and found Maggie's hand, cold and sweaty.

At the checkpoint, Ricardo talked to the soldier who leaned into his window. The women were tourists, yes. Bad times, such a shame. So many enemies of law and order. Yes, absolutely. A time for strong action.

Kay turned to see Maggie's white face, her camera clutched in her hands. Ricardo sped away from the line of soldiers and jeeps. *"Hijos de putas,"* he kept repeating. "The fucking country is full of murderers." His voice trembled. "There's worse yet to come too. They'll keep it up until there's no one left to vote one way or the other."

Then he began to calm down, apologizing for his language, saying how there was certainly some explanation, how it was just bad luck to have been there for it. He turned the car toward the Norte. "I will take you to a German restaurant for lunch, the best one in the Norte."

As soon as the drinks came, Ricardo headed for the phone. Kay knew he was calling the Padrino. She knew that he felt he had lost his cool in the excitement, and that he wished he hadn't.

For the next two days, Kay and Maggie waited for word on their flight to Cartagena, where Maggie was to pick up her cruise ship with the loaded "Frenchie." Now that flights out of Bogotá had been severely restricted, they worried that Maggie might miss her connection. Unable to go out into the beleaguered city, they slept late, talked, gossiped, watched TV, read and reread magazines, talked to Rosa, drank, ate, snorted, and finally just sat around. From the mountains to the south of the city came the occasional boom of a muffled explosion.

On July 19, Ricardo called with good news. He had a "friend" at the airport who would see to it that they got through the strict airport controls for their flight to Cartagena the next day.

Ricardo picked them up and took them to the airport, talking them through the official red tape. The terminal was almost deserted. Very few flights were leaving. Maggie went to the ladies' room and Ricardo pulled Kay to him. "It's been a long time," he said and kissed her. "I don't want you to forget me." He kissed her again, lingeringly."

"I won't," she said, but her mind was on the trip and on Maggie, who was about to come out of the ladies' room.

She hooked her arm through his and steered him toward the magazine counter.

The plane lifted and banked away from El Dorado, over the serried ranks of steeply jungled mountains, and headed northwest.

The coast was a different Colombia, indolent, humid, cheerfully Caribbean. The air was steamy and fragrant and the airport officials at Cartagena joked among themselves and performed their duties as though they were there by accident.

"No one seems to have heard about the election here," Maggie said in Kay's ear.

Their cab was decorated like a shrine to the Virgin Mary. The driver, in his sixties, had a seamed brown face, and wore a loose yellow shirt with large pockets. He had a cigarette behind one ear. Kay complimented him on his English and he said in his lifting voice, "Yes, yes, Jamaican roots. We all most of us speak English and Spanish here." His name, he said, was Francisco and he reached his arm back to give them his card.

They were driving along the shore. The wind smelled of charcoal cooking fires. Several black children ran along the beach, flying kites. Chickens scratched unconcerned along the roadside beneath the massive gray stones of the walled town.

"You came for the parties?" he asked.

"What parties?" Maggie said.

"What you tellin' me? You don't know you came for a wonderful time? Independence Day today. Choosing La Reina del Mar de Cartagena. Everyone is here, from Cali, from Medellín, from Bogotá. Where do you ladies come from?"

Kay said, "We're from San Diego, but we've been visiting in Bogotá."

"Oh yes, Bogotá, the Gray City, a strange place. I have a cousin in San Diego. One time I will visit him."

A row of low stucco hotels and apartment houses came into sight around the bend. Five or six horse-drawn carriages stood sleepily around a fountain and a little farther on was a white hotel with blue doors and a sign, HOTEL CARIBE.

In the center of the high-ceilinged lobby, four harassed clerks manned a huge circular reception desk of polished mahogany. From behind this elegant fortress they tended the wants and needs of the rich Colombian families who had come to town to escape the politics and weather of the interior.

Kay and Maggie followed a bellhop along mossy stone paths past the gardened patios and splashing fountains. The electric blue of a swimming pool winked through the greenery. To one side, three floors of arcaded stone balconies rose up into the breezy canopies of giant trees.

As soon as the bellhop had pocketed his tip, Kay checked the room and balcony. Robberies were common even in the best hotels and the Frenchie was, after all, worth thirty thousand dollars. Then she went into the bathroom for a shower and a couple of lines, while Maggie sat on the balcony looking through the room-service menus.

When she came out, her wet hair in a towel turban, it was to the euphoric ringing of a steel band. She joined Maggie at the railing and they looked down together as men in blue-and-white uniforms strung lanterns around the pool, stitching them through the green trees and hanging them in the stone recesses of the patios.

Darkness came and a candlelight dinner of grilled fish and tiny Caribbean shrimp with brown bread and wine from Chile.

The lanterns glowed in the dusk, and a bar and dance floor had been set out poolside.

The music had begun to heat up, the steel band alternating with guitar and horns in a raucous Caribbean beat, urgent and brassy. A few couples moved skillfully around the dance floor.

"You look like a horse at the starting gate," Maggie said.

Kay was leaning her arms on the railing, watching the dancers. Maggie had her feet up on a chair. She had brought out a lamp and a book and her hair stood up a little on one side where she had absently been pulling on it.

"Oh, for God's sake, go ahead and case the joint," she said. "I'll stay home and baby-sit the Frenchie."

"Thanks, Mags." Kay bent down to kiss her cheek and went inside to dress. Forty-five minutes later, she reappeared in a red-and-white off-the-shoulder print, strappy heels, and silver jewelry. A red flower from the vase in the room shone in her hair. As a finishing touch, she had done two lines of coke and she stood in the balcony doorway ready to go, feeling a raw, nervous excitement quivering in the pit of her stomach. The sound of the music lured her on.

Maggie looked her over. "You don't exactly fade into the background," she said. "I thought we were here on a job."

"Don't be bitchy, Maggie." There was a warning note in Kay's voice. While she heard Maggie's concern and even understood it, it left her cold. Maggie was cut off from her, like someone on the other side of a glass wall. The cocaine froze her feelings. She was cresting on the high, nothing was real but the wave.

"I'm not bitchy," Maggie said sharply. "It's just that I don't understand why you're so high-profile."

"I need a good time," Kay said and walked away toward the door, her heels clipping loud against the wooden floor.

"Jesus, Kay, what's going on?" Maggie called after her.

In the lobby, two young Americans approached her. They were dressed in sandals and jeans. The man's hair was tied back in a long blond ponytail.

"Are you an American?" the woman asked. She had a bad complexion and overly friendly eyes.

Kay shook her head and said severely, "No. German." She knew they were looking to score, and the next question would have been did she know where to get some pot or cocaine.

On the stage of the ballroom the candidates for the title of La Reina del Mar de Cartagena were lined up in their long pastel gowns and their white elbow-length gloves. The crowd sat buzzing at the tables below them. Kay watched from the door as the candidates wet their lips and smiled for the flashbulbs.

And the winner was . . . Señorita Felicia Ortiz. A wild cheer erupted from one of the tables and a bullet-shaped man, flushed and jubilant, jumped up, shouting for champagne, champagne for everyone, on him. The mother had burst into tears. The grandmother remained serene at the head of the table, a true queen, holding the youngest child in her lap.

Kay wandered through the garden to the outside bar where an excited crowd of drinkers and dancers celebrated beside a shimmering blue pool, above them a spotlighted high diving board.

A Venezuelan businessman asked her to dance. Kay surrendered to his expert, close lead, and to the Afro-Coastal drums, and the deep, scratchy rub rub of the guaracha. Then he took her back to his table and his friendly wife and family and they drank endless toasts of champagne to the new Queen of Cartagena, to each other, and to the Day of Independence.

The sweet night scents of the garden filled her with nostalgia and a perverse desire to abandon caution completely. Buoyed by champagne, she danced and laughed with a shifting blur of faces and bodies, moving into the leafy shadows for the dreamy acceleration offered by a vial and spoon from an anonymous hand.

Coming back from the bathroom, lolling down the path, pleased with the thin moon and the humid air, she felt a sudden whispering, a warning tingle of scalp and skin. Turning, she saw a man.

He was about fifteen feet away and the light shone on the gold buttons of a dark blue formal blazer. He turned off and disappeared down another path.

There had been something disturbingly familiar about him. She stood still under the trees, tensed, her ears straining. There was no sound but the night creatures whirring. Her heart lurched painfully in her chest. The moon shone like a scimitar blade, and, a little distance off, the music started up.

There was something about him—something squat and

short-legged, like a man she had seen around the Padrino's house.

She began walking toward the music. There was nothing to be done. If he was the Padrino's man, it was too late, he would already have been watching her all night. If it was just a fit of cocaine paranoia, it wouldn't matter tomorrow.

She had done nothing wrong, she reassured herself, except have a good time for once. She had no reason to fear the Padrino, even supposing it was his man. But if it was, why then was he here? And why did she feel guilty?

She would think about it in the morning. The band was playing beside the pool and she spotted two Japanese business-men sitting at a table with what were obviously two young Cartagena call girls. They all looked bored, and impulsively Kay went over and sat down with them.

The men admired Kay's jewelry and there was a great deal of smiling and "Very nice, very nice," and attempts at conversation in broken English as the two girls tried to join in.

Finally, Kay tired of all the politeness. She wanted to make contract with the women and began talking Spanish to them while the men sat smiling and uncomprehending.

"Can I buy you a drink," she asked with a bold grin, "or would you rather have the cash?" The girls laughed and exchanged glances. The ice was broken.

They both had children, they told her. Their mothers were baby-sitting. One of the girls leaned back in her chair and looked up at the moon. "Too bad these men don't dance," she said.

Kay said, "Would you like to dance? I dance."

She got up and took the girl off around the pool for a giggling samba while dawn came up over the diving board and the staff began to clean up. A few minutes later, after the band had packed up their instruments, Kay walked into the lobby. On the way upstairs to her room, she felt the raw burning of a blister on her heel and, dropping down on a carpeted step, took off her shoes.

She woke to find she was still dressed. The morning light hurt. She closed her eyes again. A strange sound came from the garden outside. *"Whoeee? Whoeee?"* It was a bird call, fresh and outrageous. Behind her closed lids, her head was full of fire. She sat up with care and blew her nose, trying to relieve the underwater pressure of her sinuses. Through the billowing curtains she could see Maggie out on the balcony.

Kay knew the antidote to what ailed her. In the bathroom she opened her makeup case and took out a metal nail file. In a minute, everything would be fine. With the file, she broke open the lining of the case, pulled out a sealed plastic bag, and was busy punching a hole in the bag with the point of the file when she heard Maggie at the door.

"Oh no," Maggie said.

"Just a little hangover medicine," Kay said. She took the rounded end of the file and shoved a load of cocaine straight into each nostril, watching in the mirror to guide it home.

Maggie's reflection remained blocking the doorway behind her. "Am I supposed to feel guilty?" Kay said, turning. "Is that it? This is your run, not mine, Maggie."

Maggie lowered her head and said nothing, standing there in the oversized blue-and-white-striped T-shirt that she wore for a nightgown. Through the open door came the call of the bird again: *"Whoee? Whoee?"*

Kay despised the look on Maggie's face, concern edged with a kind of helpless fear. It disgusted her. She pushed past her and went to lie down on the bed again.

Kay laid one arm across her eyes. From a chair by the window Maggie finally said, "You're right. There's no point in saying anything to you."

Kay's hands and feet felt icy cold.

"You know yourself what's happening," Maggie's voice went on. "I know you do. How much are you doing, anyway? A few grams a day? Three? Four? More?"

Kay didn't answer. The songs and calls of other birds had joined the first.

"You don't have to answer, I know. It's more. But think of it this way, Kay—even if I didn't give a shit anymore what you do to yourself—even if I stopped caring—I'd still have to worry. Because when you start losing it, girl, it's my skin, too. It's me they bust right along beside you."

Kay's anger broke apart painfully, her heart beat irregularly into her ears and she felt like crying.

"I'm sorry, Mags. It was just this time," she said from behind closed eyes.

"It's okay, puss. Come home for a while."

"No. I hear what you're saying, but I can't leave right now. I can't, that's all." She opened her eyes. "Please trust me. It'll be all right."

Rosa wasn't there when Kay got home. The apartment was cold and lifelessly clean, the curtains drawn at all the windows. There was a note from Ricardo on the kitchen table: "*Bonita mía,* we have moved operations out of Bogotá to the *finca* and to Medellín. I have taken Rosa back home to stay with her mother. Pack up and call me when you are ready. I will come for you. I embrace you tenderly, *tu* Rick."

In the tick-tock silence of the white kitchen, she realized that she was disappointed. She had been looking forward to seeing him.

The move was no surprise. The Padrino had talked several times about getting the family out of Bogotá's danger zone and moving his operations closer to the cook's kitchens and Medellín's many small airstrips.

He owned a hundred-acre coffee and orange *finca* on the outskirts of a small Andean town two hours by car from Bogotá, and a larger horse-breeding farm closer to Medellín.

Horses were a passion with him and he was knowledgeable about them, trying constantly to involve Ricardo in the game of breeding and bloodlines. Ricardo was more interested in someday managing a soccer team, but like a dutiful son, he leaned about his father's Paso Finos, the special and fiery breed of horses particular to Colombia.

The plan, Kay assumed, was to move her to the *finca* temporarily till a new base was set up.

Maggie was in transit and Kay could not leave for the *finca* until she had received her Stateside all-clear call. Shifting between fatiguing boredom and restless anxiety about Maggie, she felt like a dog unable to find a spot to lie down. She thought constantly of home, played Simon and Garfunkel and The Grateful Dead over and over. Several times she went to dial her grandmother, but in the end, she never called her or anyone else.

She was continuing to indulge in two to three grams of pure cocaine a day and refusing to acknowledge the habit. To pass the time, she experimented with radios of various sizes, pulling the batteries in and out to see how much coke could be carried without damaging the workings. Tinker and toot, tinker and toot. Finally, the call came. The phone connection was bad.

"I love you, Maggie," she shouted over the wires. There wasn't much else to say.

The prospect of escaping Bogotá for the *finca* lifted her spirits. At 9:30 P.M. she decided to leave her den and drive to the Norte for a light snack. Maybe her coke-abused stomach could handle a little soup.

Downstairs, the door attendant in his glass cage said, "*Buenas noches, Señorita Wolff.* Will you be returning soon?"

She smiled. "In a few hours. Where's your little boy?" she asked.

"Oh, he is at home." The man's name was Victorio. Usually he had his shy little son with him, and a big, easy smile for Kay, but today he seemed nervous and unhappy.

Once out of the glass doors, Kay turned to look at him again. He was on the phone. She felt sorry for him. It was no life.

Halfway to the restaurant, Kay's stomach began to cramp. She rummaged with one hand in her purse and then in the glove compartment. Damn it. No Maalox. She turned the car and headed back, parking in front of the house. It would only take a moment.

The attendant's cage was empty. She went up the elevator, her head buzzing with the usual paranoia, but the door slid open to reveal a vacant corridor. She unlocked the door and went straight to the medicine chest without bothering to turn on the living room lights. The curtains were open and the dim evening light shone peacefully in from the balcony.

As Kay stood in the bathroom drinking down the Maalox in a toothpaste glass, a sound came from the living room. She stopped breathing, standing absolutely still. Silence. Then it started again, a rasping metallic sound. She switched off the bathroom light. Glass still in hand, she moved along the wall until she could look into the living room.

There was no one there. The sound seemed to be coming from outside the apartment door. She put the glass down softly on the coffee table and moved to the couch, taking up a position behind its upholstered back. Peering over it, she could see straight across the small entrance hall to the front door.

In the dim light she made out a small sliver of a silver object shoving through the door to the left of the heavy Schlage lock.

It withdrew and then reappeared, a tiny saw biting its way in a slow circle around the lock.

In a dream, Kay found herself in the bedroom at the phone. She dialed Carlos, willing him still to be in town. "*¿Hola?*"

"Carlos," she whispered, "it's Kay. There's someone at my door trying to break in. What should I do?"

"Protect yourself. Help is on the way." He hung up.

In the drawer was the loaded gun. She got it and retreated behind the couch, holding the gun trained on the door. Her breathing quickened, her tongue was dry in her mouth. The patient blade continued to saw until, with a soft thud, the lock fell forward onto the carpet. Through a circular hole light streamed in from the hall outside.

The door opened and she saw the man outlined against the light. He was holding a small, snubby pistol in one hand and the door handle in the other. She fired, her eyes widening, closing, the gun bucking like a living thing in her hands.

The man's gun exploded almost simultaneously, a shot into the ceiling, as he went crashing down, screaming in surprise and fear. The light poured in through the unobstructed door and Kay crouched, clutching the gun, her mind going fuck fuck fuck, oh God, oh Jesus.

From the floor by the entrance she could hear him fighting to breathe. It sounded like dying. She didn't want to hear and started whispering, "Shut up, shut up."

Then there were voices and footsteps running down the hall outside the open door. Carlos was behind the couch with her and the lights were on.

He told her to go into the bedroom and pack a few things. He said everything was all right. She was a good shot, even in the dark. It was all over for the son of a bitch; he was dead.

She stood up, numb, the words not registering. Roddy and Miguel were talking excitedly in the hall. Something in her wanted to look and something else didn't and then it was too late. She had seen.

She put on a pair of old jeans and a jeans jacket and sat down on the bed. The clock said 11:20. Carlos knocked and came in. "We need some blankets," he said. After a while he came back.

"*Bueno,* we have cleaned up. Miguel will take you now, and

then Ricardo will pick you up and take you the rest of the way to the *finca*."

Kay couldn't just stay in the bedroom. She came out while Carlos and Miguel were taking her bags downstairs. She saw that the Maalox glass was still on the table, half full. There were two guns next to it, her own and the snub-nosed one.

Roddy was sitting on the couch. He looked up, grinning when she came in.

"*Tienes cojones, Kay.*" His eyes were admiring. "You killed him." He was congratulating her as though she had just brought down a twelve-point stag.

She said, "I'd better go." The floor by the entrance door had a dark spot, wet and clean. She fled down the corridor to the elevator.

Through the glass doors she could see the Mercedes waiting, parked behind her car. The attendant was back sitting at the desk in his little booth, his head down on the newspaper in front of him for a short siesta. As she passed him, she saw that he was not napping. He was face down in a pool of blood.

Miguel stood at the open back door of the Mercedes. "Get in. *Súbete, en nombrew de Dios.* Hurry up." The car jolted as he pulled away, shouting at her to get down. He threw his leather jacket over her.

With her face pressed to the nubbly floor, Kay felt a sudden intense nausea and saliva began to collect in her mouth. She tried to sit up, and before she could say anything her stomach turned and she was retching and vomiting.

"*Carajo,* my good leather jacket," Miguel said angrily. He tore down streets and around corners at high speed. Finally, they were out of the city, and he told her she could sit up on the seat.

"How are you?" he said, looking at her in the rearview.

"I'm okay, but I'd like to clean up. I'm sorry about your jacket."

"Yes, so am I." He sounded grouchy but not unkind.

They stopped in the foothills just outside of town, the sky paling into a misty dawn. Miguel pulled over on a grassy shoulder by a pump and horse trough. They got out, opening all four doors of the car.

Drying her face on the jeans jacket, Kay said, "Did you

know the man? Did Carlos know him?'' She still felt a trembling in the core of her body.

''No.''

He had spread his cleaned jacket on the grass and was sitting beside it. ''It could have been anyone. It could have been for many different reasons.''

''What reasons?''

''Robbery.'' He shrugged. ''Someone paid to look for something. Bad luck. Whatever it was, you came back too soon for the poor bastard.'' He looked at his watch and got up. ''Time to go. We have to meet Ricardo.''

''One more thing,'' she said, not wanting to hear the answer but compelled to ask. ''Did you kill the watchman?''

''Yes, of course we did. He betrayed his trust.''

Kay remembered the watchman on the phone, the fact that he wasn't at his post when she had returned for the Maalox. Had he made a deal with the intruder?

She started to shiver again in the damp morning air. Miguel put a hand on his hip and looked at her. ''Here, skinny one, wear my jacket that you have already christened and sit up front with me. Unless you are too afraid of my famous charm.'' He was trying to pick up the old bantering tone of their first days in the packaging warehouse.

The road twisted farther up into the mountains. After twenty minutes, they pulled into the parking space of a roadside inn.

As soon as she saw the blue VW she started crying, bowing her head and covering her face with her hands. It was as though the killing had released a flood of pain in her—all the pain she had ever dammed back.

The men didn't know what to do. Standing in the rain, Ricardo held her and Miguel said, ''Kay, you're acting like a woman.'' When he got no response, the two men just looked at each other.

Kay shook her head, the tears brimming and spilling. She compressed her lips and tried to stop.

Ricardo guided her into the VW. He opened the door on the driver's side, and before he got in, he and Miguel shook hands and Ricardo sad, ''*Gracias,* my brother.'' Then Miguel leaned into the car and touched Kay's cheek. ''This life is a son of a bitch,'' he said. He pulled his head back out and Ricardo started the motor up.

They drove along in silence and then Ricardo said, "*Bonita, mi vida,* do you want to talk about this or not?"

"I don't know. Yes."

"Even my father thinks it is completely regrettable. In all ways he blames the watchman. He was either in a conspiracy to rob or he was not at his post when he should have been. We will probably never know which. But my father will not rest until he knows as much as it is possible to know about what went on in his building." Ricardo paused, and when Kay didn't say anything, he said, "That I can promise you."

She stared out of the window, glassy-eyed. She had done a couple of lines, but that detached feeling she was craving never arrived. "I remember the man's little boy," she said.

"There's nothing to be done now, Kay. If he had been killed defending the building against intruders, my father would have taken care of his wife and all his children for the rest of their lives. There would be no question. My father is more than a fair man. But the man was disloyal. He knew exactly what would happen if he was caught away from his post and he took the risk anyway. What happened? He lost. He took the responsibility himself."

Kay was silent. "*Por favor, mi vida, no te preocupes más.* I am just thankful you are alive today."

Suddenly he pulled the car over to the side of the narrow road and put his arms around her tightly. At his touch something like a hot ball inside her chest burst open, and she wept, out of control, like a child increasingly frightened at the sound of its own sobs. He held her head against his chest and stroked her hair.

Back on the road she finally fell asleep, waking only when the motion of the car stopped. "Let's get out," Ricardo said.

They were at the foot of a giant range of mountains completely covered with thick vegetation except for a narrow winding road that led upward, disappearing around a curve.

The car was parked on a windy roadside shoulder beside a small cave hollowed out of the mountainside. Inside, on a candlelit ledge of raw rock, the Holy Mother and her Child stood above a mosaic altar beautifully constructed of concrete and mountain pebbles. She was flanked by the round shapes of two truck tires painted red and white, like two decorative drums. Above the cave a red sign said PARE (Stop).

It was very quite. A hawk circled overhead. Beside the shrine sat its keeper, a toothless old Indian woman, on her head the characteristic black bowler of her people. Chickens scratched around the gunnysack at her feet.

"We are going up into the pass now. The road is very narrow and dangerous, so people always stop here for a blessing and to pray for protection," Ricardo said.

He gave the woman some coins, and she drew two candles out of her sack.

"*Dios les proteje,*" she intoned in a surprisingly strong voice. Her eyes had the sightless blue of cataracts and she touched Kay lightly on the arm.

Kay knelt beside Ricardo at the wooden prayer bench before the shrine. Her mind was empty, nothing but the pull of the wind in her hair and the sound of birds.

Chapter
Nine

With the rise of Castro . . . a new threat to [Colombia's] internal security appeared in the form of ideologically based guerrilla groups dedicated to the overthrow of the National Front government which they saw as an arrangement benefitting only the nation's elite. . . . The most important of these early Castroite groups were led by students and intellectuals, and although they were short-lived, their ideologies and many of their members were picked up by other guerrilla bands. . . . Although several attempts were made to unite their forces, ideological differences that reflect the schisms among world Communist governments prevented unification. . . .

The rise of leftist guerrilla activity during the 1960's strengthened the bonds between civilian and military elites, and the armed forces increased substantially in size and in the scope of their activities. With the help of United States military assistance . . . the Colombian armed forces became one of the world's premier counterinsurgency forces during the 1960's.

—*The Area Handbook of Colombia,*
United States Library of Congress
(1969, 1977)

THE SMALL TOWN lay in coffee country, halfway up the folded, sharp hills of the central Andean Cordillera. The rains came off the blue mountains beyond the town and the steep countryside was lush with crops and trees. Giant bamboo and thick grass that smelled like celery clustered in tall groves beside muddy, noisy steams. The sun came out, sudden and strong, drying the paths through the coffee groves, and turning to dust the windy dirt streets of the town. Three thousand feet below, power lines glinted in the broad, tropically hot Magdalena River valley.

The car wound above deep gorges choked with palms and the flat leaves of banana plants. Ten-foot poinsettia trees blazed red among the green, and wild orchids bloomed everywhere. They drove through the town square past the Spanish church with its twin bell towers and the clock looking down onto the men drinking warm Pilsen beer in front of the *tiendas*.

The journey had lulled Kay, and by the time they reached the *finca* a few miles out of town, she felt nothing but a calm exhaustion. The car turned off at a thick cluster of poinsettia trees and continued down a long driveway to a massive wrought-iron gate painted red and white, the traditional colors of the Colombian country home. A seven-foot fence of iron bars, white with sharp red points, stretched around the property to either side. Two armed sentries waved to Ricardo and swung the gate open, parting the giant red "A" that marked the gate's center.

The large house was white adobe with red grillework at the windows. Under the extended eaves of the tile roof was a spacious veranda comfortably furnished with wooden tables and chairs and a bar. A wide view swept across cultivated groves outward to the Andes and on into the sky at the top of the world.

Flora and Roberto were waiting in the living room—a cool tile floor, black-and-white cowhide chairs, and tall vases of flowers everywhere.

"I'm so sorry for your trouble," Flora said, genuinely solicitous. Kay wondered what she had been told.

The Padrino nodded. "She needs rest," he said.

"*Ay,*" Flora said as she took Kay's arm, "you're so thin, you look like a spaghetti."

Upstairs there was a sitting room with a door opening onto a balcony that faced the back of the house. Two bedrooms and a bath also faced the back with views toward the river across orange groves and rows and rows of pineapple and coffee plants.

Kay's room was hot and bright. She could feel the pulsing pressure of an oncoming headache. Flora drew the curtains closed and said she hoped Kay would rest as easily here as at her own home. She was welcome to come downstairs and have lunch with the family, but if she was too tired, Guadalupe would bring up a tray.

A few minutes after Flora had quietly closed the door, there was a knock.

Kay sat up on the bed. "Are you Guadalupe?"

"*Sí, señorita. A sus órdenes.*"

With her hands folded in front of her, she looked abnormally short, like a thirty-five-year-old child. Her eyes, questioning, anxious, were set wide apart in a dark, broad-featured Indian face.

Did Kay want her to unpack the suitcases, she whispered. No, Kay replied, she didn't want anything.

The next day Flora and the children left for Medellín. At least Medellín was a city, Flora said to Kay over morning coffee on the veranda. Here, there was nothing but coffee beans.

Ricardo, sitting with them, stared morosely into his cup. Cheese floated sticky and white on top of the coffee. Kay's stomach turned and she covered her own cup with her napkin. The cheese was a Colombian breakfast custom she could do without, but she had forgotten to ask for hers plain.

Ricardo was driving his family the two hundred miles to Medellín in the Mercedes.

"His father wants him there; he is needed," Flora said, watching Kay over the rim of her cup.

"When will you be back?" Kay asked him.

He shrugged his shoulders. "I don't know."

A white horse grazed in the field in front of them and a man weeded in the garden nearby, bending and straightening along a high stone wall enclosing rows of trumpeting red amaryllis. Kay felt a listless interest in the scene and in what Flora was saying about shopping in Medellín.

At noon, the men swung open the gates and the Mercedes pulled out with the two *finca* dogs barking and racing along behind in a cloud of dust. The Padrino invited Kay into his private wing. There were four bedrooms and a study; all the rooms, even the bathrooms, were hand-painted in trompe l'oeil style to imitate formal eighteenth-century gardens with classical stone statues and birds perching on the rims of fountains.

Kay stared at the Padrino as he opened the door to his study. Why had he tried to make an Italian villa out of an Andean farmhouse? She looked around at the long library table and the shelves of books and caught an amused gleam in his eyes.

"I have left everything as my father had it," he said, holding out his arm, beckoning her into the cool enclosed patio. Coffee had been set up at a table in the shade.

He congratulated her on her behavior and handed her an envelope. Later she discovered he had given her five hundred dollars. "I am proud of you, my girl. Most women would not have fared so well." The dead intruder, he told her, was a thief. There had been a robbery in the building just a few weeks earlier using the same methods. But she had put a stop to his career.

Kay felt bad about the doorman and his little boy, but she didn't want to risk talking to the Padrino about it. Neither did she want him to get the impression that she was soft. She had a feeling that the less she seemed to know about what had happened and the less the Padrino understood about her, the safer she would be.

At least she knew for certain now it had not been someone from the trade come gunning for her, someone with a personal grudge against the Alvarez family or jealous of her position. But of course, the voice of her paranoia whispered, you never really knew. Not about anyone.

Though the mail was delayed and sometimes didn't get through at all, in her loneliness, Kay wrote to Maggie anyway.

August 15, 1970

The Boss had thought of everything. My closet is full of everything I need for the job. I work in my room and come down to sit on the veranda. The Boss blew in and out. He's busy traveling, consolidating. I'm thankful for Guadalupe in this all-male world. The finca men treat me with contempt, respect, comeradery. We joke. . . .

I'm trying to make friends with Guadalupe. She's about 25 but looks 35. She's married and she tells me she lives with her husband, her three kids, her sister and her sister's family. Seven kids and three adults all in one room at the back of the house. They have a garden of some kind, but of course for me it's Strictly Forbidden Territory. The whole finca is like an armed camp with a fence around everything, but the servants quarters are outside the fence and at night they're locked outside of the circle of protection. . . .

The local people look strange with anticipation and all the rich finca owners are afraid of their own servants, scared they might be related to the guerrillas holed up in the mountains, terrified of being murdered in their beds. The Boss regularly searches the servants quarters for guns and signs of disloyalty.

Six years ago "La Violencia" hit this area hard. The army came up here and wiped out local terrorist bands like Sangre Negra, Desquite, and Trazan, who were killing and robbing for food, money, and medicine. And now, with all the election turmoil, the big fear is that these bands are springing back up. No surprise either, what with not enough field work at less than a dollar a day to go around. . . .

I'm in a hammock having my coffee thick and black and sweetened with dark honey. The sun is coming out, the Andes are steaming from the night's downpour. I wish you could see the mountains, like Grand Canyon full of banana trees. A hummingbird is visiting the lilies and the roses.

Today I am going to concentrate on clean living: fruit, honey, and health, I tell myself, but will I really listen to what I'm saying? . . .

Guadalupe takes long cleaning my room because she likes to look at my American things, my magazines, my hairdryer, travel iron, transformer. Yesterday, when she came to get my laundry, I tried to explain to her that I was accustomed to washing out my own underwear and silk blouses and slips. (She goes down to the river with the other women and pounds the laundry to pieces on the rocks.) So as I'm talking, I see that she is very upset, holding back tears, she is desperately afraid the Boss will catch me doing my own laundry.

So I take her in the bathroom to show her how I use the Woolite and how to wash the things in the tub. And as I'm scrubbing she keeps getting down and trying to push me aside so that she can do it. So I let her take over and she just keeps grabbing my hand and thanking me over and over again for letting her do my laundry.

You can't imagine what it's like, Maggie. She's like that

about every little thing she does for me. Things that are the simplest to me, mean life and death to her. . . .

The Indians here are Catholic, but it's all mixed up with their own superstitions and lore. Guadalupe says there are evil devils in the river water. I was going for a swim and she begged me not to. "Las animitas," she said, would get up inside of me and make me sick and ruin me for having babies. She's right, of course—parasites, amoebas and God knows what else play around in that water (I even brush my teeth in beer now). She knows about all the ancient herbal remedies too—brought me aloe leaves when I got sunburned and she brews a bitter, dark tea that tastes like shit but works for menstrual cramps.

I've been sneaking her little gifts, bars of fancy French soap and a few dollars once in a while for her kids. She wears pieces of tire tied to her feet for shoes, so I gave her some beach sandals, but she has them hoarded away somewhere and goes on wearing the tires. She acts like this stuff is the crown jewels. We're both getting more relaxed, but she still goes quiet if there's a sound from outside my room, which plays right into my paranoia—the walls have ears etc. . . . but of course here they really do.

Yesterday she brought me a wooden cross to protect me and she wanted to put it up on the balcony for me. She was surprised to find out that I'm not a Catholic. She thought the Indians were the last people in civilization to receive the good word. . . .

The lamps have started to flicker. In a minute the power will go off for the night and I'll be writing by candlelight. I know letters from you will not arrive for weeks and my isolation is strangely complete. One moment I float over the Andes, the next moment I am already dead and buried. I can see the grain of the wood on the coffin lid.

By this point Kay's addiction had hollowed her down to ninety-five pounds and only her fear of needles kept her from shooting up. She had finally begun to admit to herself that the drug, with the reputation of being a magic servant, had become an exacting master. She was learning the lesson early; six years later, in 1976, *The Washington Post* was still reporting that most medical studies did not find cocaine physically addictive, though there were indications it could create emotional dependence.

Kay was sleeping later and later in the mornings, working and snorting alone in the silence of the Andean night. The Padrino knocked at her door one day, waking her around noon.

"Kay? It is necessary for me to see you, please." She recognized the tension in his voice and rushed into a robe, her mind flooding with nameless guilt.

When she opened the door he looked past her at the disheveled bed.

"*Con permiso,*" he said, stern, formal, "let us talk on the balcony."

"Just a moment, please," Kay said coldly. "I will dress first." She was on the ragged edge of irritation, strung out on her habit, sick of his manipulations and the implied blackmail of his temper. He lifted his eyebrows, turned, and walked toward the balcony.

She dressed hurriedly, annoyed that she had chosen a skirt because she knew he did not like pants on a woman. When she came out to the balcony, he stood up and held her chair for her. Even his studied politeness grated. He sat down again and began unwrapping a little bundle of newspaper.

"I would like to ask you about these," he said, taking out a bar of packaged soap, three American dollar bills, a broken gold chain, and some bits of jewelry. "Did you give these to Guadalupe or did she steal them?" Suddenly, there was nothing polite about the way he was looking at her.

A tongue of fear licked up inside her head, touching off a smoldering anger, a balky stubbornness.

"I gave her the things myself. The jewelry is from my trash, things I didn't want anymore."

He pointed wordlessly to the rest of the things, the money and the soap. Good, Kay thought, at least the shoes weren't there, and two of the dollar bills she had given Guadalupe were missing.

"Oh, yes, I gave her the soap, too, when she was helping me in my room, and the money was for her kids."

He jumped up. Kay gripped the sides of her chair and ducked her head in terror. Suddenly, he was screaming. His pale eyes were bone-chilling, at once mirthful and enraged, as though he were on the verge of becoming demonically out of control.

"Stupid woman! This is my house. These are not beggars in the streets of Bogotá. These people are not your concern, nothing to do with the servants in my house is your concern. Do you understand that?"

Kay sat and clenched her thumbs. Defiance burned in her chest. She didn't want to answer; fear prickled in the small of her back.

"I will not tolerate this behavior from an ignorant foreigner," he yelled. He leaned down, breathless, his face close to hers. "I will not tolerate it, is *that* something you understand? Answer me."

"Yes." She looked at the ground, avoiding the eyes bubbling with fury, as though she and he were sharing some awkward and terrible secret that, any moment, would push them over the edge into violence.

He turned his back on her and stood at the rail of the balcony. "Good, then," he said. She watched his back numbly and after a moment of utter silence, he turned around to her again.

"You will abide by the rules of my house while you are in it even though the customs of my country may remain a mystery to you." His voice softened. "Please, Kay, for me, I want you to try harder not to indulge in your weakness for sentiment."

He's talking himself down, she thought.

"You behave like one of the missionaries. But of course you are much prettier," he laughed and put his hand on her shoulder, a truce. "All I have ever wanted is that you understand us."

She controlled her desire to flinch, and stood up, smiling. A missionary, she thought. The congregation back home would love that one.

After that, Guadalupe was very careful. Sadly, Kay felt a new reserve from the other servants as well and realized that they were distancing themselves as much to protect her as themselves. The Padrino, when he was there, treated her cordially, as though nothing had happened. He was kind and sat in his private patio with her, drinking aguardiente and lime. They discussed many things, racehorses, art collections, famous women, Europe, Los Angeles, but he always returned to his favorite topic: ideas for packaging and concealment.

He loved telling her trade gossip, laughing at the bizarre and horrible things that had never made it through customs: the giant deep-sea fish stuffed and packaged as a trophy, the huge cage full of spider monkeys with the cage floor littered with dead stuffed birds as though they had died en route, the body of the priest shipped to Canada with a stopover in Chicago for "disemboweling."

He got a particular pleasure out of the failed smuggling attempts of men powerful in the trade, men he had thought above such insanities. Though he swore the stories were all true, Kay thought he slipped in a few heightened details because he enjoyed teasing her.

"How would you like to test your packaging skill on a dead priest?" he asked.

"No thank you," Kay countered. "Sounds more like work for a man. I think *you* should try it."

"Well, of course I would, but Flora would be upset. With her devotion to the Church she would probably leave me and go to live in Miami."

Sometimes Kay caught his eye resting on her, appraising her thin frame as if she was one of his horses showing signs of going bad. She had been having thoughts of going home lately, but before he would allow that, he would put her "out to pasture."

He never said a word to her about the obvious cause of her weight loss. He was a polite man. Besides, he thought of addiction as an American weakness. She wondered how much longer it would take before his eyes would be forced open to Ricardo's escalating use.

It was late September and Kay had been living in Colombia for one year. The rainy season had just begun, a cloudy patchwork of damp days interspersed with sudden flashes of sun. One afternoon, she jumped up and fled the solitary confinement of her room and the endless unfinished suitcases for a cool walk by the river.

She had gone halfway when she saw Guadalupe running toward her. The Padrino had seen Kay from a window and had sent the servant with a hat and a message. He didn't want her wandering past the *finca* gates to the river by herself. The times were too dangerous. It was better to stay within sight of the house. Kay looked back. The veranda and garden were empty, the windows glowed blank and fiery, reflecting the sun.

Kay wanted to keep Guadalupe with her. Quickly she suggested a walk in the orchards. "I want you to help me pick some oranges," she said, making up a service that would permit Guadalupe to stay. They walked down a row of orange trees, the fruit hanging bright against the sky. Kay pulled down a few and sat under a tree.

"Would you peel these?" Kay said, still intent on holding Guadalupe there. They sat in the dappled shade. Guadalupe pulled back the pulpy rind and parted the oranges into moist sections that welled transparent droplets onto her fingers. The tangy smell took Kay back to the Valley and Grandma's house.

Guadalupe held the slices out to Kay on the palm of her hand. Her face in the flickering leaf shadows was softer, at ease away from the prying eyes and ears of the house.

Kay told her about the orchards and farms of California. Guadalupe had never heard of California. She knew about Bogotá, that it was a big city, but she had never been there and she thought it was probably very far away. She had no idea how far the Estados Unidos was—everything over the mountain was equally far and unimaginable.

Norteamericanos didn't come here very often, she told Kay. Once some had come to the *finca* to visit the Padrino for a few days. And the ones with the packs on their backs and the long hair sometimes came through the town. But, Guadalupe said, the people in town hated them and she did not like them either, because they tried to pretend they were poor like the Indians, wearing no shoes and torn clothing when all the time they were really rich.

Kay said yes, she knew about these people. She lay back and looked up into the trees. It was like resting at the bottom of an ocean of leaves. Guadalupe looked at her. She said unless Señorita Kay needed her for anything she thought it would be better if she went back now. They would be wondering at the house where she was.

After that there was a change between Kay and Guadalupe, a more comfortable intimacy even in their silences, but Kay was aware always that a different life was being lived on the other side of the garden wall. She would hear children, a baby crying, and sometimes she would see Guadalupe's husband leaving for his road-laborer job or going into town for the cockfights or to drink *chicha,* the illegal but traditional, fiery Indian corn liquor.

On the last Sunday in September, the Padrino told Kay that he was planning a round of trips for her. "It's pretty here," he said, "but I am sure you could use a change. And also I am afraid that someday I will come back and they will tell me you have run away with an Indian." His face was as smooth and expressionless as an egg. Only his eyes signaled a wicked amusement.

Kay worked late into the night. The next day, Roberto was going to Bogotá for a *compadrazgo* ceremony. He was to be a godfather to yet another child. As his power had grown, he was asked to stand more and more often both by members of the extended family and by select friends. They were anxious for the social status and connections and the economic privileges his sponsorship would bring. The *compadrazgo* system was important in Colombia, with godparents functioning as a focal point in a complex network of loyalty and well-being. Kay figured Roberto was responsible for approximately one hundred godchildren.

He was gone early Sunday morning, leaving behind two men as security for the *finca.* The rest of the staff went with him to the elaborate festivities that would accompany the baptism. Kay had been invited, but it was a full day and sounded exhausting.

She woke up around eleven and wandered downstairs. The house held the reverberating silence of recent abandonment. A breeze blew in through the open windows and one of the bodyguards dozed on the veranda. The other rocked lazily in a hammock near the gate.

In the kitchen, a jug of milk covered with cheesecloth and two freshly baked loaves of bread stood on a wooden counter. Kay poured herself a glass and broke off a hunk of the bread. From behind the heavy wooden door to the servants' quarters a baby started to whimper and she moved away to look out of the window. The crying escalated into a choking howl.

"Shit," Kay said, her voice strange in the empty room. She walked to the door and hurriedly slid back the two heavy iron bolts, her ears alert for any sound in the corridor leading to the kitchen.

The first thing that hit her was the foul smell, and then it took a moment for her eyes to adjust. The room was almost dark. In the center of the dirt floor a baby sat in a cardboard box, screaming. There were flies on the wet spot where she had been gnawing on the edge of the box.

Kay closed the door carefully behind her and put her glass of milk and piece of bread down on the steps that led from the kitchen. "Shhh," she said. "You'll get me in trouble. I'm not supposed to be here." She dipped a piece of the bread in the milk and said, "Here, how about this?"

The baby stopped crying instantly and Kay bent over the box and picked her up. She was naked except for a skimpy shirt.

There was no furniture in the room, so Kay sat on the steps to the kitchen with the baby in her lap. "¿Mejor?" Kay said. The baby seemed to be about nine months old. She held the bread in one fist and looked at Kay. There were bits of red thread in her pierced ears.

Striped light came from a window shuttered up with boards. Through a door at the other end of the room Kay could see Lupe, Guadalupe's ten-year-old daughter, in a small truck garden. She was picking caterpillars off corn plants, and throwing their squashed bodies over the wall.

The room was hot and fetid. Sleeping mats were stacked neatly in one corner, and the family's few clothes hung on wooden pegs along the wall. A bucket surrounded by flies stood in a corner.

The baby, finished with the bread, had begun to cry again. As Kay dipped another piece into the milk, she noticed that Lupe was peering shyly around the door. Kay motioned her in, but Lupe ducked her head out of sight.

"Tranquila, niña. I just want to hold your sister," Kay said. "It's a secret. Come in and I'll give you a piece of bread."

Lupe came in and grabbed the bread and stood a little distance away, her eyes staring at Kay in sullen suspicion.

Kay fed the baby the last of the milk, dribbling some onto her cheek. With a furtive dart, Lupe was at her side, licking the milk from her sister's face.

Kay stood up. She wanted to get the pitcher of milk on the other side of the door, but someone could have come into the kitchen by now, so she asked Lupe to show her the garden instead.

Still carrying the baby, she stepped into a dirt yard with two benches and a crude wooden table. A water spigot dripped into a concrete trough with a ditch that hoarded the overflow, guiding it into the small patch of corn, beans, and potatoes.

Kay heard someone on the road. She tried to dart back into the room, but she was too late; Guadalupe had already come into the yard.

"Señorita Kay," she said. Lupe ran to her excitedly. "She likes the baby, *le gusta Carmenza, Mamá.*"

"I'm sorry. . . . I heard the baby crying. . . . I wanted to see your garden." Quickly she handed the child to Guadalupe.

"How old is she?" Kay said, trying to defuse the nervous complicity of the moment.

"She is thirteen months," Guadalupe said. She jiggled the baby up and down on her lap. "I have lost three others," she said, "but I don't think God will take this one. *Es mi tesoro,* my treasure." The baby continued to stare at Kay from her mother's arms.

Fifteen minutes later Kay was back in the clean, sunny kitchen on the other side of the door. The house was vacant and silent except for the refrigerator purring in its corner, obscenely stuffed with its glut of meat and cheese.

Kay went upstairs and sat on the balcony, her eyes sweeping the mountains where the guerrilla fighters hid in their green strongholds. Every day the papers held stories of their raids and kidnappings. She knew of renegade Catholic priests like Camilo Torres, who had joined the guerrillas' struggle, believing it was a Christian imperative in the face of the unending cycle of Colombian poverty and injustice. She knew of "Tirofijo" ("Sureshot"), the famous peasant rebel, who had spent a decade leading his Revolutionary Armed Forces in rural insurgency.

The more she had seen and heard of life in Colombia, the more she had felt a natural and growing sympathy for the rebel cause, even though it had been infiltrated by bandits and criminals. Now her vague feelings had assumed a focus—the faces of Guadalupe and her children. "I don't think God will take this one," Guadalupe had said of her baby, as though there were a God who decided which child would starve and which would be fed.

Staring off into the hills, she understood the anger and frustration that dwelt there, feeling it echo in herself. But, she thought, their guns and raids didn't seem to matter. They were like gnats on the back of an elephant.

In a while, she heard a sound from down below. It was Lupe sweeping the brick walk with a large, coarse broom. She was working carefully, her face calm and diligent. Behind her, in the orchards, something startled a flock of birds and they rose up and flew away, like a cluster of waving handkerchiefs growing smaller and smaller in the cobalt sky.

Ricardo came back for a few days to pick up the suitcases Kay had been working on. They had been apart for over a month, and Kay immediately felt a subtle difference. They were like veterans bonded by the shared knowledge of battle but scarred by different wars. Something had shifted. He was going through the motions, kissing her, telling her he loved her, but his attentions had an edge of sadness and there was something reserved and preoccupied about him now. When they found themselves alone in the house they did not make love and Kay was glad.

"How are things going for you in Medellín?" she asked him.

"Well, my father was right, of course, to move the operation there, but it is a provincial town. It is fine, but it is not Bogotá." He laughed. "I think I'm trying to say that I miss the big city."

"I know."

"*Bonita,* you look pale," Ricardo said. "You need some *distracciones.* You are getting too serious. If you don't come dancing with me today, you will wake up tomorrow and find you have grown old."

"I feel old."

"That's what I'm saying."

"Oh? I look old?"

Ricardo threw his arms up. "Women," he said.

It was noon. Ricardo wanted to take her to a little mountain resort for lunch. There would be a swimming pool and dancing, he told her, a lot of action. He wiggled his hips and rolled his eyes in a ridiculously exaggerated way, making her laugh, and suddenly they were back together again, the strain gone.

The town, as they drove through, seemed sleepier than ever. Old men sat in the *tiendas* at either end of the square, and a few ragged children ran with the dogs or sat on the steps of the church.

"It looks empty. Where is everyone?" Kay said. "I don't see any young men."

Ricardo shrugged. "It's so hot. Maybe they are sleeping their day away. My father says the mountain people are lazy trouble-makers, but maybe they are more happy than us Colombianos who rush around and chase the rat. Right?"

"Rat race."

"Yes. Rat race."

They went up higher into the mountains. The wickedly serpentine roads, barely more than dirt pathways, wound precipitously above the green gorges. They passed an old man with a machete who was cutting back the thick vegetation around a mountain spring. The spring drained into a fifty-gallon drum that had been cut in half to hold the spill before it disappeared again down the gorge. Barefoot women stood waiting to fill plastic buckets with water to take home.

Ricardo was wearing the L.A. Dodgers baseball cap Kay had brought him from the States and she was in shorts and a T-shirt that said "ARUBA PALM BEACH HOTEL. "Just like two *turistas* on a holiday," Ricardo said. The windows were open to the hot breeze and Kay's depression lifted, like a high and scattered cloud cover.

"I hope you will always love me, Kay," Ricardo said suddenly. His voice was wistful.

"Of course," she said. "Don't get your knees in a knot."

The resort hotel was situated between two mountain towns. Renaults, Peugeots, a few old Chevies, and a battered bus baked in the sun in the half-filled parking lot. The attendant eyed Ricardo suspiciously. "He doesn't know me," Ricardo explained. "I haven't been here in a long time."

He got out and talked to the man. The place wasn't actually private, yet they were careful about whom they let in.

Walking around the grounds, inspecting the weedy garden and the sad little zoo with monkeys and shrieking birds in rusting cages, Ricardo kept repeating, "It was a first-class place when I used to come here with my family."

The big swimming pool was crowded with yelling Colombian children. Their mothers, sitting around the pool at tables shaded by sun umbrellas, screamed names intermittently, like the shrieks of maternal birds—"*¡Jorge!*" "*¡Dolores, ven acá!*" "*¡Eduardo, no!*"

After splashing around in the pool, Ricardo and Kay walked to the restaurant. The dance floor was a round cement slab with hand-hewn tree poles holding up a giant thatched roof made of palm fronds. Rough wooden tables with brightly decorated oilcloth covers rimmed the floor.

They spent the afternoon drinking a beer-*gaseosa* mix and reading *El Tiempo* and an international *Time* magazine that Ricardo had brought as a surprise. By four, the loudspeaker was turned up. The dance music, played by a whirling tinny organ, sounded exactly like the skating music at the rink back home in Bakersfield. Kids ran around, bumping into each other, and a few ádults took to the floor. Kay and Ricardo decided they could dance to better music at home.

Ricardo took a longer route back. He wanted to stop at a hut where an Indian family still wove traditional hand-dyed fabrics, knowing Kay would be interested. As they turned onto the road, two army trucks crowded with soldiers sped by going in the opposite direction.

"I wonder what's going on," Ricardo said, glancing after them in the rearview mirror.

They drove along in silence, and for a while Kay dozed. When she opened her eyes, they were descending. She looked down to the steep road below and saw the charred skeleton of a bus. Several Indian women stood around it as though in shock. The air had begun to cool down in the long shadows of twilight.

Had the bus been fire-bombed? She was curious about the scene but didn't feel like talking. Ricardo, too, seemed remote again; his eyes read the road mechanically but were turned inward, lost in his own thoughts.

About half an hour from the *finca*, they came to a roadblock, a small stone guardhouse with a pipe gate obstructing the road.

"*Mierda,*" Ricardo said, pulling the car to a stop. The lounging soldiers straightened up and one came over to the car.

He was small but powerfully built, with short black hair and intense dark eyes.

He leaned his face in at Ricardo's window, "Identification papers, *por favor*."

With a sigh, Ricardo cut the engine and got out.

The other soldiers had come over to the car and were leering in at Kay. *"Ay, blondie, me gustas, vente, vente."* A face ballooned at the window right beside her, chapped lips, angry eyes.

She fought the desire to roll up her window, and sat calmly, ignoring them. Through the window on the driver's side, she could see Ricardo's sweatered midsection and the uniformed torso of the examining officer.

"What's wrong, *capitán?*" said Ricardo's voice.

"Your papers are fine, but there will be a delay for several hours. The military are clearing a problem up ahead."

Neither man was paying any attention to the soldiers, who had begun whistling and catcalling.

"A long delay? That is most unfortunate. I am here on an errand for my father, Señor Roberto Alvarez." The magic name, Kay thought. "Of course, I understand and respect the necessities of your difficult work . . ."

Ricardo's hand dipped into Kay's line of vision and snaked into his pants pocket for his wallet . . . a pause . . . then "Thank you for your understanding, *capitán*."

Back in the car, Ricardo accelerated out of the gate before the soldier had even swung it entirely open.

"Don't mind the men," he said shortly, "some of them have never seen a real blond woman before."

"True?"

"Verdad," he replied.

A few miles down the road, they came across "the problem." Four American army-surplus jeeps were parked beside an open field just up ahead. A yellow Ford bulldozer, the kind Kay has last seen in the fields of California, was rumbling jerkily along, gouging a large hole in the earth. A second dozer slowly pushed a tangled head of garbage and rags toward the hole. Some kind of a dump, Kay thought.

Ricardo slowed to pass.

Then, with the sickening horror of a razor slash to the bone, the vague image of heaped garbage focused—and refocused. Kay lifted her hand to her mouth.

A twisting stack of gray and filthy cadavers, the massed agony of splayed and naked corpses, turned and tumbled in the giant maw of the bulldozer. Churning forward, mutilated stumps rose up briefly to be plowed under again in the mangle of half-clothed, broken human remains. Headless bodies slipped obscenely one upon the other while uniformed men with rifles watched from the encircling fields.

A man in a peaked cap, featureless behind a kerchief, stood directing the action. Dust rose around him. A body slid off the pile and fell to the ground. The man signaled but the driver remained unaware and the dozer continued to push its burden forward.

And then it was gone. The wind was in her hair. On one side was nothing but the wide valley and the empty sky, and on the other a dense, sweet-smelling wall of vegetation.

Ricardo was speeding, sitting forward in his seat.

"You saw—I mean, back there, you saw it?" Kay said.

She wanted him to so no. A trick of the mind. Cocaine paranoia. Anything.

He lifted his hands and banged them viciously on the steering wheel. "Yes, of course I saw it," he shouted. "Do you think this has never happened in the world before? Where have you been?"

She sat in stunned silence.

"*Hijo de puta,* don't you understand!"

He was gripping the steering wheel as though he wanted to break it off. "The priests will go on getting themselves martyred and the *campesinos* will go on robbing and killing in the name of progress, and that is the way it is in Colombia."

Kay looked out of the window. "You don't answer," Ricardo said. "You think I'm hard. My grandfather was a Liberal. He was killed in the Bullring Massacre in 1956, gunned down, and his brother to, and hundreds of others. Why? Because they didn't cheer loud enough for Rojas. You can't believe that, can you? You thing we should all be 'doing something' about the 'situation.' "

His body beside her was charged with tension and he was taking the hairpin curves at fifty miles per hour.

Kay didn't care. She wanted to cast off, to set her boat adrift. The first star had come out, a tiny bright speck of light in the deep blue over the Andes. She concentrated on it, trying to erase the horror she had witnessed, but the terrifying images kept coming back, not to be buried or denied.

PART
TWO

BLANQUITA Y ESPERANZA

Chapter
Ten

Why Medellín? First, its strategic location in Northwest Colombia and excellent air connections. Then too, the outstandingly good cover provided for clandestine cocaine laboratories by the rolling hills that surround it. The town's industrial tradition guarantees the availability of chemicals needed for cocaine processing. Finally, a slump in its crucial textile sector in 1970 thrust onto the streets thousands of young men, many of whom became "mules" or "guns" for the traffickers.

As their empire expanded, the new capos were at first predictable, covering their flanks by paying off local police and políticos and exhibiting their new wealth in cars, aircraft and fine horses as well as haciendas and mansions. But their real dream was to buy respectability, to be accepted in traditional circles. And, perhaps to their surprise, Medellín society was delighted to enjoy their wealth without publicly questioning its source.

—Alan Riding, "Cocaine Billionaires,"
The New York Times,
March 8, 1987

THE NEXT MORNING around noon she opened her eyes to a red rose on her pillow. Its thorny stem was wrapped in a note: "*Lo siento* [I'm sorry]." Ricardo had left for Medellín.

She sat on the balcony and watched the coffee pickers moving through the surrounding fields, their heads bent under the shadows of their straw hats. Strange, she had come all this way from the Valley only to live among pickers again. The house was still, Guadalupe had gone, probably to the *tienda*.

She went downstairs and got herself a cup of coffee. Except for her day with Ricardo, she had worked concentratedly for two weeks. Now the loaded garment bags were on their way to Medellín with Ricardo and there was nothing to do. She should be working on a bag for a pass with Maggie, she thought, but instead she took her coffee to the garden and sat on the bench in the sun.

The two *finca* guards were bantering back and forth, playing their endless game of horseshoes, wearing their .22 automatic pistols strapped to their legs. Kay sat and stared at the mountains and listened to the clang and thud of the metal and the groans and cheers whenever one of them made a hit.

When the man called Luis went inside to get beers, the other one, Jorge, came over and said, "Do you want a Costena?" He stood in front of Kay and squinted into the sun.

Kay shook her head no. Jorge always dressed in black. He was very small, about five foot one, in his mid-twenties, and had a reputation for being irresistible to women.

Luis came out. "Do you want a beer?" he asked Kay.

"You are too late. I asked her that already," Jorge said.

Luis was middle-aged; the cords in his neck stood out strongly and his skin was taut and yellowish with very dark circles under his eyes. He had been with the Padrino for years and there was nothing he didn't know about guns. Kay thought the two men were a classic duo, a Latino comedy team.

"Maybe she wanted something else," Jorge said. He stood with his hand on his hip and looked at Kay solicitously. "*¿Un poco de jugo* [Juice]?"

Kay held out her cup. "I have coffee," she said. "Thank you."

"Why don't you come with us into town. It's market day. The Indians will be coming down from the mountains with things to sell—the kind of things you like."

She smiled at him, and he smiled back brightly. He was definitely trying to cheer her up. Also, she thought, he was looking for an excuse to go to town for a couple of beers. While the cat's away . . . Well, why not? She stood up and felt her head swim from the sudden movement.

They went to town in the old black *finca* Chevy, the dogs panting along behind. The square was crowded and vibrant with color and noise. Tinny music blared from the *tiendas* and fruits and vegetables were piled everywhere.

Vendors sold handwoven Indian baskets side by side with

plastic ones made in Japan. People squatted down bargaining with sellers whose wares were spread before them on blankets: second-hand pots and pans and tools, clothing, glasses, cheap toys, leather goods, Indian herbal remedies.

A half-man with no legs rode an old plank with wheels, pushing himself along the ground with two wooden blocks. He was selling hats and wore them piled in a stack on his head, yelling *"Sombreros, sombreros."*

Kay sat with the two men at a table outside the *tienda* at the north end of the square, opposite the church. More than just stores, *tiendas* were community gathering places, dark, musty rooms crowded with chairs and tables and shelves of supplies like bread and spices, candles, *panela* candy, flour, fabrics, and needles. A narrow wooden counter bleached and worn from many washings separated the staff from the patrons.

Outside, the Saturday crowd sat on wooden boxes and played *pite,* a penny-pitching game, with beers bet on the results. Four old campesinos at the table next to her had begun showing off, talking loudly over their card game and pretending not to notice her.

Jorge ordered beer and a plate of greasy *chicharrones.* The two men discussed the forthcoming Saturday-night cockfights and watched the girls go by, while in the shade under the table the *finca* dogs panted, waiting for handouts.

Kay's attention drifted away to the square, to the cook tent selling fried bread and chicken and to the meat stall a few feet away. Above the display of bleeding pink-and-red slabs, a row of cows' feet swung in a cloud of flies. Kay suppressed thoughts of the bodies piled beside a bulldozer.

She had already noticed that there were very few young men in the milling square, but what she had witnessed in the field seemed inconceivable now, in the full sunshine of the afternoon. It was as though the missing men had all simply gone to a football game and would be home in time for dinner.

Kay fastened her attention on a group of five or six *gamines* fighting each other for position around a food cart where the woman had given one of them some scraps. Kay watched as the two littlest ones gave up and walked away.

A little distance off, they stopped, and the smaller of the two hunkered down to play with something she had found, stones maybe. The bigger one stood still and cased the square, a tiny figure, belly protruding, eyes scanning the crowd for business. They could not be much older than three or four, Kay thought.

After a moment the bigger one spotted Kay, the perfect prize, a strange blond señora eating and drinking in front of the *tienda*. Kay watched her shade her eyes, stare over toward her table, hesitate.

They made their way across the square, glancing worriedly to see if the other children had noticed this new prey. They sidled up to the table.

"Váyasen, váyasen." Jorge waved his arms at them, but the two girls had locked in first on Kay and then on the plate of pork rinds, which sat at their eye level on the table.

"¿ Centavos, señora, chicharrones?" The bigger one asked. She was brazen, sticking out her hand and looking Kay in the eye. The other one hung back, glancing nervously at Jorge.

"¿Regalos, por favor, señora?" the bigger one said, making her voice high and whining, her eyes pleading.

They looked to Kay at that moment like every sad kid that had ever called after her in the streets or leaped out at her begging outside the shops and hotels. Except these two had been abandoned young, like day-old kittens.

Impulsively, Kay pulled a beer box up to the table and turned it over.

"Siéntense, niñas," she said to them. Jorge and Luis exchanged glances. Luis shrugged. Jorge moved his chair off slightly to one side.

The children sat down on the edge of the box, tentative and watchful, and Kay held out the plate of pork rinds. "Eat," she said.

"Carajo, my pork rinds," Luis said.

"Order some more, then," Kay said.

The two *gamines* grabbed at the food, gnawing it down in seconds. The bigger girl carefully held her greasy hands away from the shirt she was wearing, an outgrown baby chemise, with a row of faded ducks marching cheerfully across the chest.

"¿Cómo te llama?" Kay asked.

"Blanquita."

Kay looked questioningly at the smaller girl, who hung her head. *"Se llama Esperanza,"* Blanquita said. *"Es mi hermana mayor."*

"Your older sister?" The older Esperanza was not only

smaller, but they didn't even look like sisters. Blanquita had Spanish features, Esperanza's face was darker, broader, more Indian.

"*¿Dónde está tu familia, Blanquita?*"

"*Están muertos,*" she said with pathos and a hopeful look at the empty plate.

"Huh!" Luis made a skeptical face.

"*Sí. Están muertos,*" Blanquita said angrily.

"*¿Entonces, dónde vives?*" Kay was digging in her purse for candy and change.

"*Allá.*" Blanquita pointed to the church steps where the beggars sat in the shadow of the doorway.

"*Vámonos,*" Jorge said, tiring of the whole scene.

The men got up to go, but the two kids stayed put, their grimy, bare feet dangling down the side of the box. They stared up at Kay with an anxious, overeager attentiveness that reminded her of strays waiting for a handout. They had the best hustle yet, she thought.

But the next moment she was squatting beside them, looking into their startled faces.

"Would you like to come with me?" she heard herself saying.

There had been no conscious decision, no thought at all. She simply couldn't turn and walk away one more time.

"What are you doing?" Jorge said. "You can't take them."

The girls were standing up now, fearful, holding hands, and on the verge of running away.

"*Niñas,*" Kay said, "we will got to my house, there will be *dulces* and *panela* and you will sleep in a real bed. There will be *carne* to eat as much as you like." She took their sticky hands and began walking toward the car.

"I do not think the Padrino— This is—" Luis began.

"Don't worry, I will take the full blame," Kay interrupted.

"I don't know," he said doubtfully.

"Let her alone," Jorge said, "she wants to be a mama."

Kay looked at him and laughed. "Of course," she said, "anyone can see I am the perfect choice for motherhood. No, I'm going to fatten them up and then find them a home. *Finito,* that's all there is to it."

At the car she bent down to pick up Blanquita, feeling the shocking lightness of the child's body, weightless as an insect husk. She put her in the back seat and then climbed in beside her, holding Esperanza on her lap. Soundless tears rolled down Esperanza's cheeks. Her eyes were closed.

Kay half expected to see someone coming after them, running and shouting, but there were only the *finca* dogs racing along behind the car's exhaust, ears flopping, jaws gaping in the wild effort of keeping up. Jorge turned on the crackly radio to a bright blare of music, *"Por ti contaría la arena del mar, por ti yo sería capaz de matar [For you I would count all the drops in the ocean, for you I would be able to kill]."* Esperanza stopped crying and opened her eyes.

At home Kay took them straight to the bathroom and stripped them. They stood naked beside the tub like two pot-bellied bird skeletons, staring raptly at the miracle of a bubble bath.

In the doorway, Guadalupe gaped in shock, opened her mouth to blurt something out, and quickly closed it again.

"Do you know these two *bebés?*" Kay was certain she had recognized the girls.

"No, Señorita Kay." She had recovered, her face was a polite blank.

Kay stood up from her kneeling position by the tub. "But you looked like you did recognize them, Guadalupe."

"No. I think maybe I have seen them in the square."

"And you are sure you don't know their family? Because that is very important to me, you understand?"

Guadalupe bent down and busied herself picking up the children's few rags from the floor.

Blanquita ran to her. *"Mi camisa, mi camisa,"* she screamed, grabbing onto her shirt with the ducks.

Kay knelt down again. "You will have a nice new *camisa* to wear, a clean one, much bigger and prettier."

Blanquita shook her head and refused to let go of the shirt. *"Entonces,"* Kay said, lowering her into the water, "your shirt can come with you into the bath and get washed, and your sister too."

Guadalupe lifted Esperanza into the tub and she sat in the water hugging herself tightly and rocking rhythmically. Guadalupe spoke to her in a gentle Indian patois, rubbing her back and shoulders with soap. Kay realized that the child had not yet said a single word, and the disturbing thought crossed her mind that she was mute.

After their bath, the girls sat on Kay's bed, their eyes darting around like those of anxious monkeys. She had dressed them in two of her clean T-shirts and sent Guadalupe out to buy clothes.

While she waited for her to return, she worked a comb carefully through the matted hair on each of their heads, giving them bracelets and earrings to distract them from the pain of the snarls. They submitted quietly, tensing with the effort not to cry, not to displease her.

The thought of doing a line crossed her mind but passed again like a cloud. For the first time in many weeks she had gone six hours without a hit.

Guadalupe came back with red plastic sandals, print dresses, and white cotton underwear. At the sight of them the girls burst into a hysterical frenzy, screaming and jumping as though electrified, running from one corner of the room to the other. Kay stood by, amazed, not knowing what to do except to wait for them to burn themselves out.

In the next few days the two strays alternately shocked, charmed, and saddened Kay. They invaded her completely. They stole all of her time and took all of her thoughts. It was worse than falling in love, she thought.

Wild creatures, they plunged their hands gleefully into the toilet, ate the toothpaste, hid in terror from the hairdryer. Blanquita was afraid to take her new shoes off and wore them to bed. Esperanza, convinced each meal might be her last, secretly stuffed the pockets of her dress with scrambled eggs. She kept food stashes everywhere, desserts in the closets, lumps of rice in drawers, bits of cheese and crackers under her pillow.

The children's devotion to Kay was total and consuming. They clung to her like the drowning to the rescuer, creeping out of their bed at night to fall asleep across the threshold of whatever room she was in. Any closed door awakened the terror of possible abandonment and they imitated her slavishly, aping her every move in the overwhelming need to be worth keeping.

That first evening, they ate dinner on the veranda. Kay felt high, celebratory. She had dressed in a slim, long skirt and put a red carnation in her hair. The children sat on cushions, their chins barely clearing the tabletop. Esperanza stared at the door through which the food would come while Blanquita experimented with a napkin on her head. Kay shook her head no, and she dropped it so fast, it fell to the floor.

Guadalupe brought soup. Ignoring their spoons, they fell doglike upon their bowls, lowering their faces into the soup.

"Miren, niñas. . . ." Kay picked up her spoon and demonstrated. Serious, attentive, they lifted splashing spoonfuls to their mouths.

With the second course, a beef roast, their eyes went wide with astonishment—were they really going to have two dinners? Guadalupe put the roast down on the table.

"Carne," Esperanza breathed, a whispered benediction, her first spoken word.

Kay was dreading Roberto Alvarez's return, but several days went by without word from him. Finally, one morning Luis was gone—to Bogotá, Jorge said. By evening he was back, sitting on the veranda with a beer. The flowers glowed in the dusky garden, the air was still day warm.

"So, how are your little *gamines?*" he asked. He leaned back, took a drag on his cigarette, and blew a perfect smoke ring. Kay watched it hang, a cloudy doughnut in the air before, slowly, it began to dissipate.

"Asleep. You'll be surprised, Luis, they look different already."

"I'm sure," he said. There was a pause. "Well?" Kay said.

"He already knew about them," Luis chuckled.

"What did he say?"

"Nothing. He wants you to go to Medellín. They're moving the fabrication works there. I heard he's going to sell this *finca* and buy an even bigger one there." He shook his head. "With all the *jefes* moving to Medellín, there will be no one left to kill each other in Bogotá." He laughed a rattling laugh, enjoying his joke, throwing back his head to reveal a mouthful of gold teeth.

"Did he say when he wants me to go?"

"Day after tomorrow. Franco and Miguel are coming for you." He looked at her curiously. "What will you do about the *niñas?* Will you take them?"

A thin moon had risen and appeared to be balancing on the rim of the mountains. For the first time that day she really needed a line. "All I know is I have to go upstairs and start packing now. *Hasta luego*," she said.

After several hours on the balcony, she heard the sounds of the house quieting down. Wired and alone in the Andean night, she smoked one cigarette after the other.

Supposing she took the girls with her—she would be lifting them out of their neighborhood, cutting them away from their roots. They would be fully her responsibility. And what if there *were* living relatives? Would that mean trouble later on?

Too, there was the question of Roberto. It was impossible to guess his reaction to her appearance in Medellín with two street waifs.

He could throw her off a hotel balcony as easily as he could greet her with affectionate sarcasm or calm indifference. It would be a fine opportunity for him to distance his son from her, to point out to Ricardo just how flaky and unpredictable the *norteamericana* really was.

Or he might simply turn a blind eye, as he did to her habit, allowing this latest craziness because it didn't infringe on his territory or his servants. He might even see it as helpful for her depression.

There was no telling. She rubbed her arms in a sudden gust of nighttime cold, and went inside to get a jacket.

The children were curled together in sleep. Blanquita had piled all her new belongings into bed with her. Esperanza's breath wheezed slightly, her hair clung to her forehead with the dampness of an unhealthy night sweat.

Looking down at them, Kay thought, maybe I should just take them and walk, tell him I want out—But as soon as she thought it, she dismissed the idea. The Padrino would never allow it.

She lifted Blanquita's arm, tucked it under the blanket, and went out to the balcony again. A mistaken cock crowed briefly in the darkness somewhere beyond the wall. I'm not mother material anyway, she went on thinking. Just go back to work and figure it out and keep her mouth shut, that was the way. Fatten them up and get them civilized and look for a home for them in Medellín. Maybe some tourist couple at the Intercontinental would take pity on them.

She paced the balcony smoking, nervous, wanting to stop the thoughts that left her feeling helpless and off-balance. The star-peppered sky had shifted above her head. She thought of her grandmother, pictured her out in her garden tying back the chrysanthemums. What time was it now in California?

She looked down from the balcony and out across the dark field to the black outlines of trees against the luminous sky.

She got little sleep, waking at dawn after a few hours to pack the two garment bags she had loaded for the next pass with Maggie. After their breakfast, she gave the kids a big Vuitton purse and a straw bag. "These are your bags to pack your things in. We are going to go on a vacation, a holiday."

They stared up at her, their faces smiling, alert, totally uncomprehending. She took Esperanza onto her lap and put her arm around Blanquita. "We are going to go away for a while," she explained.

"Are you coming too?" Blanquita said, worried.

"Oh yes, all three, we are all three going."

Esperanza slipped down onto the floor and refused even to look at the bags, covering her eyes with her hands and singing to herself. She was older then Blanquita, had seen and suffered longer. Kay wondered what wordless memories lay buried inside her small head. Watching her rocking and humming, Kay felt a flicker of irrational fear.

Blanquita had come close to the bed to monitor Kay's packing. After a moment, she ran to the bureau and pulled out the drawers, emptying a jumble of clothes and cookie wrappers onto the floor. She began dancing around and jamming her new possessions into the Vuitton.

"*Mira, Esperanza*," she said brightly. "Come and pack your crackers and your oranges and your shoes and your socks and your dresses . . . *todas las cosas.*"

"We are going in a car," Kay said. "You can bring your *dulces.*"

Esperanza took her hands from her face and looked up.

"Will there be music?" she asked.

Miguel and Franco arrived at noon in the Padrino's green Fiat station wagon. It stood in the driveway, crammed to the ceiling with tools, plastic sheeting, and other fabricating supplies, while the men argued with Kay.

"*Por amor de Dios,* there is no room in this car," Miguel said impatiently. "Use your eyes for yourself. There is room only for one and that one is you."

Franco looked uncomfortably at the two children who stood holding hands, their bags at their feet. "*Lo siento,*" he said, spreading his hands out in a gesture of helplessness.

"Please?" Kay touched Miguel lightly on the arm. "I'll help you repack the car. I want them with me."

With showy resignation, Miguel gave up. "*Bueno . . . pues,* if that is what you really want. Everyone says you are crazy and this proves it to me, but what more can be expected from a woman." He went on mumbling as he and Franco opened the doors and began unloading the car's back seat and trunk.

When they were done, they had rearranged the load to permit a cramped place by the window for Kay and a seat on top of a box for the girls. Kay went back to the house to look for Guadalupe. She had realized the night before that if the *finca* were sold, Guadalupe and her family would be part of the sale, like the *finca* dogs. She wanted to leave Guadalupe with some insurance and some hope.

She found her in the laundry courtyard hanging up the wash. The sun dazzled from white walls, its reflected light highlighting her face.

"Guadalupe," Kay said, and handed her a large cold-cream jar stuffed with a wad of bills, "here, bury this, it's your *banco.*" Suddenly she had her arms around the squatness and smallness of the woman. "I'll be back," she said.

"*Gracias,*" Guadalupe said. Her strange, wide-apart eyes brimmed a sad passivity, patient and creaturely.

"Will you help me get the *niñas* into the car?" Kay said.

They walked through the house together, and when they got to the front door, Kay put her hand on Guadalupe's arm. "Do you think I'm right to take the *niñas?*"

"Oh, yes, Señorita Kay, I am glad for them. It is a very, very great good fortune for them."

"Then if you know anything about them that I should know, send me the information in this envelope." Kay handed her a white envelope on which she had printed the name and address of the Intercontinental Hotel in Medellín.

Guadalupe flushed and hid the envelope quickly in the pocket of her loose-fitting dress.

"No one will ever know that you sent it to me," Kay said.
"I swear to you. Now you swear to me that you will send me
the information if you should hear anything. Get the priest to
write it down for you."

Guadalupe nodded.

The distance to Medellín didn't look like much on the map,
but it took fourteen hours to get there on the tortuous mountain
roads.

It was after midnight when they rolled up to the glass and
mahogany entrance of the Intercontinental, like a bunch of tired
Okies pulling up at a mansion, Kay thought. The new hotel
floated like a boxy palace behind a circular driveway lined with
spotlit international flags. Kay could hear them snapping in the
humid breeze, halyards chiming against aluminum poles. Her
body felt drowsy and heavy; they had descended from the
crisp, thin-aired world of the heights to the fecund, greenhouse
climate at five thousand feet.

Franco carried one sleeping child and Kay the other into a
cool lobby full of chrome and plush. Discreet music and chatter
drifted from the open door of a bar. Emeralds, leather goods,
and designer sports clothes waited behind brightly lit show-
cases.

With the rise of Medellín as a hub for cocaine activity, the
Intercontinental had taken on a double life: it was both a
world-class sports resort and the unofficial, clandestine "con-
vention center" of the Colombian cocaine trade. In one wing,
wealthy South American families occupied whole suites and
children ran shouting through the halls, in the other wing a
twilight hush prevailed and smugglers and dealers attended
"executive meetings," sending out for room service in the late
hours of the night.

The great levelers were the Olympic-sized swimming pool
and the professional-caliber tennis courts. Here, guests mingled
freely and there was no way to know whether the man in tennis
whites playing a friendly game of doubles had made his money
selling Argentine beef or Bolivian flake.

The gardens and landscaped grounds were entirely fenced in,
and security at the hotel was strict. The only access was
through the entrance driveway, and all visitors were tactfully

but scrupulously checked. The staff, in well-pressed, spotless brown-and-yellow uniforms, were everywhere.

The desk clerk, in his brown jacket with the small yellow crossed keys on the breast pocket, stared at Kay with a worried expression. He looked back down at the reservations book in front of him and then up again at Kay. Esperanza's head lolled sleepily against her shoulder.

"A thousand pardons, señora," he said, wringing very clean, very pink hands, "but we show a reservation for a single señorita only. It distresses me, it molests me very much. There must have been some mix-up with Señor Alvarez's reservation"—he threw a terrorizing glance at the young clerk beside him—"and I beg your indulgence for one night. Please also convey my sincere regrets to Señor Alvarez and we will do our particular best tomorrow to give you and your daughters a very pleasurable stay and a special suite."

He rang the bell for the porter with a smart movement of his hand and came around to the other side of the desk to see Kay and her party off on the journey toward her room. "A thousand apologies," he said again.

The bellhop thanked Kay for the tip with a solemn, almost mournful respect and bowed his way out of the room. As a single female and a foreigner, Kay had grown used to sly stares and open appraisal from almost every Colombian male from waiter to senator. The children, she realized, had lifted her into a new category. To the outside world she was a señora now, a mother, an object of veneration and deference. She had achieved status at last.

Looking into the bathroom mirror as she tissued off her makeup, she examined her face for blemishes and considered the multiple ironies of the situation. That woman in the mirror a mother? And everyone fussing over a couple of *gamines* they would have brushed away in the street. Well, one thing was for sure anyway, it was obviously a great cover. With an amused little snort, she clicked off the bathroom light.

The little girls didn't take up much room in the double bed. She got in beside them, feeling their warm breathing in the darkness and fell instantly into a deep sleep.

In the morning, two chambermaids and a porter moved Kay into a third-floor suite. The balcony faced out across the flowering grounds to the Andes. Down below was an enclosed children's play area complete with wandering pet llamas.

Kay brought the children to the playground to stay with an elderly Indian baby-sitter provided by the hotel. The woman tried to be polite and not ask questions about a blond señora with two mestizo daughters. The *niñas* ignored the slide and swings. They stood, crying and hanging onto Kay's dress while the woman tried to comfort them, repeating in a singsong voice, "Mama will come back soon, Mama will come back soon."

Kay dragged herself away, turning once to look back. They were standing at the fence staring after her tearfully. God, Kay thought, "Mama Kay." They were losing no time in staking their claim.

Carlos waited for her in front of the hotel in a light blue Renault. His bulky frame in the small car reminded Kay of a bear squeezed into a baby carriage. He didn't see her right away and his face above the rumpled Hawaiian shirt was sour, but when she opened the door he brightened immediately.

"*Hola, norteamericana,*" he said. "*¿Qué tal?* I am truly glad to see you. How do you like this piece of *mierda* they call a car? That is what they have given old Carlos to drive, as though I were a young *sardina.*" He shook his head in disgust. "You're very thin—you better get into this shit heap before you dry up and blow away in the sun."

Carlos was taking her up into the mountains to the cook's *finca* where the Alvarez fabrication shop was temporarily housed in an old barn. The day poured sunlight and heat from a cloudless dome of sky and the town of Medellín, a million strong, had none of the haunting mystery of Bogotá.

The main square, palm-shaded, was several centuries old. Lights were strung around the perimeter and old men sat talking and smoking on curly Victorian benches. Couples strolled along with arms around each other. It was much more like a town, Kay thought, than a city.

Medellín was the capital of the mountain region of Antioquia. It had been a closed town for centuries, Carlos told her, established by the Jews. In Bogotá, anyone could come looking for blow and casual deals and be welcomed. Here, they didn't like Americans and jailed the hippies, extorting money from them by planting drugs on them, charging outrageous lawyer's fees, and then sending them packing. Sure, they were becoming more modern, letting in a little South American tourism. Yes, there was a business boom here now and the students at the university were just as wild and Communist as anywhere else in Colombia. Maybe a little more. But on the whole, Antioquians were a close-knit bunch.

"Are they really Communist?" Kay asked.

"Who? The Antioquians? No, they are very anti-Communist, very anti-Castro."

"No, I mean the students."

"I don't know about Communists, they are just young and still believe that life can be made to be fair."

"*Entonces*, things have been a little difficult for you lately, no?" Kay said.

"Things, yes." Carlos sighed wearily and brought a beefy, freckled hand up to the back of his neck. They were driving past raw-looking new housing, past Medellín's first shopping centers, and the construction going on at the airport.

"I hate this move," he said, picking up speed. He was a terrible driver, leaning on the horn at every opportunity.

"My wife does nothing but complain, the children are wild because I am never home, Roddy is becoming a hippie. And my brother . . . I don't know . . . I hope he knows what he's doing. He's playing games with that *malparido* of a cook whose shack I have to go to every day to work. It is a humiliation. Do you know what he called me? A laborer. *A laborer, hijo de puta!*"

Carlos lowered his head, stiffened his arms till they pushed straight down on the steering wheel, and pulled his chin in toward his neck.

"But what exactly is happening? Why did he call you a laborer?" Kay pressed.

"Why? Because I told the truth."

They had begun to rise out of the valley, passing men driving horses loaded with sacks of produce and firewood. Kay wished Carlos would keep his eye on the road instead of constantly looking over at her as he talked.

"He defended himself with an insult to make me look low in front of my brother. He already receives more than any cook in Colombia, but now with sales rising *como el diablo* he has become swollen with his own importance. He feels he deserves more. He is becoming greedy. So I said to him, right in front of my brother, I said, 'What do you want from us? You already take what you need in what you skim from the base with your cuts, not to mention the other business deals you are growing fat on behind our backs.' And that is when he said, 'There must be a mistake. Perhaps you do not understand business dealings. After all, no offense to you, but you are a laborer.' '' Carlos mimicked Don César's Antioquian accent to perfection, then spat out of the window into the wind.

"I had blood in my eyes, I wanted to kill him, but my brother, he put his hand on my arm. And very relaxed and friendly, he said to Don César, 'Oh, please, do not concern yourself, Don César. I have had a batch tested.' And then he dropped the subject. He fixed that son of a bitch so he didn't know *which* direction the wind was blowing from.''

Carlos drummed his fingers on the steering wheel and asked Kay to light him a cigarette.

"Oh yes, my brother can play the game,'' he said. "He tells Don César how it is important to be working in harmony together now that all the competition are slitting each other's throats. Meanwhile, he is surrounding Don César, buying up all the land around him including a big new *finca* just up the mountain from him. And Ricardo's engagement just binds the whole thing closer. Because Flora has a cousin—''

Kay interrupted him. "What engagement, Carlos?'' she said, feeling a slight tightening behind her eyes.

Carlos gave himself a slap on the forehead. "What a stupid ass of a man.'' He glanced at her. "I am sorry, Kay,'' he said quietly. "I thought you knew.''

"Is Ricardo marrying the daughter?'' Kay remembered the two girls giggling in the bedroom on her first visit to Padrino's house.

"Isabella, yes.''

So Ricardo was going the traditional route, honoring his feudal duty, the family above everything, a marriage cementing business interests.

They drove along in silence. Carlos didn't know what to say. He was waiting for a sign from Kay.

Now Ricardo would never have a chance to develop on his own, be a regular young guy, hack around the world by himself, learning things. Kay saw how, inevitably, he would be funneled straight into the heavy life, trapped in a world of rigid rules, deals, and sudden executions.

She looked out the window and sadness descended over the bright day like a veil. It was over, she had expected that, but this was not the way she had expected to feel.

For a while they had passed grand *haciendas*, obvious coffee plantations, but now the terrain had changed to dense vegetation with small, nameless roads veering off into the wild. There were no road signs, street names, or any other means of orientation.

"How do you keep from getting lost up here?" Kay said finally.

Carlos laughed. "In these mountains you don't blunder around like a dumb tourist. If you don't know what you are doing here, you don't come. Up here the *finca* owners are the nervous kind, they do not like surprises, *tu sabes*?"

"Sí, Tío Carlos."

He swung sharply onto a narrow road marked with a vine-covered column of rocks and cement topped with a corroded wrought-iron lantern. The road was just wide enough for one car, and curved steeply upward, with massive banana plants and a two-foot-high stone wall on either side. At the top was a gate and gatehouse—brand-new, Kay noticed. She noticed, too, that the guard was armed not only with a rifle, but a holstered pistol as well. A sign of the times, she thought.

They parked the car and walked along a gravel path lined with multicolored roses heavy with scent and bees. Cool, green expanses of clipped lawn swept down a hill to a swimming pool hidden among giant philodendrons, like a deep blue lagoon. Kay heard the faint buzz of a transistor radio. Two girls and a man lay motionless on the wooden deck by the pool. Up ahead, the gravel path wound on beneath ancient trees. Orchids bloomed among pots of narcotically sweet jasmine.

The main house was comfortable-looking, but not as imposing as the grounds. It was stone, wrapped in verandas with stone colonnades and a slate roof. Carlos led Kay out of sight of the house through orchards of avocado trees toward a cluster of barns and a propagating greenhouse.

The largest barn had a few wheelbarrows filled with oranges out front. A sentry leaned against the wall, seemingly taking a siesta. An entirely credible country scene.

"Processing sheds," Carlos said, waving a hand. The Indian sentry looked up from under his hat and nodded at Carlos. "*¿Qué tal?*"

"You want to have a look?" Carlos said. He shrugged. "Go ahead. Have a look at the cook's kitchen."

The scene inside was factorylike. Beneath naked light bulbs, rows of Indian laborers raked and turned mountains of lumpy white coca paste stretching from one end of the building to the other.

They left, and Carlos unlocked the door of yet another outbuilding. A dank odor assaulted them as they came into the darkness, moldy, like an unused vegetable bin. "Welcome," he said disgustedly, turning on the switch to light up the bare overhead bulbs. "Here you have it, the temporary headquarters for the Alvarez fabrication plant. *Muy feo,* eh? Pretty piss-poor." Cardboard boxes of tools lined the walls. Ghostly, unrecognizable shapes stood around, wrapped in plastic sheeting as protection against the dust of the dirt floor.

"Why me, eh?" Carlos hitched up his pants and looked at Kay. He looked away again quickly, and began fooling with a tape machine that stood on a rickety table.

"Kay, my girl," he said, concentrating on the tape machine, "my brother is giving me one of the buildings at his new *finca* for myself, you understand, to do with whatever I please. But there are problems, problems." He shook his head, sighed theatrically, still not meeting her eyes.

"I am behind schedule with it. I am running my *cojones* off like a crazed bull all of the time. It's 'Go to Bogotá, go to Barranquilla, we need new packaging ideas, go to Cartagena, go back to Bogotá.' The wife is pregnant again, and so on and so on—" He stopped.

"You are good with organizing. I want you to arrange the new place, take it off my hands, figure out the tables, the production areas, put in the best lighting, you understand?" He was staring at her with pained embarrassment.

Kay understood. Carlos desperately wanted a slick-looking interior, an impressive environment to gain prestige and recover lost face, but he didn't know how to go about it. He was recruiting her to help him, to be his private ally.

"*Seguro*, Carlos, I can do that," Kay said.

. . .

The Padrino's continuing silence, Kay figured, was a perfect piece of diplomacy. He was allowing the episode of the children to slip by without comment. He had what he wanted, the engagement of his son, and he had decided to mollify Kay by closing his eyes to her latest eccentricity.

As a silent signal of his goodwill, he sent Kay a surprise from Bogotá—Rosa. The children hid behind the door to their room, afraid it might be someone to take them back to the square, but Rosa coaxed them out.

"*¡Ay, qué angelitas!*" She talked to them in Indian patois, and finally had them sitting on her lap, one on each knee, their eyes carefully checking Kay for approval.

Blanquita opened a plastic drawstring bag she wore around her neck and pulled out a pair of shoes. "*Mira,* Rosa. These are mine," she said.

The hotel set up a narrow cot for Rosa in the children's room. When room service came, she hovered around the table, pouring Kay's coffee and cutting up the girls' food. Kay asked her to sit down at the table with them. Rosa shook her head no.

With a swift movement Esperanza plunged both hands into a dish of oily sausages and deposited them dripping onto an empty plate.

"There. Eat," she said.

After that, Rosa ate her meals with them and they began to drift into the comfortable habits and daily routines of a family. The Padrino receded into the background of their lives, the rumble of distant thunder on a clear day.

The most difficult thing for Kay to cope with became her withdrawal from cocaine. To Kay's mind, cocaine and children did not mix. She had known for some time, could see in the mirror, what her habit was doing to her, but she had been unable to find her way out. The answer came with the children. On their very first night at the *finca*, she decided to make a stand: she brought out her entire personal stash and flushed it down the toilet.

Cocaine withdrawal is totally different from withdrawal from other drugs. At first Kay spent a lot of time sleeping. She was utterly exhausted. She would curl up with Blanquita and Esperanza and all three would sleep away the day in the long sleeps of healing.

Then came the rounds of insomnia and the craving, a subtle and psychological hankering rather than a desperate physical pain. Every small problem of the day was enormously magnified and sent her mentally running for a line. Every challenge created an instant hunger for the drug until she wanted to scream, "Leave me alone!"

In Medellín, when Kay went back to suitcase work, the constant presence of cocaine was an added torment, which she gradually conquered with a stream of inky cups of *tinto* that lacerated her already injured stomach, and with a continual inner monologue—"Listen to the children's voices in the other room. You need to be in control. Don't numb your brain, don't freeze your head . . . willpower not white powder, the power of will."

Throughout the entire process, she fought a sense of personal failure and powerlessness that made her feel guilty. In those early days of drug innocence when cocaine was still being touted as nonaddictive, Kay believed that it could not have been the drug that was strong, but herself who was weak.

She fought back by imagining the cocaine as a death-dealing seductress and herself as invincible behind the armor of a strong will. She held the image of the children in her mind, and threw herself into every aspect of their welfare.

Health had become Kay's consuming interest. She was worried about the *niñas*. The legacy of the square had ravaged their immune systems and left them prey to constant colds and a variety of stubbornly persistent tropical parasites, viruses, and diseases, from ringworm to diarrhea.

Between visits to doctors, she drove around Medellín in a rented *carro colombiano* buying things for Carlos's new shop. She liked Medellín, found the Antioquians more relaxed, humorous, and colorful than the Europeanized Bogotanos.

The atmosphere, humid and bright, seemed safer than in Bogotá, and Kay relaxed her guard. But one day, on returning to the hotel, she found a long, clean knife slit in her bag and a few of the things inside missing. The thief had moved on her without her ever feeling a thing. It was slick—a reminder from below the surface that all was not paradise.

A week went by. Flora phoned but did not invite her to the new *finca*. The Padrino, Kay heard, had used a combination of veiled threats and an open checkbook to amass one hundred acres bordering on the cook's property.

Returning to the hotel one noon, Kay found an envelope waiting in her mailbox at the lobby desk. The handwriting was familiar—it was her own. She stood by the elevator and tore the envelope open. The message, written in pencil on brown wrapping paper, was nearly illegible: *"La madre es Manuela— Puerta Verde—Barranquilla."* Elated that Guadalupe had kept her promise, Kay turned the piece of crumpled paper over, but there was nothing else.

Upstairs, as she inserted the key to her room, she heard the murmur of a young man's voice inside. Her heart did a little butterfly lurch.

Ricardo was standing so close to the door she almost bumped him with it.

"I was just leaving," he said.

The girls pushed past him in delight and attached themselves to Kay's legs.

After Rosa had taken them down to the playground, Kay offered him a drink.

"Sí, por favor," he said stiffly. "Aguardiente. You're not going to keep them, are you?"

"I don't know." She smiled, and turned away to get two glasses and the bottle.

"You look great with a tan," she said. He looked taller and leaner somehow—very sexy, she thought ruefully, in his well-cut Italian pants with the thin alligator belt and the cuffs of his long-sleeved shirt rolled up.

"You look good, too," he said carefully.

She put the glasses and bottle on a tray and led the way out onto the balcony.

"Congratulations." She raised her glass to him. He raised his. "Thank you," he said, still formal.

He lit a Marlboro and crossed his legs. "It is the correct thing, Kay. She is a nice girl. You would like her if you knew her."

"I'm sure." Spare me, she thought. "Do you love her at all, Rick?"

He glanced up at her, his eyes pained. I'm being a bitch, she thought, but so what.

"Yes. In a way. But I don't think it is something you can understand."

Kay shrugged. He leaned forward suddenly and grasped her arm just above the wrist. "It is you who makes things impossible," he said tightly, "especially now, bringing home your half-breed *gamines*." He was holding her a shade too hard. She twisted her arm out of his grip, feeling a rush of fury.

"Oh?" she said. "You want me to throw them out again?"

He flipped his cigarette over the balcony rail and jumped up to stand with both hands shoved deep into his pockets.

"You pick up two kids from the gutter and then you give yourself congratulations and think it makes a difference." He stopped, and lit another cigarette. In the heavy silence he blew out the smoke and waited for Kay to say something, but she sat looking down into her lap.

"There are thousands more out there," he burst out. "Will you save all of them too?"

"I'm not big on saving the world. I'm just trying to find a way to live in it without going crazy. *¿Entiendes?* It's that simple."

A plane droned overhead. They didn't say anything.

"And what about me?" he said, finally breaking a silence that had become painful.

"What do you mean, what about you?"

He went to the rail and stood looking down, his profile to her. Down below, a uniformed waiter carried a loaded tray down a gravel path. "I still want to be with you, Kay, to sleep with you. You are a free woman . . . We could see each other . . ."

"Jesus, Ricardo, you're getting married. Are you trying to turn me into Olivia? I am not Olivia."

"*Bueno,* I think it is time for me to go," he said.

"Wait." She ran in from the balcony behind him and they stood looking at each other across the large double bed.

"*Lástima,*" he said. "It's too bad."

At the door, she put her hand on his shoulder and said, "Friends?"

"Friends?" He laughed and said, "You Americans." And then he bowed and kissed her hand with elaborate formality.

After he was gone, she stood on the balcony and watched him walking away until he disappeared behind the building. Against her will, and knowing it wouldn't happen, she hoped he would turn around and wave. He didn't.

She went inside and did the first line of cocaine she had had in a month.

Chapter
Eleven

Colombia is entering an uneasy period that could well last three years. But nobody knows if the country could withstand uncertainty so long.

Opinions in Bogotá that the government is paralyzed and the economy stagnated are widespread. And although this nation has survived instability before, now fear of the future heavily reflects on present tensions.

—*The Miami Herald,*
November 21, 1971

IT SEEMED TO Kay, sitting in her temporary quarters at the Intercontinental Hotel in Medellín, that the fall of 1970 was a season of wild instability, even by Colombia's volatile standards.

Mid-October brought rains, high winds, and earthquake to the rich cattleland of the north. To the south, the worst storms in forty years inflicted floods that took four hundred lives and wreaked millions of dollars of damage.

Peasants in the poverty-stricken rural areas, tired of unfulfilled promises of land reform, had begun a wave of violent land invasions, and the newly formed Pastrana administration was seething with plots and counterplots.

Even the relentlessly successful *coqueros* in the now runaway cocaine business were affected by the treacherous political waters. As Roberto Alvarez had correctly foreseen, government agencies were rife with double agents and doublecrosses as former employees in high places were replaced and those under the new regime vied for positions and negotiated bribes.

As a result, a sudden rash of arrests and indictments broke out in the United States. For example, *The New York Times* of October 23, 1970, reported that a former Colombian vice-consul had been indicted for smuggling five million dollars worth of pure cocaine into the United States. Carrying thirty-five pounds of cocaine, he had been surprised at Kennedy International Airport by federal agents who had obviously been tipped off.

As world attention and demand accelerated and the supply of cocaine developed into a multi-billion-dollar global enterprise, new safer methods for smuggling became imperative. For entrepreneurs like Roberto Alvarez, the personal carry and the "mule" were a thing of the past. The only way to keep riding the cresting cocaine wave was to inaugurate new routes and more sophisticated, volume-efficient means of transport.

Roberto was planning on moving one hundred kilos of cocaine a month. He had already made deals with several orchid growers in the Medellín area and would soon be smuggling his white magic concealed in the false bottoms of boxes of the frilly and exotic blooms.

Knowing that diversification was the best and only sure way to protect himself, Roberto had involved Carlos in a number of secret missions to Barranquilla on the coast, where Carlos had hinted to Kay he was looking into the custom building of fiberglass boats. Kay's guess was that he was dreaming up a way in which the cocaine could be hidden between the wooden core frame (which used large sheets of plywood for the flat areas) and the exterior fiberglass lamination. You could hide a ton of coke like that, she thought.

Roberto had also begun talking about the feasibility of liquid cocaine, a technique in which the cocaine would be dissolved in solution (approximately a half kilogram per quart), and smuggled via cruise ship in sealed liquor bottles of various brands. Since the solution was the exact color and clarity of genuine liquor, it was impossible to detect.

Kay had been keeping track of these developments through Carlos, but it was not until the last week in October 1970 that she received a phone call and a summons from the Padrino himself.

It was late afternoon. She had finished supervising the installation of track lighting in the new fabrication studio and had returned to pick up Rosa and the children in the little hotel playground. The hotel was crowded and an overflow conference of European coffee buyers had been temporarily quartered in Kay's wing.

Kay herded the children into the elevator, worrying that they would feel smothered by the forest of tall adult bodies crowding in on them. Glancing down, she saw that, far from being frightened, Blanquita was dipping her small fingers deftly into the pocket at eye level in front of her.

A brown leather wallet slowly slid into view. Kay shook her head vigorously. *No*. Blanquita's fingers lingered, a bee around a flower. She looked up at Kay.

"No?" She formed the word silently. Kay shook her head again and mouthed, "No!"

A little bell dinged, the doors slid open, and Blanquita's eyes followed the man regretfully as he pushed his way out and beyond her reach forever.

Back in the room, Kay said, "Blanquita, *mi corazón*, you cannot do that."

Blanquita's eyes were puzzled. "Why? Did he see me?"

Kay stared at her. How could she even start to explain? "Because you don't have to anymore," she said finally.

Rosa took the girls into the bathroom and Kay could hear her telling Blanquita that God could see everything she did and if she stole He would punish her and that was the real reason she shouldn't do it. Kay strained to hear more, but the rest of the conversation was lost in the sound of running water. She sat down to read Maggie's latest encoded letter.

When the phone rang, she was deciphering Maggie's news that the last of the coke was almost gone and it was time to arrange the details of the next pass. "*¿Sí?*" she said, expecting Carlos.

It was the Padrino. "*¿Cómo está usted?*" he asked formally.

She sucked in her breath; once again he had caught her off-guard. She hated it. "*Muy buen. ¿Y usted?*" she countered.

"*Gracias a Dios, muy buen.*" He paused and then asked how her *hijitas* were. He had heard they were quite pretty and doing well. Yes, Kay told him, they were doing very well. A great little pair of outlaws, she wanted to say, but instead she asked after Flora's health. Flora was, of course, also *muy buen*.

"I would like you to attend a meeting at the home of Don

César Gutiérrez tomorrow. Five o'clock sharp,'' he said. There was a little beat while he waited for a response, and then Kay said, "Yes, certainly. I'll be there.''

"*Entonces,* I am glad that you are well,'' he said and hung up.

Kay put down the receiver, annoyed for the thousandth time by the sense of foreboding and imbalance he managed to leave in his wake.

The next day was hot and humid, and Kay coiled her hair in a sun-bleached knot at the nape of her neck. She slipped into a cool, backless dress that glowed white against the deep tan of her skin. Bare of jewelry except for silver earrings, she exuded a provocative aura at once undressed and elegant.

Don César's house had a special odor that struck her immediately, a combination of old candle wax, furniture polish, and something vaguely spicy. A servant woman led the way through the entrance hall, empty but for a giant pot of red flowers with aggressive yellow stamens.

The servant opened the door. Grouped around a massive fireplace above which hung a family crest and a large Austrian flag, were six men: the cook, Carlos, the Padrino, Ricardo, and two strangers. They held tall glasses of cold beer in their hands and turned to stare at her, entranced. Kay felt a cool surge of pleasurable power.

Then the Padrino was moving toward her, taking her by the elbow, complimenting her on her health, her beauty, joking in a half-insinuating way about motherhood. Over his shoulder she exchanged glances with Ricardo.

"What a beautiful room, Don César,'' she said. She wanted to court the cook a little, show him she didn't take sides against him.

"I am pleased that you like it.'' He was melancholy and as thin as Don Quixote.

The room had the flavor of an old-fashioned hunting lodge, with fish and game trophies and comfortably worn leather furniture. A glass cupboard held rows and rows of hand-carved, antique chessmen and their checkered wooden battlefields.

"Señor Ruiz, Señor Calderón, may I present Kay Wolff, our North American designer from California.''

A servant brought her a cold beer and then began loading the long table with a buffet spread.

The man called Ruiz was fat. His fly strained over a globular belly, his small fine features lost in the fleshy sag of his face. Kay thought there was something familiar about the other one, Calderón, but she couldn't quite place him. He was in his forties with a receding hairline—but something in the way he stood, stocky in his navy blue jacket, reminded her of something.

Her guess was that these men were important new connections for paste supply. With the increase from thirty to one hundred kilos a month, the Padrino needed new sources of raw paste to stock the cook's refining kitchen.

"Please," Don César said, "come and have some food." He gestured toward the table. Kay commented on how particularly delicious the *arepas* were, partly to distract the others from the fact that she had left the dish of beans swimming in pig fat strictly alone.

"Miraculous," the Padrino said, "you have lived for several weeks in Medellín. And yet you have escaped a lecture on the celebrated Medellín *arepa*, which was, of course, invented here."

Kay laughed, and the cook said, "No, no, it is true, the *arepa* is an Antioquian specialty. The trouble is with all the poor imitations you have obviously had to endure."

Ruiz said he, personally, didn't care who invented the *arepa*, as long as it tasted good. His voice had a suffocated quality and he pronounced his vowels in a flat way, like someone whose first language was Portuguese. Kay wondered if he was Brazilian.

Sighing, he wiped the sweat from his neck with a balled-up handkerchief and took off his jacket, tossing it carelessly onto the couch. Strapped under his left arm was a gun in a brand-new leather shoulder holster.

Ricardo had been very quiet and had seated himself as far away as possible from Kay. Now he got up and asked Don César something in a low voice. Kay had seen Ricardo spill a bit of food on his pants and she knew that he wanted to wash it out immediately.

Don César was politely solicitous. Later, Kay imagined, he would laugh and tell his wife that his new son-in-law was a true

Bogotano, a real *rolo* (dandy). The men of Medellín had no time for clothes and aftershave.

After dessert, the cook excused himself and disappeared for twenty minutes with Ruiz. Right, Kay thought, the new paste connection. Carlos had risen to follow along, but at a glance from his brother he sat down again.

"Did you hear about the Seligman bust in France?" Calderón said, lighting a Marlboro. "There have been quite a few European suitcase busts lately." He squinted through the smoke at Roberto.

The Padrino smiled. "Are you saying that I should be worried?"

"But no, of course I am not," Calderón said. "We have a good man over there in Reynaldo. I was merely mentioning it."

"Correct." Roberto was still smiling.

After Ruiz and Calderón said their good-byes, coffee was served in a small back room, a kind of library. There was an entire shelf of illustrated botany books. Don César had once taught biology and chemistry and Kay wondered if in his quiet, meticulous way he had been a good teacher. Had cocaine processing begun as a hobby with him, a small sideline worked at in the evening after dinner? She looked up to find him watching her.

"*Empecemos* [Let's begin]," the Padrino said. "I thought it was time for all to sit down together and discuss the changes in our organization." Kay wanted to hook Ricardo's eyes, but he was having none of it.

"I would like to clarify," the Padrino was saying, "the future directions we will be taking in the hope that we can then lay to rest, *de una vez por todas* [once and for all], our disagreements and doubts."

Kay always marveled at the Padrino's tone in any meeting related to the business. He seemed to think it necessary to sound like a chief executive officer addressing his board.

"We need to move forward," he went on, "with absolute unity of purpose and mutual assurance in these times of difficulty and, more important, of enormous possibilities."

The cook shifted in his chair.

"In the next months we will be taking a giant step. Greatly expanding our operations, we will be moving into the volume business, carrying via cruise liners and freighters into Canada, the Caribbean, and the North American Gulf ports of Texas, New Orleans, and Florida.

"As you know, we have been experimenting successfully with flower-box packaging, and in the future this transport line will include not only orchid shipments, but carnations and roses as well, tripling our volume capacity while opening a new and safer use of air routes. Ricardo will be coordinating these new routes."

He paused and looked around. Ricardo nodded, lowered his glance, and crossed his legs. Carlos fiddled with a pencil.

"So, though we are honoring our remaining suitcase commitments, personal carry has become too risky and uneconomical and will be terminated within the next two months. I would like to ask Kay, under the direction of Carlos, to oversee the completion of this phase, making sure the fabrication of the remaining suitcases is accomplished as quickly and safely as possible."

He stopped and took a sip of coffee. Damn, Kay thought, that's going to mean a lot of late nights. And when it's over? Trips to Europe, away from the kids, carrying money for Padrino's deals. She didn't like the way things were shaping up.

The Padrino put down his cup. "We are now talking about one hundred kilos processed through Don César's kitchen every month. There seems to be no limit to the *gringo*'s appetite and, impossible as it seems, the prices are rising every day. Soon they will be paying one hundred dollars a gram. So, in view of our cook's expanded and extremely central role, I have decided to make our old friend and new relation a full partner in any and all ventures."

Carlos looked up abruptly, the pencil he had been toying with motionless in his hand.

"And naturally," Roberto went on quickly, "in recognition of and in fairness to our now far more complex fabrication department, an additional ten percent of the sale of all cocaine packaged by the Alvarez organization will be going to Carlos as the head of that department."

"Very good," Carlos said. His face was a little red, but he was keeping himself in check. He'll probably make a private deal with his brother later, raise his cut, Kay thought.

Roberto placed his palms together and nodded his head

amiably. "*Así va la cosa*. Now that we have a clear road before us, let us drink a toast to the very bright and very shining future. If our host would do us the kindness?"

"With pleasure, Don Roberto." The cook got up and ducked his tall frame through the low wooden door to call the servant.

Kay was the first to leave. She wanted to avoid walking to the cars with Ricardo. The Padrino's Mercedes was parked under a tree, all doors wide open, radio on full blast. Miguel and Franco and several other men were standing around drinking beer and listening to the soccer broadcast.

She walked by and waved. Miguel made a thumbs-up gesture. "Two to zero," he called, and Kay returned the gesture and called back, "*Bueno.*" She was glad the Millonarios, the Bogotá team, was winning, because the boys had really made a soccer fan out of her.

To her surprise, she saw that Miguel was wearing his gun in full view over his short-sleeved shirt. Then she saw that all the men were carrying.

She had heard of the bad times between rival families in Bogotá, but she had felt safe and secure in Medellín. Now, as she climbed into her car, she thought of her own gun left behind in Bogotá.

She turned left at the stone pillar marker toward town. A few miles later she passed a new black Renault sedan and glancing at the driver, thought she recognized Calderón, still wearing his very correct navy blue jacket. What *was* it about him? She tried to imagine where she might have seen him before—why did the man give her such a tingle of apprehension?

At least these days, she said to herself, she could count on the fact that it wasn't cocaine paranoia talking.

She clicked on her headlights, catching the quivering dance of gnats and tiny night insects in their sudden beams. The meeting, so cordial and optimistic on the surface, disturbed her deeply. There were underlying currents. It was obvious that the Padrino had organized this little show mainly for Carlos—to get things out into the open, to mark clear boundaries for each player.

But would Carlos sit still for his brother's plan, or would he consider it a final humiliation, lose all control and fall out with the cook? Patience wasn't exactly his strong suit. Suddenly, she was icily aware that her security was tied to Carlos in the same way it had once been to Ricardo.

She had watched Ricardo at the meeting. She was pretty sure he would disappoint his father in the business. He had no real stomach for it—he was too dreamy and he had none of the necessary killer instinct. But he had cut her at the meeting with such determination, she worried that his passion for her might have turned vengeful.

Something else about the meeting bothered her—the fat man, Ruiz. Her intuition told her that the Padrino had met his match there and that if the two were to lock in combat the Padrino might even lose. And that would leave her without any protection at all.

As she turned onto the dirt road leading to Medellín, small pebbles spraying and pinging at the sides of her car, the full realization hit her like a burglar alarm going off in the dark—her life in Colombia had turned dangerously precarious. And she had two kids to worry about. For the first time, she thought seriously of going home.

The last letter Kay had received from Maggie confirmed their next pass for the island of San Andrés. Kay had chosen the island because though it was one hundred and fifty miles off the coast of Nicaragua, it was Colombian territory and she would need no papers to bring the children there.

She wanted Maggie to meet the girls. She had written to her about them, but she knew nothing could prepare Maggie for the way they were, so different from any concept of childhood she could possibly have.

After this pass, Kay too would be abandoning the dangers of the suitcase carry, transferring her own concealment operation to an import-export business in art objects. The recent busts had made her jittery for Maggie's safety, even on this fairly routine run. Always, she reminded herself, but especially these days, there was no such thing as "routine."

The small island of San Andrés, only two and a half hours from Miami, was destined to become a center for a variety of smuggling operations. In 1970, however, it was still mainly a shopping free port, a popular place for Colombians to pick up TVs and toasters while taking a few days of sun and fun amid the reefs and palm trees.

Kay loved the island because it was unique in the Caribbean, a throwback to a more innocent, pretourist, pre-Hilton time. Conditions were rough, with accommodations little more than shacks, but Kay didn't care in the turquoise, sea-warm mornings and kerosene-lamp evenings, whether the hot water ran out or the electricity failed.

She loved the austerity of the triangular-shaped wooden houses, the garden walls made of gray driftwood and pink seashells. And she loved the quiet pride of the natives, whose black skins, occasional blue eyes, and Welsh surnames spoke of their mixed past as did their soft lilting voices, which slipped easily back and forth from Spanish to English to an island patois that combined them both.

Kay arrived first and rented a wind-worn, pastel-blue house tucked into the cove of a shoreline deserted but for fishing nets and seabirds. Someone had splashed graffiti on a decaying wooden fence: GLORIA IN EXCELSIS DEO.

The planeloads of Colombians, she discovered, never ventured past the small town at the head of the island, where they crowded onto the strip of main beach and into the duty-free shops, amusing themselves in the evenings at the two ramshackle casinos on the main street.

Maggie had four days. Kay picked her up at the airport.

"My God, Kay, you look human again." In the laughter of their embrace, Kay breathed the familiar fragrance of Maggie's hair, a smell like apples.

"And look at these kids. I had no idea there were so *small. ¿Hablas inglés?"* Maggie asked them.

They hung their heads and pressed against Kay's side.

"They're learning," Kay said, putting her hand on the top of Esperanza's head.

At the blue house in the cove, Maggie unpacked two talking dolls for the girls and they fell into their usual fit of frenzied appreciation.

"They always do that when they get presents," Kay said.

They spent most of the first two days on the beach. Kay had bought a red-and-yellow-striped umbrella to shade the children, and they stayed close to her, dumping sand from one pail into another, digging holes, burying and unburying themselves.

Kay was worried about Esperanza, who had begun to wake

up with nightmares. After the first few hours of sleep at night she would sit up in bed, screaming. It would take a long time to soothe her back to sleep.

"I think she remembers something that happened, something more than abandonment," Kay said. She turned over on her back on the towel and then sat up, blinking in the white heat of the sun. Down the beach, a flurry of gulls wheeled and dived, picking at something in the sand.

Maggie took a mango from the picnic basket. "So tell me. What are you going to do with these kids?"

Kay leaned over and, holding Maggie's wrist steady, bit into the mango. She wiped her mouth and looked at the girls.

"I don't know. What do you think?" she said.

The children were hunkered opposite each other, heads bent, staring intently into the hole they had dug. Their shadows on the sand were round and small. A little distance from them, tiny birds skittered back and forth like spiders before the breaking waves.

"I've been wondering about adopting them," Kay said, trying to sound casual, even to herself.

"What?" Maggie said. She put down the mango and stared.

"I've had weeks to find them a home, but I haven't even bothered to look—I just keep thinking up excuses. Since I can't seem to say good-bye to them, it looks like I'm stuck with them and they're stuck with me."

They watched Blanquita struggle across the sand lugging a pail of water with both hands. At every careful step water splashed out onto her red bathing suit and scrawny legs. Her face was stoic.

"Have you gone as far as thinking about the procedures? I mean, what about papers? Isn't it a terrible hassle?"

"I don't know. I think I can find the mother—I think she's alive in Barranquilla somewhere."

"And then? Let's say you did legally adopt them. They have to go to school and all that, don't they? You want to raise them down here? I mean—'my mother the smuggler'?"

Kay picked up a fistful of sand and let it run, cool and fine through her fingers. "You don't have to say it, Maggie. I know I can't go on dragging these toddlers around like this. But how do I get them back home? I've already done a little investigating at the American embassy. They gave me the runaround and told me there is a six-year waiting period on all immigration from Colombia.''

Maggie's face was pure innocence. ''So? Are you telling me you don't know how to get around that? What's the problem?''

Kay laughed, jumped up, and stretched, feeling the wind lift her hair off her neck. ''Problem? There's no problem. All I have to do is smuggle two sickly *bambinos* across seven international borders without getting killed or caught.''

Maggie squinted up at her. ''Oh, is that all? Jesus wept,'' she said.

Kay had heard that certain beaches on the Texas Gulf were accessible. They discussed the possibility of hiring a yacht. She would sail up the coast to a point offshore, then row in with the children. Maggie would be waiting with a car. It seemed plausible. They decided on a dress rehearsal to see how the *niñas* would do in a boat.

Johnny Key, just off San Andrés, was a small reef outcropping with extraordinary snorkeling. Only inches from its palm-fringed beach, schools of Day-Glo fish darted nonchalantly among the coral under the fins and goggles of *turistas* from Bogotá.

A weather-beaten twenty-foot motor launch with a small cabin and several rows of chairs took the curious back and forth on the twenty-minute trip. Captain Giro—his name stitched in blue above the visor of his dirty white cap—lifted the children tenderly over the guardrail and onto the deck of his domain.

''Very nice daughters,'' he said, obviously interested in their Indian looks.

''It takes two to tango,'' Maggie said.

''You childrens want to come drive?'' he asked. They shook their heads, no, and he went into the cabin and started up the engines with a coughing sputter, an old man in a loose white shirt and dirty, baggy shorts. A pair of high-powered Bushnell binoculars dangled from a short strap around his neck.

The deck was crowded, every seat taken. Five minutes out, the boat began to rock and wallow. Waves splashed and sprayed over the deck, soaking the passengers and making them scream with laughter.

The *niñas* one on Kay's lap, the other on Maggie's, had become what Kay thought of as ominously still. Blanquita, with a peculiar look of stern concentration on her face, slid rapidly off Maggie's lap, just as Esperanza lifted both hands to her mouth. Seconds later, Kay and Maggie were at the railing, each holding a sobbing, retching child over the side.

"Cancel Texas beach assault," Maggie said.

Kay loaded the children in the back seat and drove Maggie to the airport. Kay had an extra day before she had to return to Bogotá, where the Padrino wanted her now. The kids fell asleep while Maggie stared pensively out the window.

"I never feel like leaving these little island dream worlds," she said. "I didn't tell you, things are not too great at home. My parents have cut me off. We're not even speaking right now."

For years, Maggie had been receiving sizable checks from her grandfather's trust fund.

"On the night of my birthday they read me the riot act, no pun intended." She smiled bleakly, "I didn't even get to eat my cake. I had to get up and leave.

"According to my father, my grandfather would be spinning in his grave if he could see the way I throw his money away. My mother told me I looked terrible, I was 'letting myself go.' My father told me the money was supposed to be for a fine education, for looking smart and not like a rag picker, for traveling and not for me to open my house and purse to a bunch of crazy, hopped-up Communist dupes."

Maggie tapped Kay on the knee with a forefinger. "Communist dupes, that's what he said, Kay, and both of them are very upset, he said, to see that I've fallen for Soviet propaganda. Do you believe this? Soviet propaganda?"

"I'm sorry, Mags," Kay said.

"Oh, they're sorry too. They're sad, even, but they said they're only trying to do what they think is best for me." Maggie took out a tissue and began wiping at the dusty windshield. "Don't worry," she said, "there are other things to think about right now, like what's going on in Cambodia. The sons of bitches haven't done enough 'Vietnamization.'" They have to escalate to Cambodia."

"Even Nixon can't go on forever," Kay said.

"Don't count on it, maybe *he* can," Maggie snapped.

Kay admired Maggie's courage but didn't know how to say

so without sounding corny. She had always been ambivalent about what she called Maggie's "soft background," but now she wondered what she would do if she were Maggie and her parents cut off her money. She had no easy answer.

Flying to Bogotá, Kay tried to think about the problem of the children, but sitting back with her head against the seat, cocooned in the never-never land of the airplane, she had a hard time focusing. She closed her eyes, relaxing into the steady drone. Papers first, she thought.

Roberto Alvarez wanted her back in Bogotá for a while. He had a number of small custom orders for her to work on in her apartment. The young *gringos* traveling to Bogotá, he told her, would keep right on wanting suitcases, and he didn't mind producing the packaging as long as his own people were not involved in the carry. Though he had moved his base to Medellín, he still kept in constant touch with the capital, hiring a private plane to fly back and forth, maintaining his Bogotá house and properties and a low-profile business doing small "packaging only" orders and supplying the middlemen in the major hotels.

"After you have finished with this order, you go to Europe for a money pickup," he had said. "Perhaps I will meet you in Paris afterward. We'll see about it later." Kay knew he had been investing large sums buying paintings from a famous Paris gallery.

He was probably sending her to Frankfurt to meet Reynaldo again. A few months earlier, on a brief three-day visit home, Reynaldo had been formal and correct, eyeing her with a pointedly cool haughtiness, and telling her about the German film star from UFA he was dating. Clearly, he was trying to gloss over the embarrassing memory of their last encounter at the Frankfurt airport.

They were sitting on the apron patio in front of the new fabrication house Kay had created for Carlos, a large white barn with red doors. Inside, she had designed an environment as impeccable as a laboratory, and Carlos had gratefully presented her with two very perfect fire emeralds.

Reynaldo was sunning himself in a striped beach chair. "I hope it goes well with you," he said from behind closed eyes. "I hear you have become a . . . what? Shall we say Mama?"

Kay said, "Yes. It keeps me home and out of trouble."

"Chacun à son goût," he said, shrugging, and produced a

small glass vial with a silver top and a tiny spoon from the breast pocket of his linen sports jacket. He held the bottle out, offering her a toot. His fingers and nails were clean as bone.

"Thanks, no," she said.

He raised his eyebrows. No?

"My nose."

"Aha," he said blankly.

Carlos called to her and she got up to go inside. At the barn door, she turned for a moment to look back. Reynaldo was staring fixedly up into the trees, his silvery blond head tipped far back against the chair rest. His arms hung limply to either side and one hand trailed, palm open on the ground. Feeling her gaze, he straightened quickly and sent her a tiny, embarrassed wave, like that of a guilty child.

When she came out again, he was gone and three days later he was back in Europe.

Kay found Bogotá quiet, the soldiers less in evidence. On November 14, the new President, Pastrana, had lifted the state of siege that had been in effect since April 21. Kay wrote to Maggie:

Nov. 20, 1970

The beautiful baskets have left on a huge truck going to the Pacific port. I really hope the import bizz will do well. Am writing this on the roof where I like to come to get a few minutes alone. There is a little wash room up here and a door out onto the roof with lines and lines of washing billowing against a big sky with the Andes in the background. I know how much you would like to wrap your camera around this.

I don't leave the house for the next four days. Again, isolation, but strangely, among friends. We are a Spanish family. The girls are gaining weight. They look like "rich kids" now and they are crazy about "I Love Lucy" in Spanish. I think about my earliest days in this city, so extreme, the hotels, the work, the people. I think about you and I'm grateful. . . .

Time to banish words for work.

She went back downstairs to the smells of chicken frying and the sounds of television coming from behind the closed apartment doors. Expectantly, she fitted the key into her own lock, but no children came running to the open door. The living room was vacant, a mute clutter of dolls and toys and empty plastic cups. Panic. Something had happened.

The door to the kitchen was closed. Opening it, she saw Rosa with Esperanza on her lap and Blanquita stirring cake batter in a big earthenware bowl on the table. Esperanza slid down and leaped into Kay's arms, clinging like a spider monkey.

"She saw something on the television," Rosa said. "It frightened her."

"Do you know what it was?" Kay asked.

"It was a car," Blanquita said, licking the big wooden spoon with which she had been stirring the batter. "It went *boom.*" She spread her arms wide. "And then there was a big fire. Esperanza didn't like it and she started to cry."

"No se vaya," Esperanza murmured into Kay's shoulder.

"No, mi corazón, no me voy," Kay said. "I won't go." It felt heavy to her, as she said it, like a vow, and it scared her to death because she knew she could never back out of it now.

Chapter
Twelve

Dr. Gutiérrez has spent 23 years studying family backgrounds and structures in Colombia and has won two Guggenheim Fellowships on the subject. . . . The anthropologist broadly attributes the growing problem of gamines to poverty, population pressures, the low status of women, and the Latin male machismo.

It's a patriarchal society, and although the woman is the center of the family unit, she is relegated to the hardest, lowest-paid domestic chores.

"In downtown Bogotá it is not uncommon to find 60 people sharing a house with two or three families to a room. . . . There is little hope for a family structure to survive in these conditions.

"When the man finds the financial demands of a family too great, he deserts, leaving the woman with even less chance of coping.

"The children become refugees. As soon as they are able they are sent out to fend for themselves. That is if they don't run away to join the street gangs first."

[Dr. Gutiérrez] said that in a Latin slum a woman's best hope is to find a man to support her. "The girls marry young, perhaps at sixteen, and get pregnant. If the marriage breaks down, as it commonly does, the society provides very little opportunity for the woman and child to cope. Eventually the woman's only option is to find another man to support her.

"But if she does, the new husband will often say 'why should I support another man's children?' He will drive the children of the previous marriage away, refuse to use contraception, which he considers to be an affront to his masculinity, and renew the cycle."

—Ian Steele,
The Christian Science Monitor,
May 20, 1977

KAY KNELT ON the floor so that Blanquita, younger than Esperanza but taller, could stand behind her and reach up to brush Kay's hair. It was short now, a blond cap cropped close to her head. Kay had cut it herself, because frequent dyeing for her disguises had left it stripped and dry. The brush fluttered through her hair, tentative as a gentle breeze.

"It's okay," Kay said in English. "You can do it much harder. I like it." She spoke to them often in English now, when she knew they could understand what she meant.

Behind her, Blanquita was breathing through her nose, concentrating. A moment later, the bristles of the brush came scraping painfully across her scalp.

"Ow," Kay said, and Blanquita poked a worried face around to look at her. "*¿No es bueno?*"

On the rug nearby, Esperanza sat with a cup of water in front of her. She was, she said, making soup, mixing in little packets of sugar and salt crackers she had squirreled away among her toys. She would stir until the water became cloudy and pasty, and then would happily drink it down. Making soup was one of her favorite things, she told Kay.

Kay had taken most of the last two days off, wanting to spend some time with them before her trip to West Germany. When she got back, it would be the first week in December. Almost Christmas.

In Colombia, Christmas Eve was La Nochebuena, "the Good Night." There would be no snow, no Christmas tree decorated or stockings hung, no reindeer. Instead, there was El Niño Dios, the Baby Jesus who left toys for the baby Colombians while firecrackers exploded in the cold and dusty streets.

In Colombia, the big event came later, in January, the Festival of the Three Kings marking the pilgrimage of the Wise Men. The festival was beautiful, Kay thought, but it made her homesick. She wished she could take the kids home to her grandmother for a real American Christmas.

The phone rang. It was Olivia. Kay was surprised at how glad she was to hear from her. Aside from Carlos, she now had little to do with the social side of the Alvarez clan, and though she didn't like to think about it, she missed Ricardo.

"*¿Hola, qué tal?*" Olivia was cheery as a cricket. "I am just in town for a few days. Would you like to go out for a dinner with me?'' She paused for a moment, and then in a lower voice, added, ''I'm going to be moving soon.''

''Oh? Where are you moving?'' Kay was playing the required straight man. She enjoyed the way Olivia always managed to create high drama out of her life.

''Medellín. *Finalmente*. He rented a nice apartment for me and Estrella. I hear you took up some *gamines* and now you have daughters too?''

''Yes, but I think it's more that they took me up.''

''Oh, how nice,'' Olivia said politely, and went on to ask, in an overly casual voice, whether Kay had heard anything from anyone.

Olivia was obviously fishing for information, but Kay couldn't figure out what she wanted. Smiling into the phone, she played along—no, she hadn't heard anything.

After a pause, Olivia wanted to know what she thought of the engagement announcement in *El Tiempo*.

Kay had missed it.

Well, Olivia said, the photo of Isabella was good, but of course she was much prettier in real life. The wedding was going to be held in June, La Basílica, Bogotá's largest church, and she wished she could go, there would be so many important people there.

''Good,'' Kay said, ''I hope they will be very happy.'' It wasn't as though she had ever wanted to marry Ricardo, but she felt like choking Olivia. ''Why tell me all this?'' she said coldly, ''I don't see him anymore.''

''Oh. Excuse me. I am sorry. I thought . . . you would still be seeing him.''

''No.''

''Well . . .'' Olivia sighed. ''I thought you might have heard something.''

''What, exactly, is it that you think I might have heard?'' Kay said.

''I am a good mother,'' Olivia burst out. ''I want what's best for my child. It's only natural I want her in the best school in Medellín.'' She sounded belligerent, as thought she were expecting an argument. ''He should care, no? After all, she's an Alvarez too, not only his other children.

''So I went to the priest and I told him that I wanted to enroll

Estrella, and that her father, Roberto Alvarez, would be happy to give the school a big check for their building fund.''

"*¡Tienes cojones, Olivia!*" Kay said.

"What do you mean? It is my right. I knew Roberto would do it. He would have been ashamed not to. And so he gave the donation."

"You have *mucho coraje.* You finally got Estrella into a good school."

"Yes. Everything would have been just right, except that the stupid priest called Flora." She was gloomy now.

"He called Flora?"

"Yes, the stupid man made a mistake and called up to tell Señora Alvarez her daughter Estrella had been accepted at the school. Also, he wanted to thank her husband for the generous check."

Olivia snickered and said, " 'Her daughter Estrella.' Can you imagine Flora's face? She was so angry she took Eva and went to Florida and made him pay and pay just charging new clothes as fast as she could. I know she has been pestering him for a house in her name in Miami, and now he'll probably have to buy it for her to make up for the humiliation."

"To me, it sounds like a good thing for everyone, no?" Kay said.

"Yes, but Roberto is so angry. He hasn't spoken to me for a week. I wondered if you had heard anything." Her voice was briefly muffled as she covered the phone to say something to someone in the room, then she was back.

They talked on for a while until Olivia said she had to go and see her mother, but Kay couldn't put Olivia out of her mind. Did she understand at all that she was an amateur playing hard ball with a professional?

The next afternoon at about four o'clock Carlos phoned. "There will be a meeting tonight at the usual place. Nine o'clock. Be there on time. *Adiós.*"

"*Pues,* Carlos, wait a minute."

"Something went wrong and it is very bad, understand? I have no time to talk." He hung up.

Kay sat still and stared around the bedroom. Under the ceiling light things looked overly bright and hard-edged, the glinting brass knobs on the bureau, the wrinkles in the bedspread, a pair of white gloves thrown carelessly on a chair. The moment had a sickening déjà vu familiarity, as though she had known all along it would happen exactly this way.

Something went wrong and it is very bad. Was it something she had done? She sat there, scalp taut, hands clammy. Behind closed eyes she tried to check her past actions, watching herself packaging, cutting the plastic sheets, working at the gluing, the drying. If a mistake had been made, she couldn't remember it.

She opened her eyes. There were so many variables. In the other room the children ran back and forth, their footsteps an exuberant clatter on the bare floor of the hall. This is really bad, she thought.

The security at the Padrino's house was tight. That night the guard at the gate nodded, recognizing her car, but a second guard leaned down and looked in the window to check the back seat. The driveway and garage were crowded with parked vehicles.

Old Luisa opened the familiar door with its carved ram's-head knocker and wordlessly took Kay's coat. In the courtyard, shafts of light streamed out from the upper-story windows, illuminating the shrubs and blue-tiled walls. The fountain splashed serenely, and in the silence Kay was acutely aware of the missing voices, the missing laughter and music of meetings gone by.

The living room was half empty. The food laid out on the table had not been touched. Kay looked around; there were only a few men talking quietly, and she didn't recognize them. Most of the others must already be upstairs, she thought. There were no women except for Flora, who hurried toward her and held her hand in a nervous grip.

"Kay, my dear," she said, a peculiar sheen to her eyes. She handed Kay a cup of coffee laced with Cognac. Under her Miami tan, she looked strained and old.

Upstairs, most of the men had settled into their places. The mood was somber, no conversation, and the Padrino sat smoking and looking down at a pile of papers on the table in front of him. To one side of the overflowing ashtray was a half-empty glass of Scotch. Ricardo, sitting next to him, looked up when Kay came in and nodded at her. He was a stranger now.

To her surprise, Reynaldo was there, slumped in a chair near the foot of the table. She slipped into the empty seat beside him. His eyes were closed, his chin leaning on his hand. From across the table, the cook bent his head, acknowledging her.

The Padrino shuffled the papers in front of him. He took a sip of his Scotch and, still looking down at the papers, he began, "An organization is only as strong as its men. An obvious truth, one would think."

He paused and looked up and down the room. A chair creaked. "This business, the safety of this family, depends on the judgment of each and every one of you. It depends on trust. There can be no accidents, you understand? We cannot afford even a single act of carelessness. Not a single act."

Kay clenched her hands; his voice had begun to rise. "There is no room for failure in this business."

He held up the papers in his hand and shook them. "Yet I have received unbelievable news. On November twentieth, fifteen kilos were seized in Paris. Fifteen kilos! Unbelievable! Hundreds of thousands of dollars lost. Big money, big money. But do you know what that money is compared to the breach in security we have suffered?" He waited—as though anyone would have broken the silent tension in the room. "Zero!" he bellowed.

Beside her, Reynaldo grabbed onto the edge of the table. The Padrino had turned toward him. "Did you check out the connection?"

"Yes," Reynaldo said. He was leaning forward, pressing against the table. "They were recommended by Colombians in Germany and everything went smoothly there. . . ."

"Wrong," the Padrino roared, "what you checked out was Interpol"—he leaped up, reaching into his jacket now, screaming—"*and they checked you out!*" And Kay hunkered down in her chair, seeing it coming up now in his hand, the black shape of the Magnum, and with it the flash and the deafening hollow crack and Reynaldo's chair crashing backward while something warm went splashing on her arm.

She looked down. Reynaldo's body still sat in the toppled chair but his forehead was gone, the top of his head smashed and open like a ripe fruit. She pushed her chair back, her dress dipping into blood-gush, seeing his scattered brain matter, like bits of crumbled pink cauliflower among the pink-and-rose patterns of the Persian carpet. Up and on her feet, she had to get out of there, but the Padrino was coming around the corner of the table, screaming.

"Sit down and shut up," he shouted, his fist exploding into the side of her rib cage. Air rushed sickeningly out of her lungs, and then a second blow knocked her back down into her chair. She had heard a crack and now pain flooded her chest with a white, excruciating heat.

"Are there any other women here?" he shouted. There was total silence.

Carlos was there by the body. Still no one said a word. He and Miguel worked swiftly. They scooped the pieces of Reynaldo's brain matter into a plastic bag, pulled the filled bag over the shattered head, and closed the whole thing up into a tight package with a wide strip of tape. Kay, shivering with shock and nausea, couldn't help but think of the grisly expertise of the packaging job. She wanted desperately to turn away but couldn't.

In the silence, Miguel removed the blood-spattered chair, and he and Carlos quickly rolled the corpse with its grotesquely shrouded head into the carpet and carried it out the door. Kay saw that one of Reynaldo's black loafer shoes had fallen off and lay in the doorway.

"I am sincerely sorry," the Padrino said, his face very red, "that you have had to witness this and that I have had to do it. He was my own brother-in-law"—he tipped his head back and drained the Scotch in his glass—"but there was no other way. Let no one miss the message. This is a dangerous business. Mistakes are deadly, and you can trust no one on the outside."

The meeting went on. Kay tried to control her shivering. The searing agony in her chest kept getting worse while at the same time she felt a giddy, insane euphoria at being alive. Her vision seemed to dim, closing down on the shiny surface of the table, the green tie of the man across from her, a ring on someone's hand. She concentrated on her breathing. The Padrino was saying something about Europe and California. The pain bit into her.

People were filing out of the room and Ricardo stood beside her chair. He bent down, "Are you all right?"

"No. I can't get up." The pain was burning. She tried to keep her breathing shallow.

Now the Padrino was there. She avoided his face, training her eyes on his waist and silver belt buckle.

"I am sorry, I hope I have not hurt you badly. It was necessary—to show my control. You got up, you were challenging. There can be no challenging." He put a hand on her, which made her wince. "You cannot question what I do. I do it for the good of all." She willed her body not to shrink away from his touch, unable to utter a word.

"I am needed downstairs," he said wearily, withdrawing the terrible weight of his hand. "It is going to be a long night. Please . . . Ricardo, you will see about this. . . ." And the hand came back again, warm, and then was gone.

In the hospital X rays showed one broken and three cracked ribs. "You are lucky you are so thin," the doctor joked, "this will be easy to set." The broken rib had snapped out of position in the rib cage, and as the doctor manipulated it, pushing it up and back into place, Kay blacked out.

They strapped her into bandages and a corset brace. She felt someone holding her hand, whispering to her, stroking her hair. Ricardo. They shot her full of morphine and she woke up in a white hospital room with two empty beds. Ricardo must have paid for her to have privacy. The bedside light was on, and behind the lowered window shade the sky was beginning to pale into dawn.

A crucifix hung on the wall directly at the foot of her bed. It was very graphic. Blood poured from Jesus' hands and feet and dripped on his agonized forehead. Kay turned her head away. Why do they have to have that in a hospital, she thought.

She heard the nuns rushing around in the hall outside and remembered—the children.

"*Hola*," she called out loudly. One of the nuns poked her head in the doorway, a round young moon face in a starched white wimple.

"I have to use the telephone," Kay said. She threw her legs over the edge of the bed and tried to get up, but the nun pushed her firmly back. "*Tranquila, señora, tranquila.*"

"No, no, I have to telephone my daughters," Kay said, frantic.

"*Más tarde, señora.* The doctor wishes you to stay in bed." Another nun had come into the room. She was older and wore a white-striped apron over her long white habit. "*¿Qué pasa* *aquí?''* she said severely. A bunch of keys hung on a ring beside the beads at her waist. The young nun had backed away and stood near the door.

''I have to leave,'' Kay said loudly, in English. ''I can't stay here.''

They called Ricardo, who had gone home, and an hour later an ambulance took her through the early-morning streets to her apartment.

Rosa was drinking a cup of coffee when they brought Kay upstairs. Blanquita and Esperanza, still dressed in their overalls and sweaters, lay asleep under the living-room table. As usual, they had refused to go to bed while Kay was out.

Kay had left the hospital in the green gown they had given her. She did not want to see her blood-spattered dress and no one had mentioned it. As soon as Rosa saw her come in, supported on the arm of the ambulance attendant, she began to cry.

For a week, Kay was totally immobilized. She lay among the beribboned baskets and the elaborate flower arrangements the Padrino sent daily, and stared out the window at Monserrate. Carlos had visited. ''My brother would like to express his profound apologies,'' he had said, ''a necessary accident, but an accident all the same, and is there anything he can do for your recovery?'' He sounded odd and flustered with his brother's message on his lips.

She had sent her thanks for the well wishes but there was, of course, no longer the slightest doubt in her mind. Her season in Colombia was over. Her time was up. In fact, she thought, it was just about one minute to midnight.

She had understood from the beginning that a smuggler's professional life in Bogotá was fleeting—a few years at the most. Usually the end came with a death execution-style or a jail sentence of seven to twenty. But Kay had come to Bogotá a loner, responsible to no one, confident that she could walk away a big winner and believing that the gamble was half the game.

Now, lying in bed, she knew that the stakes had gone up to a price she couldn't pay. It was no longer her game alone. If anything happened to her, the two children whose voices she heard jabbering away in the living room would find themselves instantly back among the living garbage of the streets. At best, they would be prostitutes by age ten, at worst, they would be dead.

She wanted desperately to take them home, to see them finally safe in the back-yard haven of her grandmother's house.

Ever since her trip to San Andrés with Maggie four weeks earlier she had been trying to decide on the best method, but now there was no more time for indecision. Guadalupe's note had placed the children's mother in Barranquilla. The first thing to do was to go there and find her. Taking the children out of Colombia without at least trying to get legal permission from the mother was asking for trouble.

And if she never found the mother, or if the mother refused to sign . . . well . . . she would run with them anyway.

The Padrino's words came into her mind, "There can be no room for failure." She pushed the memory of what followed from her mind, took a pain pill, and began to make notes on a pad she dug up in the mess of newspapers and magazines on the bed. She wrote:

bank
jewelry
papers: passports, adoption papers
(call Carlos re lawyer)

By the time she started a letter to Maggie, she was filled with a sense of sharp, clear elation.

The kids had fallen in love with Lucille Ball. They loved having Kay a captive in bed, and sat on either side of her to watch the show, careful not to lean against her. Kay had heard Rosa telling them to be careful or *Mamá Kay* might break again.

Rosa came in with a cup of the sickening tea she said was good for making strong bones. Kay sniffed at it and made a face. Esperanza eyed her sympathetically. "Do you want me to drink it for you?" she offered after Rosa had left the room.

"Listen. I want to tell you *niñas* something," Kay said. She lowered her voice to a whisper and they leaned their heads in close to hear. "It's a secret. You can't tell anyone else. Only we three will know." Their faces were attentive and still. "Okay?" she said in English. They nodded.

"We are going to go away. We are going to the Estados Unidos, where Lucy and Ricky live."

Blanquita grabbed Esperanza's hand and squeezed. "*¿Hoy?*" she said excitedly.

Kay lifted her finger to her lips. "Shhhh. No, not today, soon." She put her finger back to her lips, and they imitated her, conspirators.

Carlos knew a lawyer who was good in "domestic matters," he told Kay over the phone. She had called him in Medellín. He had sounded pleased to hear from her, and then tried, with clumsy tact, to find out when she was coming back to work. He hoped she was over "the regrettable accident," and asked after the children. Yes, she told him, they were fine and that was what she was calling about.

"I'd like to adopt them—legally," she said.

There was a pause, she could see him scratching his head, imagine him sizing up the situation, wondering whether she was getting ready to run, or whether it was the emotional aftermath of her brush with death.

"*¿Sí?*" he said.

"Yes, I've had time to think since 'the accident,'" she used his term, "and I want to have a document, a legal will, you know? So that they will be provided for—should anything happen to me." She let the words hang between them, knowing they would embarrass him, yet also strike him as reasonable.

"I need a lawyer," she went on, "please help me, Carlos. I really love them, and I don't know who else to turn to."

"All right." He sighed. "I will call my lawyer friend."

The next day, she had a date to meet the lawyer at 5:00 P.M. at the Hilton. She went first to the travel service in the lobby and booked four tickets to Barranquilla, two children, two adult. The chest brace that encased her from armpit to crotch was bulky and hot, her ribs ached unremittingly, but it felt good to be setting things in motion. She felt as though she had just woken from a deep sleep.

The lawyer sat waiting for her on one of the sofas in the lobby just outside the Bar Inglés. He got up as she came toward him, a man about sixty with gray hair, his briefcase worn, his manner polished, his suit Colombian-made.

"Señor Cárdenas?" she asked.

"*Sí.* And you are the friend of Carlos Alvarez." He smiled, his teeth the stained yellow of a lifelong smoker, and extended his hand. "Shall we sit in the bar?"

How strange, Kay thought, looking around in the familiar dimness and sinking into a wing chair, to be sitting here talking about adopting children.

Señor Cárdenas had taken out his pack of Piel Rojas and put them on the table. He shook out one of the stubby cigarettes and lit it. The brand was unfiltered and strong, and the pack showed the bright red profile of a North American Indian wearing a feathered war bonnet. Kay had always thought it was a strange trademark for a Colombian tobacco company, but she guessed it was no stranger than a pack of Camels back home.

Cárdenas ordered a beer and Kay a soda water.

"I can't drink today," she apologized, patting her purse, "I'm on medication." She wondered if he knew about the "accident."

He opened his briefcase and began taking out papers. The drinks came, and he took a sip of his beer.

"So, you want to adopt two children from the street. How unusual," he said. He closed his eyes and pinched the bridge of his nose as though with weariness. "Have you had them completely checked over by a good physician? They may be harboring a variety of diseases." He took a drag on his cigarette. "Are you certain they are mentally sound?"

His voice was calm and practical, but Kay felt herself bristle. She tried to suppress her irritation. After all, she told herself, he was just being thorough, doing his job.

"Thank you for your concern, Señor Cárdenas. The children, naturally, are already receiving medical attention. I have made a final decision and I want to proceed. I think the mother may still be alive. A servant gave me a name—Puerta Verde, in Barranquilla."

"That is a whorehouse," he said, "which doesn't surprise me. You must be prepared, she will ask you for money. Certainly she will sign the papers, but she will name a price, and be assured, she will try to extort the highest possible amount."

"*Por favor, Señor Cárdenas,* she could have had a reason for leaving the children. Maybe she left them with someone else and doesn't even know they were abandoned. We have no idea what really happened or why.''

He looked at her as if she was a naïve schoolgirl. ''Señorita Wolff,'' he said dryly, ''I will not attempt to give you a social analysis of our country, the Church, the state, or the collective morality concerning abandoned and unwanted children. The sheer numbers are too staggering, the situation too complex.'' He pressed his cigarette out in the ashtray.

''Just believe me, she will see you as a mark, she will try to extort the maximum from you. She has already walked away and left her children to the street, and probably she will do it again. Trust me, I have seen more of this than you can imagine in your life experience.''

He tapped the papers he had put on the table between them. ''So now, here you have the papers. I have marked the places where she will need to sign. Remember, don't give her more than five hundred U.S. dollars for each child, you understand?''

Kay said, ''Yes, thank you,'' and put the papers in her purse.

''Call me when you have the signatures and I will arrange any other papers you may need.'' He finished his beer and asked if Kay wished another soda. When she said no, he looked at his watch, asked if she had any further questions, and excused himself. His good-bye was cordial yet professionally neutral.

Afterward, Kay went into the lobby news shop and bought a small map of Barranquilla. Cárdenas's words had left her glum. She glanced down into the showcase at the display of jewelry there. Necklaces, thin gold chains with tiny emerald pendants, caught her eye, and impulsively she bought one for each of the children.

PART THREE

THE LAST RUN

Chapter
Thirteen

You look far away beyond Buenaventura, far out to those cragged mountains on the horizon with their heads wrapped in turbans of white clouds where lies Bogotá, as unreal as a place you see in your dreams.

But you know you will always be different because of Bogotá, different as an American stamp is different after it carries a foreign cancellation, different because of the power that has come to you from the knowledge of another way of life, different because of the aloneness of Bogotá and the strength you have drawn from it.

Your aloneness comes from having left so much of you in Bogotá. For part of you will always be the beggar on the street . . . Mercedes at the market . . . the owner of the cantina.

Your strength comes from understanding.

—Virginia Paxton,
Penthouse in Bogotá

BARRANQUILLA IS A busy commercial port on the Caribbean coast close to Cartagena. As always, Kay took a suite in the best hotel in town, the Spanish Colonial—style Hotel Prado. She had passed some money at the desk and asked for a mature, responsible woman who would be free to spend the night baby-sitting for her *niñas*. She was attending a late-night party, she said, and didn't want the woman to have to travel home in the morning hours.

The woman had knocked on the door of the suite promptly at nine o'clock. She was large, and her dark face was crowned with two crinkly white braids that crossed over the top of her head. Her manner was soft and easy, a coastal Colombian.

The children liked her instantly. They were eating dinner when she arrived, and Esperanza speared a forkful of meat from her plate and held it out to her. "Here, for you," she said, as though she was conferring a major award. The woman laughed and said, *"No, gracias, preciosa,"* and Esperanza looked relieved and quickly put the fork into her own mouth.

Kay dressed for the evening ahead in a denim mini-skirt, sandals, and a red tank top under a lightweight loose shirt knotted at the waist.

The boys were waiting for her at a table in the bar, two long-haired young dudes from Seattle she had picked up on the beach that afternoon, perfect escorts for a lady who needed an entrée to a Colombian whorehouse.

They sat opposite her, drinking potent Caribbean rum and exotic juices in tall glasses, very pleased to be hanging out with this rich American lady. Neither of them spoke a word of Spanish and neither one of them had any idea of where Kay was leading them.

Her cover story: she was an American married to a Colombian and living in Bogotá. Her husband, she had told them, had brought her and the children with him to Barranquilla on a business trip.

"Man," the skinny one called Sonny said as he sat down, "do we need to talk to you. How do we get visas to Peru? Every time we go for one, they give us some hassle and say we need some other piece of ID or some bullshit like that."

"You need to pass a bribe, that's all. In Colombia, nobody does their job for nothing," Kay said impatiently. These boys should have looked around and dug the scene by now, understood that they were in S.A., not Seattle.

Then, relenting, she said, "Anyway, don't go to Peru, Machu Picchu has become touristy, everyone is going there right now. You boys would do better in Ecuador. It hasn't been discovered yet and the people are good to you. It's cheaper and it's beautiful."

After the third round of drinks, she told them her husband was out on business for the evening. The guys weren't really so bad, talking about their trip—starting out in L.A., hearing the Beach Boys at the Whiskey A-Go-Go. Besides, she needed them.

She looked up from the bar tab she was signing and smiled,

flashing the nicked dimple in her left cheek—how would they like to join her for a taste of Barranquilla nightlife? They exchanged glances, that would be cool.

They cabbed from club to club, in and out of a haze of colored spotlights and smoky perfume, from all-black steel bands to fandango dancers to small rooms loud and hot with the Afro-Coastal beat. The rum drinks multiplied, until at last Kay thought the moment was right. They had just left the last club and were standing outside. A warm wind blew down the street carrying a whiff of industrial waste, a sickly sweet odor like a mixture of gasoline and molasses.

"What do you say to one more stop," Kay said, "the Puerta Verde."

"Sure, babe." Dave was drunkenly enthusiastic.

Sonny flung out his arm. "Take us to your leader," he said thickly.

The Puerta Verde was in the vicinity of the harbor. As the cab rattled through a shantytown *barrio* of narrow lanes and dank one-story houses, Kay could sense the docks nearby, the smell of rotting wood, tar, and sea water. She looked out at the ill-lit streets and chewed nervously at her lip.

There was no neon, no signboard, just a wooden door painted parrot-green. "Hey," Dave said suddenly, "is this safe?" But a small window in the upper part of the door had already opened and a man's face appeared.

The eyes looked at Kay surprised, suspicious. *¿Sí?"* the head said. She just wanted to bring in her two friends, she said, talking fast in Spanish, the rich American boys who were looking for a good time—they wanted to dance, drink, spend money on women. She stuck a folded American ten-dollar bill through the opening.

"*Espera,*" the face said and disappeared.

After a moment, another face appeared in the window, a caricature of Simone Signoret, the eyes heavily lined and lids puffy under blue makeup.

"Why do you want to come in here?" she asked. Kay winked and shoved another ten dollars through the opening. "My two friends want a good time, *me entiendes?* And I don't want to wait outside here in the street."

The woman looked at them all speculatively. Kay could see her figuring. "*Sigan, entonces,*" she said and opened the door.

The room inside was rowdy and blaring with music. At one end of the busy bar was a window that opened into the kitchen where an old woman sold fried potatoes and chicken wings. On the jammed dance floor some of the men were so drunk they remained standing only because they were draped over their dance partners. In the back by the stairs, couples stood in line two by two waiting for a turn at a room. A bunch of French sailors waved at Kay to come to their table.

Kay sat down at the bar and looked around nervously, trying to ignore the stares. A woman sitting at a table on the edge of the dance floor had Esperanza's high cheekbones and broad-bridged nose—the mother?

Kay had no idea how to approach the woman once she found her. She ordered a shot of Scotch and a glass of water from the hefty bartender, who grinned under his raggy black mustache. *"A sus órdenes, bonita,"* he said insinuatingly.

Dave and Sonny stood leaning on the bar, dazed and happy. Time to cut them loose. She was businesslike. "I need to see some people in here, so why don't you split?" She slipped each of them a hundred-dollar bill. "Do whatever, rock out, but from now on you're on your own. You get your own ride home and you never saw me before in your lives. Get it?"

They nodded. Dave shook his head back and forth. "No one's gonna believe this, man," he said. They walked away holding their bottles of beer and leaving the glasses on the bar.

"Do you know a woman named Manuela?" Kay asked the bartender.

His shoulders went up, the corners of his mouth down, he shrugged, and then, after he saw the tenner on the bar, he nodded toward a table in the back of the room against the wall.

There were five women at the table. Two of them were sitting on a bench facing the room, keeping an eye out for action, the others leaned forward talking. Kay stood and watched them for a moment, steeling herself, seeing if she could pick up anything that would help her.

They all seemed to be intensely involved in their conversation, except for a redhead in a tight blue skirt who sat back in her chair and lazily blew out the smoke from her cigarette, bored with the evening, her life—the whole thing. None of them seemed to Kay to be more than twenty-two or -three, and the redhead looked like a kid.

Kay drained the last of the shot and walked over to the table. "I am looking for Manuela," she said. "Do you know anyone by that name?"

"Why?" The woman who answered was chubby and wore sunglasses, so Kay couldn't see her eyes.

"Because I have something important to ask her."

"Sit down," the woman commanded. The redhead sat attentive in her chair now, the cigarette burning unnoticed in her hand. A waitress materialized as if at a signal. No one said anything. Kay looked around and saw that there were bottles of rum on the other tables. She ordered a bottle of Ron Medellín, ice, and Coca-Colas. The woman eyed her the whole time as though she had dropped from outer space. Then the woman who had spoken nodded at a fragile girl in a green tube top.

"I am Manuela," the girl said truculently. "What do you want from me?" She folded her arms across her narrow chest and gave Kay a cool stare.

Kay was surprised. She didn't know what she had expected— there were reflections, the skin, fair like Blanquita's, the wide Indian cheekbones—yet she could make no connection between the children and this girl.

"I think I have your children and I would like to adopt them," she blurted.

In the bristling silence, Kay realized what they were thinking—that she had come to play the judge, that she, a rich *gringa*, looked down on Manuela for abandoning her children, for being able to walk away and forget them. She knew that no matter what she said, they would take it as condescension. She felt trapped.

The waitress came and rescued her, making a big operation out of unloading her tray on the table. In the business of opening the rum and pouring drinks all around, Kay felt some of the tension going out of her.

"I have some papers with me," she said after everyone had taken a drink. She patted her bag. "Adoption papers."

The chubby one leaned down in her chair, her dark glasses gleaming. "So you want to adopt Colombian children. Why? Is something the matter with your husband?"

The red-haired one sniggered.

"Look," Kay said flatly, "if there is no family that wants them, *I* would like them."

The chubby one was about to say something, but Manuela interrupted her. "Their father is dead, my mother has other babies, she cannot feed them." She had begun to twist one of her earrings.

The chubby one with the glasses took over again. "What did you bring?" She nodded toward Kay's purse. "I hope you brought more than papers." She made a money gesture, rubbing her thumb and fingers together. "We don't just give everything away to any *gringa* who walks in here, you know."

Kay said, "I know." She picked up the bottle and poured another round.

The red-haired girl smiled, more open than the others. "*Gracias,*" she said. Kay took out an envelope with the money the lawyer had suggested—ten American hundred-dollar bills—and passed it to Manuela.

"Count it, Manuelita," the chubby woman said.

Next, Kay took out the adoption papers. The woman held out her hand for them and put them on the table in front of her. She bent her head over the typewritten sheets, reading aloud. Probably the only one who could read, Kay thought.

Finally she looked up. "Is that all the money you brought?" she asked.

"Yes."

She looked questioningly at Kay's jewelry. "What about those things?"

Besides her watch, Kay was wearing silver bracelets, earrings, and hand-wrought silver rings.

"Sign first," Kay said, beginning to strip off the watch. She handed Manuela a pen.

While the other women argued about something in a dialect Kay didn't understand, Manuela laboriously signed her name where the lawyer had indicated.

"You too," Kay said to the woman in sunglasses. "I need you as a witness."

"There's still one more thing you can do for us, you know?" the woman said scribbling her signature, Maria "Los Ojos [The Eyes]" Ayala.

"Yes, buy another bottle of rum." Kay laughed, trying to ease things up, and put the signed papers back in her purse.

The woman nodded with a tight little smile and said, "Do you have any birth-control pills?"

"If you mean with me, no," Kay said. She covered her surprise by taking out a pack of Marlboros and offering them around.

"Of course she doesn't carry *píldoras* with her," one of the other women said. She had a round face, narrow, almost Oriental eyes, and, like Manuela, she was wearing a tube top, a white one pulled low to show off her cleavage.

Maria Los Ojos ignored her. "We can't get pills and obviously you have seen yourself why we need them," she said dryly. "The Church has decided to close an eye to the pills lately, but what does that matter when a month's supply still costs more than most women make in one day?"

"Yes," the girl in the white top said, "but Father Ramón says the pill is imperialist. He says it's just another of Washington's simple solutions for us."

"Father Ramón may be a good, radical priest but he's not the one who gets pregnant," Los Ojos said caustically.

"It's easier to find a pregnant priest than a birth-control pill." The red-haired girl waved her hand airily, and everyone laughed.

Manuela took a drag on one of Kay's cigarettes, exhaled, and eyed Kay through the smoke. "How old are you anyway?" she asked.

Kay said she was twenty-eight and Manuela said something in dialect.

"She says that for your age you look good," the red-haired girl said. Manuela told her to shut up and everyone began joking, while under the table the redhead passed Kay a small packet of coke and a rolled-up dollar bill.

Kay had not done any coke for a long time, but with the stress of the evening, the temptation proved too much.

On the way back from the bathroom Kay passed the table with the sailors and they yelled good-humoredly to her in French, *"Et toi, la belle blonde, tu n'aime pas les françaises?"*

"Je regrette," she yelled back, "I'm here on other business."

One of them got up and was calling something else to her when a short man with muscle-knotted arms and a bowler hat stood in front of her blocking her path.

He reached out drunkenly and grabbed at her hair, "How much?"

Kay pulled away and tried to slip by. *"No se vende,"* she said. The blood buzzed in her ears.

"Sí, sí," the man was saying, his eyes furious, his breath beery in her face. He grabbed her arm. Out of the corner of her eye she saw one of the sailors coming to her aid from behind his table.

Suddenly the Madam was there at her elbow.

"Jairo, hijo de puta, what are you doing?" she screamed. She had shouldered aside the sailor and was standing between Kay and the man. "My girls are not good enough for you? This *gringita* is not here for fucking, *me entiendes?"*

"Carajo. ¿Porqué está aquí, entonces [Then why is she here?]*?"* he muttered.

"Leave her alone, or get your ass out of here," she said, signaling with her eyes to the bartender.

The man moved off, and she turned to Kay. "Go back to your table, *querida,"* she said. "I see you talking with Los Ojos. I will send you another bottle."

"What was wrong?" the round-faced woman in the white tube top said when Kay got back to the table. "You didn't want to fuck him?" The other women bent laughing and snickering over their drinks.

"No, *chiquitas,* he wasn't my type," Kay said, suddenly flip and confident.

"Her Spanish is not too bad for a *gringa,"* Los Ojos said.

"Why not," Kay countered, "after two years in Colombia?"

"You live in Bogotá, no?" Manuela's head, cocked questioningly, gave Kay a sudden shock. The gesture, the look, was exactly Blanquita.

"I live here and there," Kay said vaguely, lighting a cigarette. She didn't want anyone showing up at her door later, making trouble or asking for more money.

Los Ojos met her eye. "You are a *traficante,* I think." Her voice was lazy.

"I work for an export firm."

Los Ojos gave a short laugh, like a honk. *"Sí, claro,* and I work for a dentist."

She began fiddling with a box of matches on the table. "You live here, you get rich, but you don't have an idea of what goes on here."

"I wouldn't be so sure," Kay said. She was getting a little pissed off now.

Los Ojos folded her arms on the table and leaned forward. "Do you know how the *conqueros* get their *coceina* plantations? They go up to the mountain villages where the Indians have lived for centuries and push them out. If they try to fight back for their land, they are murdered."

Kay didn't say anything.

"No, you didn't know that," Los Ojos said.

Exhaustion washed over Kay. She wanted to lie down.

"The North Americans think they are putting *perica* up their noses, but they make a mistake. It's blood," Los Ojos said. She waited a moment and then she said, "And do you know why the *coqueros* stay in power? Because they infest the government like roaches in a wall. Because the Colombian government is like this," she lifted two fingers pressed closely together—"with the U.S. banks and corporations. They make money from you and then use their profits to buy guns and slaughter from you for the Colombian *campesinos*."

Kay wished Maggie were there to talk to this woman. She would have had the right words. "The American government is not the American people," she said.

Los Ojos was jabbing her finger at the table, straining to keep her voice low. "Revolution, civil war is what we need to see here."

The girl in the white top crossed her legs, releasing a little gust of cheap perfume. "My father was killed when the soldiers went through our town looking for a man who had stolen some guns from an *hacienda*. They took all the men out in the square and shot them, and then they machine-gunned the houses and set fire to them." She spoke rapidly but tonelessly.

"My brother ran away, but later we found his head in a ditch. His mouth was stuffed with his own *cojones*. Then my younger brother—"

The red-haired girl interrupted. She said she didn't want to hear all that terrible stuff again—what about the birth-control pills? Could Kay send some from the United States and could she wrap them in something so they wouldn't get stolen on the way?

Kay said yes, she would do that, and the girl stood up. She

was tired of sitting around and wanted to dance, she said, and wandered off.

"*Puta*," the girl in the white top said, but after a moment she said she thought the pills were a good idea and was Kay really going to send them? Kay said yes and asked for her pen back so she could write down the address.

The evening ended when the red-haired girl returned and whispered something to Los Ojos, who got up abruptly and left. Kay looked around. Earlier, when the town bars had closed down, there had been a last-minute rush, but now it was three-thirty and the pace had slowed.

She stood up after she had paid the bill and said, "*Entonces, adiós y buena suerte.*"

The round-faced girl nodded, friendly now, said "*Buena suerte.*" Suddenly Manuela was pressing something into Kay's hand. It was a button. Kay slipped it into her purse without looking at it and asked the Madam to get her a cab.

On the way back to the hotel, she took the button out. It was a picture of Che staring up at her from under his shovel-peaked fatigue cap. Under his bearded face, in red letters, was the word RESISTA!

Kay had seen his image everywhere in South and Central America. From airport bathrooms to cemetery walls, the graffiti always included at least one "*El Che vive.*" But in Colombia, carrying Che's image was more than a symbolic gesture; if discovered, it could also mean an immediate trip to the nearest jail.

Kay returned the button to her purse with the adoption papers. She leaned her head back against the shabby seat cushion and closed her eyes.

In the hotel lobby, a black man in a vest and cuffed pants mopped the floor to a tiled bronze sheen. The desk clerk smiled "*Buenos días,*" at her over his morning *tinto*. In the garden outside, the first birds were starting up among the fringed leaves of the trees.

"Would you like *El Tiempo?*" the desk clerk said, handing her the key to her room. She shook her head, no.

Upstairs in her room she pulled the curtains against the rising light and slid into bed. She lay on her back with her arms folded behind her head and listened to the voices in the adjoining room. The kids were getting up. The sound of their chatter soothed her, buoys in a rocky sea.

After a while she heard Esperanza's voice very loud, on the phone to room service.

"Hola hola," she shouted. *"Dos chocolates para las niñas, y un café para la mamà."*

Kay turned over on her side and closed her eyes. She thought about going home. "Home for Christmas." She knew the thought was corny, but felt it warm her heart and mind. Besides, there were sound, practical reasons for choosing to make the run during the holiday season.

Three fugitives with doubtful papers stood a much better chance of slipping through officialdom in the rush and confusion of holiday travel.

When Kay got back to Bogotá she found a message to call Ricardo.

"How did it go?" he asked. "Do you have the papers to be a mother now?"

Kay said, "Yes, *más o menos* . . ." There was an awkward pause, and then to cover it they both began to speak at once and ended up laughing.

"How are you anyway, Ricky," she said.

"I am okay. . . . I miss you." She felt the old electricity humming away; it was as though they had briefly entered a demilitarized zone.

"So," he said quickly, "I called to tell you that my father would like you to come to the house tomorrow night. We will be here for a few days and then we return to Medellín."

"What time does he want to see me?"

"Nine." Again the awkward pause.

"Will you be there too?" she asked.

"Yes."

She hung up with a fluttery stomach. She had not been back to the house since the night Reynaldo was killed.

The houses was hushed and ghostly, with drapes drawn and the furniture under protective sheets. Kay climbed the familiar stairs to the study like someone returning to the scene of a crash. She was afraid, not only of the memory, the rose-patterned carpet spattered with bloody gore, but of the man who waited up there.

The study had not been packed away like the rest of the house. Fresh flowers stood in vases, bright splashes around the room. Roberto came toward her, smiling, his hand out. "Kay, I am so glad to see you."

She shook his hand, trying to disguise the shrinking of her body. She was like a person once savaged by a dog, afraid that her very fear had a smell that would provoke attack.

"Hello, Kay," Ricardo said in English and pulled an extra easy chair over by the bar.

"Come, sit down, we have all missed you," Roberto said. "You will have a Scotch? I cannot, after all, believe that motherhood has eliminated all of your tastes for pleasure." He glanced up at her from under his brows, and gave his high soprano laugh, getting ice out of the bucket, mixing her a drink as though nothing had ever happened. No, actually there was a subtle difference, he seemed more relaxed, and at the same time more effusive, as though in his eyes, the violence had brought her closer, had made her almost family.

He put the drink in her hand, his light gray eyes shining with some sort of odd good humor that turned her cold again.

"And how was Barranquilla?" he wanted to know. Did she not find the people perversely proud of the ugliness of their city? And then he went on to tell her how the business was now in the millions of dollars. "Yes, my dear Kay," he said, "you will be a very rich woman." He raised a quizzical eyebrow, slipping in the allusion to a raised salary.

"When are you coming back to work for us? Carlos is always grumbling these days—we need you." She couldn't tell if he was looking at her sharply or not.

"We want you in Medellín," he continued his pitch. "The climate is so much better, it is much easier to be a human being there than in Bogotá—don't you agree, Ricardo?"

Without waiting for an answer, he went on. "And it would be healthier for your *niñas*. How are they doing?" His voice was kindly and indulgent, like that of an old uncle inquiring about beloved pets.

They were doing very well, she told him brightly, but Esperanza, the older one, had a strange bump on the back of her head and Blanquita's teeth were giving her a lot of trouble, so before going back to work she wanted to get their health problems out of the way.

The Padrino looked at her, nodding understandingly. Naturally, she went on, she wanted nothing but the best medical care for them, so she had made plans to take them to Miami to the doctors there.

Kay had decided that the safest approach was a straightforward one. The Padrino's men would know her every move anyway, so the best thing was simply to tell the truth about her destination. Once in Miami, she would disappear.

"You know of the lawyer Señor Cárdenas?" she asked.

Roberto nodded. *"Sí, sí."*

"He has arranged for a two-week medical visa to Miami for us. I'll be glad when it's all over. Blanquita has been crying a lot with the teeth, you know." The worried mother—she hoped she wasn't laying it on too thick, Ricardo was giving her a funny look. His eyes watching her made her uneasy. He knew her so well, knew the nuances of her voice.

The Padrino swirled the ice cubes in his glass and said, of course, he understood perfectly. But don't get lost there in Miami, he said mildly, among all the shopping and attractions. He hoped she wouldn't be tempted to stay there too long, "because we do need you, Kay."

Carlos's warning of a year ago came back to her. "The world is a small place when a Colombian is looking for you," he had said. She remembered his soft grip on her upper arm.

"Would you be so kind?" she said, holding out her glass and smiling up at Roberto.

"I'll do it, Father." Ricardo was already standing. He went behind the bar with all three of their glasses.

"Thank you Ricardo, *mi hijo.*" Kay got the feeling they had been spending a lot of time together recently. She felt a slight uncontrollable tremor in her right eyelid and hoped it wasn't obvious.

"Well then," Roberto said jovially, "I'll begin to look for a *hacienda* for you and the *niñas* to come home to. Ah"—he tapped his forehead with his left index finger—"I know just the one."

"That would be nice," Kay said, "a nice sunny yard with flowers for the girls to play in." She sounded falsely prim to herself. Ricardo lifted his head from filling the glasses, but the Padrino was satisfied. *"Eso es, exactamente,"* he said.

Then he began talking about all the beautiful new neighbor-

hoods in Medellín and his growing real estate interests. He
described several *casitas* she could choose from, how he would
bring Rosa, arrange everything, until it really began to sound
good to her, even though she was perfectly aware of what he
was doing. He was so good at it, the tender trap, the carrot in
front of the horse. It all sounded so painless, so appealing. She
wanted to believe him, and the fantasy he was spinning. . . .

He went on to ask her opinion about new ventilation for the
fabrication shop. He seemed confident that all the problems
between Carlos and the cook were a thing of the past. Ricardo
said nothing, but Kay could tell, just from the angle of his head,
that he was skeptical. It was uncanny how they could be both
so intimate and yet such strangers.

The Padrino came downstairs to the door with her to say
good-bye. He seemed genuinely conciliatory and hopeful and
kissed her the Colombian way on both cheeks. She breathed in
the faint spiciness of his shaving lotion, and realized that this
was the last time she would ever see him. Damn, she thought,
the bastard, even without knowing it he's actually making this
hard for me.

Ricardo had come down the stairs behind him. He started to
say something and then changed his mind. ''Good-bye, Kay,''
he said formally.

She wished that he had not come. She was sure now that he
suspected something about Miami.

On December 21, Kay went to the bank and stood, pen
poised over a withdrawal slip. At last she wrote the sum of ten
thousand dollars. She heaved an inner sigh. The rest of the
money in her account, one hundred and twenty-five thousand
dollars, would have to be abandoned. It was simply too risky to
withdraw more than would be normal for one of her trips.

The bank manager was a friend of Roberto Alvarez, a man
personally and profitably involved in the myriad complex
transactions of the Alvarez financial domain. Kay knew that he
kept a close eye on all matters pertaining to the family
accounts; the odds were, he would go straight to the Padrino
with news of any unusually large withdrawal from the account
of Kay Wolff.

Kay went to the ladies' room of the bank. She was glad she
was no longer wearing the rib brace and could slip the cash into

a muslin money belt at her waist. No use to get robbed on the way home. She stopped at the travel agency on Carrera 10 and picked up three airline tickets.

She performed these tasks carefully and thoroughly, as she would for an ordinary run, yet every now and then her head would suddenly lighten with an alarming sense of weightlessness. Walking past the church of San Diego and the fountain opposite the Tequendama, she knew she was saying good-bye to Colombia for the last time.

The scene around her assumed a heightened beauty, a sense of almost mystical clarity. The faces on the street, the *ruanas*, the flower stalls, the mist pouring down the mountains—everything seemed radiant with meaning. She felt a sadness streaked with joy, like Bogotá itself.

At home on Avenida Jiménez, the children were waiting for her. They bounced around on the bed as she changed clothes and took the money from the little pouch. ''Is that a lot of money?'' Blanquita wanted to know. ''Is that why you have to hide it?''

Kay said yes, the money was for going to the Estados Unidos. Tomorrow. They stopped rolling around and sat alertly on the edge of the bed.

''Is it still a secret?'' Esperanza asked. Kay said no it wasn't anymore, Rosa knew about it.''

They shouted, ''Rosa! Rosa!,'' and ran out of the room to the kitchen. Kay had felt bad lying to Rosa. It was just a two-week trip, she had told her, for the *niñas*, then they would be back and they would all move to Medellín. She would have liked to tell her the truth, but it would have been a terrible burden on her. It was safer for her to know nothing. Then later, when the shit hit the fan, there would be nothing they could wring out of her, no reason to punish her lack of loyalty.

The couch in the living room held Kay's emergency stash, twenty thousand dollars in one hundred-dollar bills. She took her canvas kit of upholstery tools and began to open the cushions. Blanquita had come to stand by her shoulder. After a moment, she sat on the floor beside Kay and began a careful examination of the tools, opening and closing the shears, watching Kay, hefting the knife with serious-faced attention, marveling over the needles in the palm of her small hand.

Kay gave the girls their own suitcase to pack, a plaid zipper bag with a pull strap and wheels. The radio blared from the kitchen, a whirling organ *valenta*, as the girls ran from room to room collecting things. They had become practiced packers.

After supper when the children had gone to sleep and Rosa was in bed, Kay sat smoking and staring out of the window at the Andes, at Monserrate brooding and mysterious beneath its floodlit church and star-spattered sky. Most of all, she thought, she would remember Monserrate. She began going over the details of the trip in her head, making an inventory of the trouble spots.

The traveling papers worried her—she didn't have much faith in them. The only legitimate documents she was carrying was the adoption agreement. The children had no formal entry papers to the United States except the forged Colombian passports and the two-week medical exit visas Cárdenas had produced for her on her return from Barranquilla. Probably obtained by bribery, she thought.

In addition, she herself was also using a doctored passport under the name of Susan Michaels. She had thought of using her own legal passport but decided against it, not wanting to involve her family if anything went wrong and she was arrested.

She and the kids were an odd match, and with the additional complication of questionable papers, she was certainly going to have to do some fast talking.

She stubbed out the cigarette with little stabbing motions and pulled the drapes. Still, it was the best way to go. She could figure no alternative. Looking at her watch, she saw it was eight o'clock in California.

After several rings, Maggie picked up. She said, "Speaking," and laughed. Kay heard a dog barking in the background and the sound of Joni Mitchell singing "Both Sides Now." It made her glad she was on her way home.

"Kay," Maggie said happily, a little stoned, "how is life?"

"Fine, is that Teddy I hear barking?"

"Yes, he's mad because we put a lock on the fridge and now he can't open it anymore. What news, Kayleen?"

"Remember that silly game I was trying to sell, the one I was going to call Texas beach assault? I'm glad to tell you I've got a new version and I'm working on the design package right now. I think this one might work. I'll show it to you when I get home.''

''When's that?'' The music was turned down now. Kay imagined Maggie suddenly alert, holding her hand over her free ear to block out the insistent barking.

''The kids and I are going to Miami. Blanquita's teeth are bad, so we're getting out on a limited health visa. We should be there on the twenty-second, but you never know. Why don't you stay near the phone for the next few days just to make sure we're on schedule?''

''Of course. Do you need anything? Is there anything little old I can do?''

''Not right now, but I'll be in touch.''

''Okay. I'll be available.''

''Thanks, darlin'. See you soon.'' Kay hung up and opened her closet door with a sigh. She was not looking forward to this part. It was going to be hard.

Authenticating her story of a two-week trip meant leaving the whole damn thing behind—the furs, the suits, the rows of shoes and evening gowns, the tastefully classic designer creations, the luxurious underwear, the accumulated wardrobe she had collected with such pleasure. She had to pick and choose carefully now, pack just enough to fill a large suitcase and a carry-on bag.

Briskly, she put regret behind her and turned on the overhead light. Businesslike, she threw discarded choices on the bed until only the top of the padded headboard showed above a mound of color and coat hangers. Then she turned to the jewelry. Quickly, she filled a velvet bag with some of her favorite pieces, thinking about her choices, exchanging a necklace for a bracelet, a pair of earrings for a ring. In the end, she had to abandon several emerald and diamond pieces and all the costume jewelry in order to artfully re-create the everyday clutter of her dresser top.

After cleaning up, she stood back. The room looked good, normal, as though she had left things in a hurried mess knowing she would be back soon. Her suitcase, one of the leftover brown Samsonites, and a carpetbag carry-on stood in the corner. Strange, she thought, to have arrived with two bags and to be leaving with two as well.

But none of that mattered, she told herself. It was trivial

compared with the thought of leaving even a single clue that might start Roberto Alvarez thinking. A well-dressed corpse is not all that impressive, she thought, laughing grimly to herself. It was 3:00 A.M. She looked around the familiar room one last time before going to bed, feeling herself already a stranger.

The flight was Braniff, leaving El Dorado at 10:00 A.M. for Costa Rica and the first leg of the journey. At 6:00 A.M., still in her nightgown, Kay gave the apartment one last going over—a search-and-destroy mission to get rid of anything that might remotely be used to trace her. She tore up all passports, photographs, letters, papers, and visas and stood watching the pieces swirl and disappear down the toilet as the gray outside the tiny bathroom window turned to a yellowish dawn.

Something made a bumping sound out in the hall. Carefully, she emerged from the bathroom to find the girls waiting in the wan light beside the apartment door. They had dressed themselves for a Caribbean vacation in white sun hats and their favorite T-shirts with Penina, the Latin TV child star, on them. The plaid suitcase rested at their feet. "Time to go?" Blanquita said.

When she burst out laughing, they looked at her with hurt, puzzled eyes and she grabbed them in her arms and hugged them. They were ready for anything. With a shock, she realized how fiercely she loved them.

Two hours later, riding to the airport in the cab, she was glad for their cheerful, noisy voices. Rosa had known. Kay had seen it in her eyes, swimming with tears as they stood at the door saying good-bye.

Then Kay was standing in the corridor as the children excitedly dragged their bag by its strap to the elevator. She waited until she heard the click of the lock as Rosa slid the bolt into place on the other side. It sounded unnaturally loud. Down the hall, Blanquita was yelling. "*Aquí, Mamá Kay, aquí está el ascensor* [The elevator is here]."

Kay had dyed her hair a dark auburn and lightened the children's by a shade. The three of them all wore the same shoulder-length cut, and she had dressed them in expensive new patent-leather pumps and twin dresses. She wanted to create a look of unified identity, a subliminal impression of respectable familial affluence.

The airport was packed with Christmas travelers carrying packages wrapped in green and red. Children crying and announcements of delays echoed through the cold air. Soldiers patrolled the area as usual, and two spiky-looking stray dogs cut through the hall, noses to the ground. Strangely, there were no porter boys.

At the check-in counter, Esperanza looked disconsolately after the plaid suitcase as it disappeared behind the flapping curtain of the baggage carousel. She could not be comforted.

"*Qué triste*, what a sad one," said the man at the counter. Kay saw him sneak a sly glance from her to the kids, doing a fast calculation on what this señora must have done to produce such Indian-looking offspring.

At the candy counter, Kay bought the girls chocolate bars and gum. She would have liked an international *Time*, but all they had was a three-day-old *Miami Herald*. Suddenly, through the bobbing heads of the crowd, she thought she caught a glimpse of Ricardo. She whirled back to the counter, her heart in high gear hammering in her ears. It was not a complete surprise—she had been half expecting him.

Yes, it was Ricardo—he was talking to the ticket agent. Why? To bring her back? Her first impulse was to fade into the crowd, to run, but she knew it was useless. He would be waiting at the departure gate. He knew all the officials.

"Come, *niñas*," she said, "*Tío Ricardo* is over there. We will go and say hello."

"Your hand is cold," Blanquita said.

Kay went right up and kissed his cheek. "What are you doing here?" she said, trying to sound light. "Have you come to make sure I really leave?"

They were standing close, she could almost feel the heat from his body. The beginning of a new mustache shadowed his lip.

"I wanted to say good-bye. I got the feeling at my father's house that I might not see you for a while." His eyes, scanning the crowd, avoided hers.

Blanquita pulled at Kay's skirt and asked if they could sit on the carry-on bag. "Of course, *querida*." Kay was effusive, bending down, glad for the distraction.

"The *niñas* look good, Kay," he said.

They both looked down at the girls, self-consciously aware of how close together they were standing. "Yes, they're doing well."

"How are your papers?" he said.

"*Meti-meti.*" She wavered her hand.

"Do you want me to come with you to the gate?" This time he looked straight at her. "It will be easier if I come."

She nodded, still feeling trapped, still half suspicious of his intentions. Was he actually offering to help her get out of the country, knowing she might never come back? Was he capable of acting against the family loyalties like that?

He bent down to the girls, and she watched them stare at handsome Ricardo, who was smiling at them and saying, "*Vámonos al avión.*" They looked at Kay and she nodded. It was all right. There was, after all, nothing tangible to fear from him. What could he prove? That she wasn't going to Miami for a couple of weeks?

He had picked up the bag, slinging it over one shoulder, and with his other hand he tucked Kay's arm close to his side in the old familiar way. The girls moved on a little ahead of them, looking at their feet in their new shoes as they walked.

How perfect, Kay thought, just a happy little family going off on vacation. She glanced at him sideways. He was squeezing her arm tighter, but his face remained impassive as he maneuvered through the crowd.

The immigration man was unctuous, keeping up a rapid-fire conversation with the young Señor Alvarez while stamping Kay's papers with barely a glance. Kay opened her purse to get out money to pay the Colombian exit tax, but Ricardo laid his hand over hers. He pulled out his wallet and paid the man himself.

Afterward, they stood at the gate, waiting. The departure had been announced half an hour earlier but there was obviously a delay. The door to the airfield was closed and Kay could hear a hard rain beating on the metal.

"Can I see Lucy and Ricky in the Estados Unidos?" Blanquita asked.

"Yes," Kay said, "but they speak English there."

"I can speak English," Blanquita said. She was looking at a

boy across from them who struggled to hold a giant blue teddy bear off the littered floor.

Ricardo reached out to touch Kay's neck. She recoiled in surprise, but he was pulling at the thin chain until the little silver heart appeared from under her blouse. He held it in his hand. "We had a good time," he said. *"Es una lástima."* He took her in his arms and kissed her on the mouth. Nothing had changed for her about his touch.

They held each other. "Remember what I told you when I bought you that heart?" he said into her hair.

"You made up some story." Over his shoulder she saw Esperanza's amazed face, her mouth slightly open.

"I told you the old legend that if you do not walk up Monserrate, you are doomed to return over and over again."

She reached under his shirt collar at the back, curling her fingers against the warmth of his neck. "There's also the old Colombian saying, *'Lo que viene por agua, por agua se va* [That which comes over the water, goes away over the water],'" she said.

"Good," he said. "I see you have finally learned something Colombian."

"And will you tell your father you saw me off?" she asked. They stood a little apart now.

"No. I am my own man, you now. I don't tell my father everything."

"Good, then. Thank you." She wanted to touch him again.

"But Kay, don't forget," he said, "my father is not stupid."

She laughed. "Don't worry, it's not something I would forget."

He pulled out a roll of peppermint candies, peeled back the paper, and offered her one. Then he put one each in Esperanza's and Blanquita's outstretched hands. In unison they said *"Gracias, señor,"* and in their singsong voices Kay suddenly heard the street again, just a few short months behind them.

The boarding announcement crackled over the loudspeakers. The stewardess opened the door, her hair blowing wildly in the rush of the wind. Outside in the rain, Kay saw a man in a yellow hooded slicker wheeling steps to the side of the waiting plane.

Ricardo picked up the bag and placed it on her shoulder, and the children grabbed onto her hands. "Take care of your Colombian daughters," he said.

The wind and rain hit them, and the children ran beside her, huddling into her legs. She turned her head once to see Ricardo, still standing in the open doorway. He waved.

Chapter
Fourteen

You can plan all you want to, but you always have to figure in the "x factor," and in the end, that's the real measure of how good you are.

—Kay Wolff

KAY WAS PREPARED for a number of problems with their exit papers, Instead it was the old smuggler's nightmare, the x factor, that was waiting for her at the El Coco airport in Costa Rica.

The flight, meant to continue to Miami, was inexplicably aborted in San José and Kay had to go through Costa Rican immigration before boarding a new flight.

"You are traveling on a medical visa," the immigration inspector said. "These children will need to be examined for communicable diseases before we can allow you to proceed."

"I have a letter here, would you like to see it?" Kay took out one of her envelopes with a hundred-dollar bill enclosed in a sheet of paper.

"I understand, señora. Nevertheless, they will have to be examined by a state doctor. Follow the signs for the medical examiner. Next . . ."

Kay couldn't believe it. An honest official? Or was an inspector watching him?

The state doctor's office was a bureaucratic green cubicle with a paper-covered examination table. An ancient changing screen of shirred yellowing material partitioned off one corner, and outside the open barred window Kay saw a line of dusty palm trees lazily stirring in the humid breeze.

The children sat stoically side by side on the table, their legs dangling, thermometers in their mouths. A nurse in a light green uniform examined their scalps under a bright light while they maintained constant eye contact with Kay.

The nurse removed the thermometers, silently wrote something on a clipboard, and disappeared through a door. A moment later, a man in a rumpled white doctor's coat came through the same door. He looked down at the clipboard in his hand shaking his head.

"I am very sorry, it disturbs me deeply, but I am not able to stamp these visas. To be absolutely frank about it, señora, your children seem to have contracted ringworm. . . ."

The man was eyeing her strangely. Oh no, Kay thought, he thinks I abuse my kids. Starvation and neglect. Though it was now four months since Kay had lifted the children out of the filth and malnutrition of the street, their bodies were still weak and puny and endlessly prey to parasites, colds, infections, and diarrhea.

"They have been very ill," Kay said. "It has been very difficult."

"Well, I am so sorry, señora, but you will have to return to Bogotá." He blinked and shook his head again. "Unless of course"—he paused—"but no, I cannot permit entry."

She reached into the side pocket of her beige linen jacket for the envelope, willing to try again. "Perhaps if we stayed in a hotel here in San José for a few days?"

She handed him the envelope. "Ringworm is not such a serious malady, no? It is Christmastime, doctor. Can you not make an exception for the *niñas*?" She smiled beguilingly, while he glanced at the three one-hundred-dollar bills.

The envelope disappeared into the pocket of his wrinkled white coat and he scribbled a prescription. "Well, after all, what can be wrong with a few days in San José. The sun will do them good . . . clear up the problem."

"*Gracias, muy amable señor. Vámanos, hijitas.*" The girls slipped quickly off the table and stood by her side. She took their hands. "*Feliz navidad,*" she said to the doctor on the way out.

Kay booked a room in the Royal Dutch, the best hotel in San José. Then she called the hotel *farmacía* and had it send up a bottle of purple gentian violet for the ringworm. The outbreak was a disaster. There was no way to know how fast the medicine would work. Sometimes the telltale little red spots remained for two to three weeks, spreading to face and body before disappearing. Sometimes it was all over in a week.

One thing was certain, though; the already dubious plan for crossing the U.S. border at Miami now seemed foolhardy. The bad luck had been a sign, Kay thought, telling her to stop and rethink.

Not only was she still worried about the traveling papers, but Miami was the Padrino's town, and though she had picked it, she had always been aware that getting out of there unnoticed by his men would be more than difficult, it would be a minor miracle. She lifted the phone receiver and ordered ice, a double Chivas Regal, and two Cokes for the kids. She needed a stiff drink.

Once out of Costa Rica, they could probably still slide their way up through Central America. But the U.S.–Mexican border would be a different story. Arriving by air meant a strict immigration scrutiny that would still involve the questionable papers. Crossing the border by car would be hard but not *as* hard. She would need Maggie's help, but she didn't want to call her until she had made more headway.

She lay down on the bed and stared bleakly at the ceiling, trying to plan the next day's move. Going back to Bogotá was out. Staying here was impossible. Her papers to continue were invalid. It was a vicious circle.

The room-service knock interrupted her thoughts. Blanquita and Esperanza had been casing the room, but now they came to sit down with her. They had been busy, unwrapping the fruit and cheese basket, turning on the television, and picking through the folder of menus and advertisements on the desk.

"*Mira, qué linda,*" Blanquita said. She held up a placard of a woman in a red flamenco dress and black mantilla. Underneath her feet was written "Enjoy the Excitement of the Royal Room—Shows Nightly Except Monday."

Esperanza had opened Kay's suitcases for her and was helpfully taking out her clothes. She was touched. They were trying to distract her.

The Royal Room was crowded and noisy and hung with gaudy papier-mâché Christmas bells. Kay was pleasantly aware of the entrance they made, an attractive woman in ice-blue silk with her two Christmas *niñas* in red velvet dresses and white fur-trimmed boots. She had tied lacy white scarves around their heads to hide the purple ringworm medicine.

The show was a "spectacular," a lavish mixture of Spanish and South American folk tradition. The dancers started with a "*bola*," stamping and shouting, wildly twirling gaucho lariats weighted with shiny steel balls.

In the darkness at the table, the children sat stiff with fear, but later when the flamenco dancer took her bow, they applauded so extravagantly she came down from the stage and presented them with glittery little stars from her hair. A bottle of champagne appeared on the table.

"Compliments of Señor Suárez," the waiter said and glided off.

Two tables away, a middle-aged man in heavy black-rimmed glasses smiled and nodded. Kay smiled back and beckoned him to join them. You never know, she thought.

"What charming little daughters, señora," he said. "You are traveling alone?"

She sighed, put on a sad expression, and gave the man her cover story. She was an American, a recent widow on her way to Mexico to join her husband's family there for Christmas.

Blanquita picked up the sparkly star the dancer had given her and turned it around and around in her hands. "Our father is dead," she added soulfully.

Kay stared in surprise at the small face, mournful beneath its white scarf. Blanquita the street *gamine* was backing her up. Señor Suárez asked her to dance. A band had come on and was playing "*Bésame Mucho.*" The girls were busy devouring steaks. They looked up briefly to make sure Kay wasn't going anywhere.

On the dance floor, Kay soon learned that Señor Suárez owned a thriving corner of the huge South American cut-flower trade, had a private plane, and was flying on a business trip to Guatemala in the morning.

She had seen the wedding ring on his finger, but his dancing was to the point, a wordless expression of his sexual hopes for the night. Kay looked over at the girls. They were talking to an old lady who had come to sit with them. Esperanza's eyes searched the dance floor, found her, and she smiled.

Kay smiled back, feeling Señor Suárez's insistent belly press against her. She sighed. There was nothing to do but to go ahead with it.

Fate had dealt her a blow and then turned around and dealt her their ticket out of Costa Rica. She should be grateful for Señor Suárez, she thought, laying her face against his smoothly shaven cheek. After a night of fun, he would be delighted to take them along in the morning, happy to give the merry widow and her children a lift to Guatemala in his little Cessna 172.

"Señor Suárez," she said, "let me put my babies to bed, and then why don't I join you for a glass of brandy?"

She left his room at 4:00 A.M. She had put the children to sleep in the big double bed. Esperanza opened her eyes and closed them again as Kay climbed into bed beside her without bothering to take off her ice-blue dress.

But sleep wouldn't come. The clock ticked loudly, she was painfully conscious of the children's breathing and the pounding of her own heart. In the past, the ultimate fear that haunted every run had always been the loss of the coke and the possibility of years behind prison bars. Now the punishment for failure would be two lost lives.

She sat up in bed and reached for her cigarettes. Traveling with false documents was a federal offense. Her children would be taken from her—she would have found her daughters and rescued them only to lose them again, to see them slip back into abandonment. She got up to phone Maggie, but she could not raise the international operator. The line rang on and on, till finally, in frustration, she went back to bed and lay awake till dawn.

The flight over Guatemala was like skimming over a green moonscape. The children sat in the back, squeezed among oblong boxes of carnations. Mesmerized, they pressed their foreheads against the window, their breath making small clouds of fog on the glass.

Through breaks in the cloud cover Kay gazed straight down into the molten mouths of active volcanos. Black smoke fumed from the center of their restless hearts.

"¿Es muy grande, no? Es una obra de Dios." The man grinned expressively and waved his hand, shouting above the engines. Kay nodded. She wished he would concentrate more on flying the plane. Her hands were cold and she clasped them in her lap, dizzy with fatigue and nerves, trying not to think of the Guatemala airport and the uncertainty that lay ahead.

The first moments after they arrived were a breeze. Señor Suárez sauntered into the busy private-plane arrivals office with cheery greetings for everyone, a regular customer. His plane was checked in quickly. He didn't bother with filling out the passenger forms and no one asked him for them. There was no customs check. At the door into the public terminal, he told Kay how much he had enjoyed meeting her and her beautiful children, wished her a happy and healthy New Year, and went off toward the exits.

Alone again, she looked around, trying to assess the feel of the airport. The girls stood quietly beside her, sensing her tension. Until this moment, she had been in familiar territory, but Guatemala was an unknown—she had not been this way before.

To her alarm, the terminal was full of police and patrolling military. Though crowded with Christmas travelers, the overall atmosphere was one of somber stillness that struck her as ominous. It reminded her unpleasantly of the tight mood she had walked into at Lisbon's Portela airport.

To Kay's experienced eye, the Guatemala airport showed all the danger signals of a government crackdown, making the safety and feasibility of bribes an open question.

Esperanza drooped, leaning against Kay's side. Across from where they stood, Kay spotted a small airport bar with red leatherette booths, a place to rest and think.

She pushed aside a soiled paper plate and an empty *gaseosa* bottle and ordered coffee for herself and milk and grilled-cheese sandwiches for the kids. They looked across at her, little girls of four and five, their chins barely clearing the tabletop. Hungry and tired, they waited, uncomplaining, for the next move. They know, they want to help, Kay thought, and realized with grateful astonishment that somewhere along the line the three of them had become a team.

She took several airline schedules out of her purse and began nervously running down Mexican destinations. As every professional smuggler knew, Mexico City was to be avoided. The customs officials were notoriously tough and ruthless, taking *gringos* off to jail for the smallest infringements. To be discovered with a false passport there would spell disaster.

Guadalajara would be better. It would be a small airport and the officials might be willing to look the other way. It was the only thing left to do. Guatemalan immigration was a gamble she was just going to have to take.

The best bet was the last flight in the evening on Mexicana Airlines. At that point, the officials would be tired. They would be in a hurry to get the job done and go home to supper and a beer. Too, there would be fewer of them trying to process the crowd.

She told the kids they were in charge of the bags until she got back, took a last sip of her coffee, and went into the terminal to book tickets, forcing herself to think of nothing but the next step.

All flights to Guadalajara were sold out. Her body felt heavy with fatigue and tension, and for the first time in weeks she really wanted a burst of cocaine energy.

The kids were waiting anxiously at the door of the bar when she got back. She had found out the name of several travel agencies in the international section of Guatemala City. The girls woke up at the prospect of a cab ride into another strange town. "Are we going to a hotel?" Esperanza asked hopefully.

Outside, the sky was yellowish and lowering. A strong wind rushed clouds over the low airport buildings. As they got into the cab with their luggage, the first raindrops had begun to streak the windshield. The girls chattered at the windows. Kay put her hand to her waist to reassure herself with the comforting feel of her money corset.

The downtown streets were empty, confirming Kay's suspicions of some sort of military crackdown. She taxied from airline to travel agency, always finding the same blank faces, the same story, planes full, no tickets, no information. The town reeked of fear, heightening her own desperation.

Finally, she found herself at a prosperous little travel agency with gray carpeting and potted palms. The children sat together in one chair, bleary and patient. Kay told the travel agent, a young woman with a shadow of dark fuzz on her upper lip, that money was no object, that relatives waited, that the children were sick. She introduced the inevitable white envelope and the woman picked up the phone.

"Señora Valdéz," she said. "This is Señorita Golance from

the *agencia de viaje*. There has been an unfortunate confusion regarding your booking this evening.''

Kay walked out into the rain with three first-class tickets to Guadalajara on the last flight of the evening.

They got back to the airport at 8:30 P.M. with two hours to kill till departure. It was after they had eaten dinner that Kay saw the man. She was sitting on a plastic chair making a list of what to discuss with Maggie. On the floor at their feet the children played with paper dolls.

She saw him by the Braniff ticket counter across the terminal, a stubby man in a dark blue blazer. He had turned away from the agent and was scanning the airport. Terror caught in the pit of her stomach and turned her cold.

She remembered him now, the shadowy man on the path in the hotel garden in Cartagena, the man named Calderón who had been at the meeting in the cook's house in Medellín, Señor Calderón, the Padrino's spy, the Padrino's hound, and now she was the fox.

She bent down to the children, feeling a light-headed nausea. ''I want you to do exactly what I say,'' she told them, trying to keep her voice calm and steady. ''Quickly put away your toys, take your suitcase, and follow me to the *baño* without looking around at all, *entiendes?*''

They nodded and followed her instructions without a word.

There was no one in the ladies' room except an old Indian woman washing the floor, dragging a wooden box of brushes and rags. She didn't look up.

''Wait a minute, *niñas*,'' Kay told the girls, and closed herself into the stall nearest the end wall. She could see their small feet standing guard on the other side of the door. With the suitcase open on the toilet, she stripped off jacket, skirt, and blouse. Her body was clammy with sweat.

He must have been on her tail since Costa Rica. She was glad now for the little .38 Astra Cadix she was packing, hidden on her thigh in a strap holster. Shivering, she pulled two hundred dollars from the corset-carry and folded the bills into an envelope. And then, she thought, when he saw that she was going on, that she wasn't turning back to Bogotá . . . he would know that something was very wrong and he would take action.

Two stalls away, someone banged a door shut. Laughter,

voices discussing the rain, shopping in the town. She clenched her teeth against the shivering and pulled on a full blue skirt and a frilly white blouse. With swift expertise, she fitted a wig of short auburn curls over her hair, opened the door, and motioned the children in.

They stared with frightened faces. She undressed them quickly, telling them there was someone who didn't want them to go to the Estados Unidos, someone they were going to have to fool. It would be a good game, she told them, buttoning them into their red party dresses.

At the sink, she made up her face, applied bright lipstick, and put on a pair of rose-tinted glasses. "When will you be *Mamá Kay* again?" Esperanza whispered unhappily.

She came out of the ladies' room, the children hanging back behind her. The man was gone. Then she saw him, walking away toward the sweet shop. She got rid of their bags, checking them through, her back tingling the whole time, cursing herself for having brought the children's little plaid one, which was so distinctive.

Then it was gone, and she held the claim tickets. Blanquita and Esperanza watched her face for clues. She withdrew again to the safety of the ladies' room. Her mind felt clear now, totally concentrated on her moves.

From behind the half-opened door of the ladies' room she saw him again, ambling past the airline counters and coming to a stop under the flight announcement board. He studied the board calmly, looking up at it and eating a chocolate bar. Boarding for Mexicana flight 102 to Guadalajara had just been announced, and a stream of people had started toward the gate.

"Don't be afraid, *niñitas*," she said, "I'll be right behind you, I promise. But don't look around. We have to fool the man now."

A large Mexican family was passing, the children slicked up in their Christmas finery. Kay pushed the *niñas* out into their midst. "Walk with them," she whispered. Esperanza turned to look at her, but she shook her head severely and followed the little distance behind, as though on her own.

The man had turned now and was watching the crowd carefully. His eyes swept over the Mexicans, moved past them, and rested at last on her. She felt a deep, cold thrill. His gaze lingered and passed over her, unrecognizingly. She kept

moving, suppressing a bursting sense of triumph until she was
well out of his field of vision.

Blanquita was talking animatedly with the Mexican children.
Kay grabbed her hand on one side and Esperanza's on the other
and walked rapidly, pulling them along on their short legs
beside her. She had to move fast now, wanting to be through
the glass doors at the end of the corridor before the man
thought of posting himself there.

"We fooled him, no?" Blanquita said as the doors finally
closed them safely into the crowded departure room.

Kay bent down to hug them. "Yes, we really did," and
found their faces hot and flushed. She pulled a bottle of
half-finished orange *gaseosa* out of her shoulder bag.

She was high on adrenaline now, speedy. Standing in the
customs line, she continued to hold the children's hands, only
realizing after a few moments that she was clutching them very
tightly.

Kay had placed herself strategically near the end of the line,
but not last. As the line of people between her and the
black-jacketed man at the small table shrank, she tried to
overhear the questions he was asking. Her body buzzed and
clamored with apprehension. She lowered her eyes and began
counting her breaths, her old smuggler's formula for stilling
panic.

Finally, it was their turn. Amazingly, the office was working
alone without attendant military. She handed over the passports, sizing him up while he examined the entries. Good, he
looked tired, a little dazed. Black mustache, wedding band,
early forties, a family man. Good, a civil servant with a family
could always use cash for Christmas.

She spoke easily to him about the holidays, about the
crowds, but he was hesitating, holding the passports in his
hands. He looked up.

"I have a letter here," she said quickly. She gave him her
travel folder with the envelope on the top.

He met her eye, glanced inside the envelope, and passed it
smoothly under some papers on the table beside him. He
stamped the passports and handed them back with a smile.
"*Feliz navidad, señora*," he said politely. She looked down at
the stamps, Guatemala–La Aurora, December 23, 1970.

Kay was cautiously jubilant but could not allow herself to

relax completely. As she sat in her first-class seat waiting for takeoff, she could not rid herself of the idea that the customs man might have kept the bribe and then reported her anyway.

At last they were airborne, and the stewardess brought them juice and blankets and small talk. From the other side of the curtain came the sound of babies crying. The plane was as packed as a Mexican bus.

Rain flooded down the portholes black with night. The cabin lights had been dimmed and the girls had fallen asleep. Kay was amazed at how Indian they looked, leaning against each other under the white blanket with the red stripe. She took a deep gulp of the Scotch on the tray table in front of her and let herself be lulled by the drone of the plane.

But Esperanza was not asleep. She had begun to rock rhythmically in her seat, keening a low song, her hands covering her eyes.

"Esperanza," Kay said.

She didn't answer.

"What's wrong?"

"*Baño*," she said. Her eyes, when she took her hand down, were inward-looking and strange.

"Bathroom? Do you feel sick, *querida*?"

Esperanza shook her head no. The first-class bathroom was *ocupado*, so they went to the rear of the plane. The OCUPADO sign was up here, too. As they waited, Esperanza looked over at a row of nuns fingering their beads. She turned away and lifted her arms to Kay to be picked up.

Her face was dark with foreboding, disturbed by something that she couldn't put into words. Kay had always felt that Esperanza had special sight, that her melancholy Indian eyes reflected a knowledge deeper and more ancient than the buried memories and pain of her short life. Holding her close, Kay felt a lick of fear.

In the bathroom, Esperanza could not pee. She seemed frantic, turning the water on and off, clinging to Kay, wanting to leave again. Suddenly, with a sickening plunge, the plane began to pitch and lurch, and the captain's noncommittal voice requested a return to all seats.

They were beginning the descent to Guadalajara International Airport, his voice intoned. For the last hour, they had been flying above a severe storm system. Now, in order to make their descent, they would have to drop down into the bad weather. Passengers would probably experience a bit of turbulence. He was sorry for the inconvenience.

The plane bounced and bucked. Esperanza and Blanquita had begun to cry as the angle of the descent steepened sharply. The plane hit the rain-slick runway with a shuddering thud, and then suddenly the lights went out. With a violent jerk to the right, they slid out of control into a smashing darkness pierced with screams and the sound of ripping metal.

"No," flashed through Kay's head and then they came to rest, freakishly tilted toward the right, still strapped into their seats. For an instant, the entire planeload of passengers hung suspended in silence and darkness. "Thank God, oh thank God," Kay breathed, "no fire."

Seconds later, the panic hit, and she sat holding the sobbing children in her lap, looking on in horror as screaming nuns clawed their way forward and old people were shoved and trampled mindlessly underfoot in the hysterical drive for the door.

A flimsy emergency chute had blossomed from the side of the plane like a nightmare carnival slide, ending in a tangle of flashing lights and emergency vehicles. Kay stood at the door with the children in her arms, looking down. A shadowy figure yelled up at her, "*Salten, salten,* jump out as far as you can."

Blanquita and Esperanza clung to her, howling, scratching her in the wildness of their fear. Half blinded by the lights, she picked them up one at a time and flung them out onto the yellow slide as far as she could. The man down below was yelling encouragement and she closed her eyes and leaped, clutching her bag tightly to her side.

It was a Mexican Federale who caught her in his arms at the bottom. A cheer rose from the darkness beyond the lights. She was the last passenger off.

Above her, she saw the twisted hulk of the 727 sunk in mud, one wing seared off, and suddenly she was hugging the Federale and thanking him over and over. The ends of his mustache dripped in the rain, his features were indistinct in the halo of light from the kliegs behind him. She kissed him, smelling wet wool mixed with sweat. Tears prickled in her eyes.

The accident had thrown the entire airport into a state of

confusion, and a number of passengers had been hurt in the panic. Ambulance sirens wailed while the Federales put the uninjured passengers into taxis for Guadalajara without checking passports or papers. Luggage was to be picked up the following day at customs.

"The Guadalajara Hilton," Kay told the driver. Mexico! She was elated, on the verge of tears. In the back seat, the little girls knelt on either side of her, trying to peer into the darkness out of the rear window. She squeezed them against her, saying, "*Está bien, todo está bien.*"

"*Sí, está bien,*" Blanquita said. Esperanza reached up and touched Kay's hair. "Right," Kay said and pulled off the wig.

Chapter
Fifteen

My love is like a seed,
it just needs time to grow.
It's gettin' stronger day by day . . .
Trust in me, baby.
—Janis Joplin: "Pearl"
"Trust Me" by Bobby Womack

As soon as Kay arrived at the Guadalajara Hilton, she called Maggie. It was finally time to ask for help. They decided Maggie would rent a car in San Diego that they would use for the last run. It would take her approximately three days to drive the car down, which would put her in Guadalajara sometime around the evening of the twenty-seventh.

"Just make sure you get down here, puss," Kay said. "I am really tired."

The Hilton was swarming with Canadian and stateside tourists celebrating an exotic South-of-the-Border Christmas, complete with exuberant mariachi bands, huge paper flowers, and folkloric dancers in multicolored skirts and sequined sombreros. It was Christmas Eve and the hotel boutiques and gift shops rang their cash registers to the sound of *"Feliz Navidad"* and "Silent Night" sung in Spanish.

Outside, the weather matched Kay's mood, unseasonable rain pocked the blue waters of the swimming pool and dripped from the tarpaulins covering the stacked-up cabana chairs.

She phoned the airport to see about the luggage and was told the baggage had been taken off the plane and was waiting in customs to be claimed. No, she thought, there was no way she was going anywhere near Mexican officialdom. Losing her luggage would have to be the price of her entry to Mexico.

She bought clothes and the necessary toiletries at the hotel shops but no special presents, not having the heart for a Hilton Christmas. The girls didn't understand about Christmas, anyway, to them it was just another wonderful hotel fiesta with more and better things to eat. They knew nothing of *Niño Dios,* the Baby Jesus who brought gifts to the good little children of Colombia. He had not come calling on them in the town square. When they got home, Kay thought, Grandma would have a tree and gifts and Santa.

All three of them slept through much of Christmas Day, recovering in the suite she had rented, like animals in a cave. But the thought of the Padrino's man haunted her, and every noise in the corridor brought her wide awake and reaching for her gun, which she had put on the night table under her purse. Afraid of public areas, she stayed holed up in the suite and ordered room service.

The children played in the bathtub and watched television while Kay studied the map she had spread out on the imitation Louis XIV desk. The best plan would be to cross at Tijuana. There was no passport control there for the hundreds of day-trippers who flowed back and forth every day. Relieved of the passport problems, they could pass themselves off as just two more California housewives shopping Tijuana for duty-free bargains.

She was thinking about dyeing the children's hair still one shade lighter when Maggie knocked.

Kay was so glad to see her that she couldn't speak.

"You been having a good time?" Maggie said, giving her a tight embrace. Her left arm was red, sunburned from the long hours of driving.

They left at dawn the next morning. The plan was to drive straight up the coast on Route 15 to Tijuana, spelling each other behind the wheel. Maggie had rented a big black Chrysler sedan with air conditioning, power steering, power windows, and San Diego plates.

"Go ahead, go crazy," Maggie told the kids when they began excitedly pulling out the ashtrays and raising and lowering the windows. "I thought it would help to have a slick car at the border," she said.

They drove out of town toward Tepic, a small city in the lee of an extinct volcano. Guadalajara was cosmopolitan, a combination of Mexico City, Beverly Hills, and Miami, but to Kay there was something heavy and brooding about Tepic.

The Indians here were different, Maggie told her, they had never been Christianized. They were into peyote and kept to themselves in the remote mountains. Maggie had heard about the beauty of their weaving, so on the way down to pick up Kay she had stopped at a folk arts shop but the woman had laughed. "The Huichols in this area don't sell their work," she had said.

Then the woman had told Maggie about the Huichol Indian who had wandered into her shop begging, holding out his hat for a few centavos. When she offered him two hundred pesos for the magnificent embroidered scarf he was wearing, the man turned his back, spat, and walked out.

"She was from the area, she should have known better than to insult him like that," Kay said. She looked back at her daughters. They were cutting out clothes for their Mexican paper dolls with blunt plastic scissors. The back seat was full of bits of paper.

"I'll tell you something weird," Kay said suddenly, "sometimes I feel as though the Indian gods of the Andes are watching over me, and the only way I can get out of all this alive is to give back as much as I took."

When they rode through Mazatlán, Kay took over the wheel. The children had fallen asleep. "Kay," Maggie said, "you've got a lot of friends back home who are going to back you in this and who love you for it."

"Yes," Kay said, "I know, I'm glad." She didn't like the careful tone of Maggie's voice.

"But I've got to tell you there's other talk around. They're saying you're so coked out you're using those Indian kids for just another border scam and when you wake up you won't know what to do with them."

"Those fuckers," Kay screamed, banging her hands on the steering wheel.

"I'm sorry," Maggie said, "I just didn't want you to get hit with it when you get home." She lit up a Camel and passed it to Kay.

"I forgot what assholes some of those people can be," Kay said, dragging on the cigarette. "And now that you mention it, I should be gearing up for what a few of the good folks in Bakersfield will say when I show up with two half-breeds—I can just imagine."

"It's not everyone, Kayleen," Maggie said. She patted Kay's arm and added, "Hey, it's tough to be a star."

Past Mazatlán, the white adobe villages dwindled and the landscape opened into a spacious grandeur. They drove through shimmering desert toward distant mountains whose reddish gargoyle shapes rose up against a painfully blue sky.

Maggie was driving. Cursing, she braked and slowed from 75 to 45, the generator warning signal flashing red. They pulled into a gas station, two Gulf pumps and a shack beside the road.

A fourteen-year-old boy in a torn undershirt immediately dragged out the gas pump while three or four scraggly urchins attacked the car with wet rags, industriously streaking and smearing the dusty windows. A woman with a baby watched the proceedings impassively from the window of the shack.

"*No, por favor.* Hey, how do you say wait a minute?" Maggie yelled. She jumped out and began waving her arms, shouting, "Broken, car is broken. You can fix?"

The Mexicans stared at her as though she was demented, and Kay began to laugh.

Maggie shrugged, furious, and raised the Chrysler's dusty hood, discovering a broken fan belt. Moodily she disappeared into the shack to borrow a wrench.

The Mexican kids completed their *"trabajo"* on the windows but remained staring in at the two rich children in the back, the smallest urchin snuffling and wiping his runny nose on the back of his hand.

When Kay returned from the filthy little bathroom, she found Esperanza giving away her precious stash of candy and crackers. *"Mamá Kay,"* she called urgently as Kay came toward her, "please can you give them centavos?"

Beside the pumps, Maggie was arguing with the boy about a twenty-dollar labor charge, *"Por lavando el carro,"* he said pleasantly. Through the windshield Kay saw Maggie turn toward the grimy Chrysler in disbelief. "Twenty dollars? Why not just pull out a gun and rob me honestly?'' she said, but she paid the boy.

Back on the road, Esperanza was silent, and after a while she asked to sit in Kay's lap.

They reached Tijuana sometime around ten at night and rode around for half an hour looking for a room. Kay's stomach had knotted the minute she saw the lights of the town and the pink neon-lit sky above it. She reached over and turned on the car heater.

The town was noisy and gaudy and full of honky-tonk holiday cheer. Kay felt as though she was on a bad trip. Her paranoia had returned full force. She could not believe she was truly safe from the long arm of the Padrino's revenge. With silent despair, she began to understand that her life would never be entirely free of fear—until she knew that he was dead.

When they finally found a room with two double beds in a second-rate tourist trap, she was in bad need of a drink. While Maggie was scrounging up a bottle of tequila, she put the children to bed.

''Tomorrow we will be in the Estados Unidos,'' she said, as much to herself as to them.

Maggie returned with a bottle of Oso Negro with a pallid worm curled up at the bottom of the bottle. ''You didn't have to get that authentic,'' Kay said.

They turned off the lights and sat at the rickety table, sharing shots out of the one plastic bathroom glass and looking out of the window. Behind them, Blanquita whispered something in her sleep.

''It's not good this time, Mags,'' Kay said in a low voice. ''I'm too scared. When things get too important to you, you blow it.''

''Bullshit. You won't,'' Maggie said.

Drunken voices went past, singing in the street below. Headlights swept across the shadowy ceiling.

''Do you want to talk about it?'' Maggie said.

''No.'' Kay reached across the table for Maggie's hand. ''Could we just go to bed and curl up like we used to?''

The crossing was planned for five-thirty in the evening. Kay wanted the kids asleep. One Spanish word from them could lead to a line of questioning that would end in disaster.

That morning, December 29, Kay and Maggie took the children to the Tijuana open-air market to shop for the crossing cover story.

Kay bought a blue ceramic yard deer, two small wooden chairs with painted flowers, a pile of sequined sombreros, a painting on velvet of a matador, and a shopping bag full of wooden Christmas tree ornaments. Then she and Maggie piled the whole shopping spree into the trunk of the car along with a case of tequila. "Looks good," Maggie said.

Kay had also bought new disguises for all of them: shorts and T-shirts for the kids, a pantsuit for herself, and a blouse and madras cotton skirt for Maggie. She was grateful to be concentrating on the mechanics of the run, keeping herself centered and calm.

After they had dressed, she threw the clothes they had been wearing into Maggie's suitcase. Day-trippers did not carry luggage and they talked briefly of wrapping the suitcase and mailing it back home, but decided it would be safer to abandon it in the street with all identifying tags and clothes labels removed.

At four-thirty they checked out of the hotel and went to a *taquería* to eat. The children dangled their napkins under the table playing with a scrawny marmalade-colored kitten, and every few minutes Blanquita wanted to know whether it was time to leave yet.

"They aren't going to be tired, are they?" Maggie said.

"They're good kids," Kay said. "It'll be all right." But in the end she gave them each a quarter of a Valium and inwardly asked their forgiveness. The risk was just too great.

Finally, with soft music on the radio and Maggie driving around the block, the girls fell asleep. Kay looked at the dashboard clock: five-fifteen. She leaned back to check the girls one last time.

They lay curled against each other in the back seat, their hair almost auburn from the fresh dye job she had given them that afternoon, their faces glowing with a light California tan she had applied from her makeup bag. They slept soundly, Esperanza's mouth slightly open.

"Okay," Kay said. "Let's go, then." She leaned over and kissed Maggie's cheek.

Both women had been through the Tijuana border checkpoint before. It was a huge, sprawling complex of pedestrian bridges and car, bus, and truck traffic lanes, twenty-five in all.

The first official they would face was the American traffic expediter whose job it was to separate the incoming vehicles into categories he then sent on to other lanes: American day-trippers, Americans with tourist visas, Mexicans, Central and South Americans, all other nationalities. Vehicles he suspected of transporting drugs or illegal aliens he sent to an inspection station where the people were interrogated and the vehicles dismantled.

Kay glanced at Maggie as they inched forward in the line. Her face looked strangely frozen. "Count your breaths," Kay said, "it'll keep you straight till our turn comes."

They were behind a blue, beat-up-looking van with six hippies in it. On the left side of the bumper was a sticker that said BURY GOLDWATER, on the right, FREAK FREELY. It seemed to Kay that the expediter took an unusually long time asking them questions. What did that mean about the man? She looked into her purse for the tenth time: it was all in order, the receipts for their purchases neatly clipped together, car license and registration in a plastic shield.

Finally, the van pulled away and turned toward the drug inspection lane. One of the hippies had gotten out and was walking disconsolately beside it, talking to the driver.

Maggie pulled the Chrysler even with the toll booth, and the agent, blond and young in a blue U.S. customs shirt and a pair of aviator glasses, leaned down to the open window.

"How long have you been in Mexico?" he said, looking them over.

"Just today," Kay said. Suddenly all traces of anxiety vanished. She had entered a familiar place, the moment of optimum risk. Her awareness was so highly concentrated that nothing existed but the limitless calm of present time, the man's face, his questions, her responses, with no room for past or future.

She had been here many times before—she knew the territory. It was as though all of her expertise, all of her experience with official borders and official faces over all of the many moths had been just practice, a preparation honing her for these few seconds.

She smiled with something that felt almost like relief.

"Big crowd today, huh?" she said.

"Yeah." he shook his head. "Long day. Anything to declare?"

"Are you kidding? You bet," Kay said.

"Okay, my friend, go on over to line A, customs."

Maggie pulled away and they joined the customs line. Neither of them said anything and they didn't look at each other. Kay turned the radio to a San Diego rock station. She checked the kids. They had not moved, sleeping like puppies, Blanquita with her head on Esperanza's chest.

As they neared the final barrier of the silver customs booth, Kay began counting again.

The customs man had a face like a friendly hound, all seams and weathered lines.

He asked for their license and registration and then wanted to know what they had bought. Maggie handed him the receipts and a neat tally that Kay had made.

"Can I have your keys, please? I'd like to check the trunk," he said. They waited. Off toward San Diego, the sky was turning a deep reddish purple.

He appeared at the window again and handed Maggie the keys back. "That'll be thirty-two dollars' duty on the liquor, please."

As Maggie reached into her purse for her wallet, he peered in at the kids. "Looks like you tired them out," he said. "Did you folks have fun?"

"Oh yes, we sure did," Kay said. A trace of Okie had crept into her voice. "Those kids can sure keep going too. I can tell you, we were glad when they finally passed out."

He laughed, and Kay and Maggie joined in.

"You ladies have a happy New Year now," he said and waved them forward.

Maggie drove smoothly past the raised barrier and they were on the other side moving away from the border.

"My God, we did it, we did it!" Maggie screamed.

The radio was playing "Lucy in the Sky with Diamonds" and Kay turned it up full blast. "Picture yourself in a boat on a river . . ." She was trying not to cry. The kids woke up and looked around with bewildered, sleepy faces.

"I want to sit up front," Blanquita shouted over the music.

Kay pulled first her and then Esperanza over the back of the seat into her lap.

"Are we there?" Esperanza asked.

Kay looked over at Maggie and smiled. "We're there," she said. "El Dorado."

Epilogue

Next to cancer, murder is the most common cause of death in Colombia and is the No. 1 cause of mortality for men 15 to 45 years of age.

—Jonas Bernstein,
Insight Magazine
August 15, 1988

The violence is largely an everybody-against-everybody war in which the lines of responsibility are often blurred: members of the armed forces are believed to act jointly with drug traffickers against leftist guerrillas in some parts of the country, while leftist rebels and cocaine barons work together against the army in other regions . . . additionally, drug-trafficking cartels often fight one another, and Marxist guerrillas are known to have had armed clashes among themselves.

—*The Miami Herald*
September 9, 1988

IT HAS BEEN seventeen years since Kay crossed the border for home with her two new daughters, but in the sunny California house that she shares with them Colombia is not forgotten. Kay's tape collection of wild Colombian rhythms is enough to rouse the most torpid of guests, and on the walls the bright patchwork patterns of native *molas* and the hot contrasts of Kay's own paintings are vivid echoes of the land that still haunts her dreams.

For the first few years, the memories brought only fear. Kay hid out in a sparsely settled area along the California coast, helped by Maggie and a close circle of trusted friends. She surrounded her house with barbed wire and slept with a gun. "We were like a fort at the summit of a mountain—you could see the road for a long way, see who was coming," she told me.

"But then, as the girls grew older, I knew I couldn't keep them isolated forever. They needed to go to a good school, to have friends and live normally. We moved to the city, I found work, and they were busy becoming Americans."

We were sitting in the living room of Kay's house. She is employed by a small university and on her desk was a portable computer and an "in" basket that contained a sleeping cat.

Fear will never entirely leave Kay. It has made her—she was already a private person—very circumspect, but the worst paranoia has receded. Although she can't prove it, she believes Roberto Alvarez is dead, probably shot to death by a rival.

"He was treading on some very dangerous toes even when I was there in Medellín," she said. "The names of the drug lords are common knowledge now. I read them in the papers—*The New York Times, Time* magazine—how the Medellín cartel and the Cali gang are killing each other, but the name Alvarez never appears. So my guess is he was murdered in the early struggles for power in Medellín."

And if Ricardo and Carlos are still alive, Kay doubts that they bear her ill will.

In the summer of 1986, partly because of her belief that the Alvarez family had been forced out of the cocaine business, and partly out of longing to see Colombia again, Kay decided to travel with me on a research trip to the areas where her story had taken place. I was flabbergasted.

She would be traveling under heavy disguise, she assured me, and she was eager to see what had become of her old haunts. Her green eyes were alive with nervous anticipation, like those of a horse before a race. Kay had changed her values and her life, but not her zest for adventure.

On the weekend before we left, I had a chance to get to know Maggie and the two children. The children are not children anymore; they are two beautiful young women in their late teens who speak English with a slight California drawl. They have no conscious memory of Colombia now, though in early childhood the scars of their deprived years were slow to heal and required visits to many dentists and doctors. They are outgoing and charming, and, Kay says, no one was ever able to resist them, not the doctors who treated them, not the concerned people and the friends who became their extended family, and certainly not their adoptive great-grandmother.

Grandma, Kay's main support in those first years, is now eighty-eight years old and confined to a wheelchair in a nursing home a few hours' drive from Kay's home. On their last visit to see her, Blanquita and Esperanza found her tearful. "Tell me about what you're doing now that you don't need Grandma to take care of you and make you pancakes," she asked.

Sitting close together on the hospital bed, they both started talking at once. "Don't cry, Grandma," Esperanza pleaded. Blanquita quickly began to reel off a list of activities: the soccer team, her job at Victor's Cafe, her boyfriend who didn't want to go to the winter formal.

Esperanza has always been interested in her Latin American birthright. "I have friends in school," she told Grandma. "One is from Ecuador. He had to walk all the way here."

Maggie remains close to both girls and comes for frequent visits from Los Angeles, where she works as a film editor. Time seems to have mellowed the relationship between the two women into a deeply familial friendship laced with humor. After "the last run" they lived together briefly, but separated when Kay moved north. "It was a draw," Maggie said to me, flashing a smile at Kay. "In the end we simply wore each other out."

True to character, Maggie worried about our forthcoming trip to Bogotá. The violence that characterizes Colombia had not yet risen to the epidemic proportions of today. Our main concern was for Kay's personal safety, but she insisted that the veracity of the book depended on her accompanying me to places I might otherwise have trouble finding.

The morning of our departure, the doorbell rang. I opened the door to find a middle-aged woman, plumply dowdy but neat in support stockings, a polyester suit, and pink-tinted glasses. She had dark, shoulder-length hair, permed frizzy.

"Hello," Kay's voice said, coming out of the stranger's mouth. I stared, completely astonished.

"Good," she smiled, "it works." Throughout our trip, Kay's approach toward her disguise was matter-of-fact—she knew it was necessary to avoid any chances of recognition, and she was workmanlike about what she called "maintenance," or keeping up "the look." But for me, spending time with a physical stranger who was also *Kay* remained a somewhat surreal experience.

At the airport, Kay was very silent, explaining later that it was best to keep still and draw no attention to herself. At one point, when I turned to ask her something, she had disappeared. I was unnerved at her vanishing powers, even though she had only gone to the ladies' room.

In Bogotá, as we stood in line for arrivals immigration, her face was calm and impassive, but from her viselike grip on my arm, I knew she was struggling with sudden doubts, with last-minute thoughts of the x factor. Could she be wrong about the Alvarez clan? Could their absence from the news headlines mean not death and loss of power but, rather, skill at subterfuge? Would some unforeseeable, tiny coincidence jiggle something in this official's mind that would link her to them? Stranger things had happened.

I found myself holding my breath. Kay's fear was contagious. I knew it was partly paranoia, the residue of experiences long past, but I had learned enough from her to understand that when the stakes are very high, the line between what is paranoia and what is justifiable vigilance becomes quickly blurred. "It's always better to be a little too paranoid than a little too dead," Kay had said to me.

The immigration men were thorough and serious and we passed through customs with dry mouths, but without incident. In the taxi from the airport to the city we were bright and chatty with relief, yet our initial mood of anxiety and apprehension had set the tone for our stay. Fear and paranoia continued to shadow us like the intermittent clouds that came down over the Andes.

The drive from the airport to the Bogotá Hilton surprised Kay. The road into the city had been completely modernized. Gone were the donkeys and tumbledown shacks, and in their place giant billboards proclaimed A MORE SECURE CITY FOR US ALL, part of a government campaign and crackdown against street crime. As the taxi turned into the international section of the city, she was even more astounded. There were almost no *gamines* on the streets.

"I know they're somewhere, but where?" she said, alarmed. "Have they been 'disappeared'? Or thrown out of the international section and restricted to the *barrios?*"

"Where are the *gamines?*" she asked the cabdriver, but he just smiled and shrugged. It was a question that was to plague Kay for the rest of our trip.

When we arrived in the Hilton lobby, Kay instantly saw that the hotel was as much a hub for the Bogotá social scene as ever. "I'm getting the creeps," she murmured tensely, and did her vanishing act, leaving me to handle our check-in. On the way to the desk I paused for a moment at the door of the English Grill.

In the dim light where Kay had once sat with Carlos's lawyer to discuss the children's adoption, two men were now drinking *tintos,* relaxing against the high-backed Edwardian chairs. The man facing me glanced up, met my eye, and smiled. *"Hola,"* he said. He was about sixty, natty in beige pants and a beige cashmere sweater. With a cold prickle I realized he could easily have known Kay, have been one of the Padrino's circle of friends.

Once in our suite on the nineteenth floor, Kay began checking out the rooms. She opened the curtains to let in the view across the city to the mountains, and then went to look at the gold-and-white bedroom. Nothing, not a thing, had changed about the Hilton, she said, and then she smiled for the first time in hours.

At the Hilton's Roof Room Restaurant the maître d' had not changed either, and encountering him gave us our first seriously bad moment. His name was Juan and he was the same man who had sometimes kept the Roof Room open after hours so Kay and Ricardo could continue to dance; the same man who had officiated at all of the Padrino's formal banquets, dinner meetings, and family nights out; the same man who had always greeted Kay warmly and who had served her on at least fifty different occasions.

Kay saw him as soon as we got off the elevator. "Oh God, it's Juan," she said and turned to get back in as though she'd forgotten something. But it was too late. The doors were swishing closed behind us and there he was, standing at his little reservations pulpit waiting for us.

Beside me, Kay made herself as invisible as possible, fading back into herself, lowering her eyes behind her glasses.

"You have a reservation, ladies?" Juan said in English. We watched his gaze slide smoothly over us without a flicker of interest. Obviously he had registered nothing more unusual than two American tourists. Nevertheless, we spoke little over dinner and left without drinking our coffee.

In the following days I saw giant double rainbows arch through the mist over the green mountains; we bought puffy *bocadillo* pastries from the food vendors, and belts and shoes from the Indians whose stalls, hung with leather goods, still lined Carrera 7. Yet to Kay, while the city's physical magic remained as powerful as ever, the sense of warmth and spontaneity that had once animated the crowds seemed strangely absent. The downtown streets were as crowded as ever, she told me, but the people seemed subdued. And tourists? Even the ubiquitous Japanese were a rare sight.

In the Norte we found that Schneider's hotel had gone and much of the cozy European atmosphere was given over to shopping centers. On certain streets, however, galleries and boutiques still displayed their elegant wares and the walled gardens of the rich still gave out the fragrance of moist earth and flowers.

We were approaching the Padrino's district, avoiding the house but circling the neighborhood. Whenever we were out in the streets of Bogotá Kay kept up a running scan of the passersby. This time she turned her head, saw three men lounging on the steps of a building, and suddenly propelled me into a doorway, her grip on my arm icy.

"One of those men knows me," she said tightly. "I just hope he didn't get a good look at me."

Immediately, I began to recite our by now familiar litany of mutual reassurance—too many years had passed, Kay's disguise was flawless, there was nothing to worry about—but my voice sounded hollow. "Who is he?" I asked, shivery.

"One of the Padrino's bodyguards," Kay said. After a minute, she drew me back out into the street and we walked rapidly and silently toward the shopping center. As we lost ourselves in the crowd, her mood began to lighten. She patted my arm and took her turn at the reassurance game. "You're right, even if it was him he couldn't have known me, and besides, I wasn't really sure it was him.'' Seeing my face, she suggested we stop for a drink with lunch.

We ate in a downtown restaurant. At the table next to us a large family was finishing dessert. Candlelight glowed reflected in the wineglasses; the children were quiet and immaculately clean; the grandmother sat in state at the head of the table.

"Watch them," she said to me, "they're just like the Alvarezes."

After lunch I wanted to see the Plaza Bolívar—the central square with its ornate seventeenth-century churches and eighteenth-century façades facing the more recent monolith of government architecture, the Palace of Justice. The square had been the scene of Maggie and Kay's encounter with tanks and troops in 1970, and in 1985 it had become a horrific battlefield between the April 19 guerrilla group, M19 (named after the allegedly fraudulent election of 1970), and the Colombian military.

In November 1985, President Belisario Betancur's partially successful attempts at negotiating a peace between the government and the guerrillas had broken down, and the group had seized the palace and its occupants, holding them hostage and demanding the release of documents that would prove the consistent violation of peace agreements by the military.

The military had stormed the palace in a counterattack, pounding it with tanks and rockets that partially destroyed some of the archives and left more than a hundred people dead (including twelve supreme court magistrates) in what is now referred to in Colombia as "the Holocaust."

Kay and I stood in front of the burned-out, shell-pocked building. Cumulus clouds hung peacefully over Monserrate. I lifted my camera; a man in a uniform approached and told us that we would have to move on. I asked him for five minutes in the square, and he strolled off to observe us from a distance.

Kay's eyes gazed sadly from behind her dowdy makeup. "Poor Colombia," she said.

Later, standing in the eucalyptus-scented mist atop Monserate, she recounted the legend Ricardo had told her—how those who did not climb the mountain on foot were doomed to return.

"And here I am again," she said, "and let me tell you, it's very eerie."

"Do you think you'll ever come back after this time?" I asked.

"I don't think so," she said, "but then how do we know? Back in '70, when I left with the kids, I thought for sure I'd never see Colombia again."

We were silent, looking out over the red-roofed city with its green parks and cluster of skyscrapers. From our perch on top of the mountain it was astonishingly beautiful.

We came home unsettled, with questions on our minds. Kay's major concern on the trip had been to find out what had become of the *gamines*. We continued to see very few of them, yet on our return we learned from UNICEF that there were still thousands of children homeless and starving in the streets of Colombia. An Americas Watch publication informed us that in a wave of violence unknown assailants had been killing prostitutes and petty street thieves.

"Prostitutes and petty street thieves," Kay said, "that's *gamines*. And 'unknown assailants'?" She left the question hanging. Her fear continues to be that the *gamines* are being systematically murdered, "disappeared" into jails, or forcibly restricted to the hovels and shanties of the *barrios*.

And what of the continuing escalation of drugs and violence, a scourge upon the people of Colombia as well as on those outside their borders?

While it is true that Colombia supplies eighty percent of the cocaine used in the United States, the Colombian government claims that fifty percent of all the cocaine produced in the world ends up in the United States. In a three-quarter-page advertisement published in several of our leading newspapers recently, and obviously directed at our own administration, the Colombian government stated that "stopping the drugs at the U.S. border is not enough . . . without demand, there is no supply . . . the menace will not go away until demand goes away."

Our aim with this book has never been to judge the Colombian people, among whom Kay found so much gaiety and warmth and pride and humor as well as tragedy and violence; nor do we pretend to be able to untangle the many complex skeins that form the Colombian experience and destiny. Our hope is only to awaken others to care, because, after all, that is always the first step toward making a difference.

We must look to ourselves as well as to Colombia.

—Sybil Taylor
March 1989

SHOCKING STORIES OF TRUE CRIME

___FROM CRADLE TO GRAVE
  Joyce Egginton 0-515-10301-2/$5.50
One by one, Marybeth Tinning's nine children died—of mysterious causes. This startling <u>New York Times</u> bestseller takes you into the mind of a mother who committed the unspeakable crime.

___WHEN RABBIT HOWLS The Troops for
  Truddi Chase 0-515-10329-2/$4.95
The #1 <u>New York Times</u> bestseller. A world of 92 voices lives within her. Here a woman journeys back to the unspeakable crimes she suffered, to discover where the nightmare began.

___DARK OBSESSION Shelley Sessions
  with Peter Meyer 0-425-12296-4/$4.95
Shelley seemed to have it all, with her good looks and millionaire father. In fact, she was abused for years, the object of her father's obsession. In a dramatic courtroom trial which led to a $10 million settlement, Shelley took a stand against her father. This is her story. "Powerful . . .Vivid."—<u>The Kirkus Reviews</u>
